Japanese Grammar

Essential Sentence Patterns
for Everyday Communication

A WORKBOOK FOR SELF-STUDY

MASAHIRO TANIMORI

TUTTLE Publishing

Tokyo | Rutland, Vermont | Singapore

"Books to Span the East and West"

Tuttle Publishing was founded in 1832 in the small New England town of Rutland, Vermont [USA]. Our core values remain as strong today as they were then—to publish best-in-class books which bring people together one page at a time. In 1948, we established a publishing office in Japan—and Tuttle is now a leader in publishing English-language books about the arts, languages and cultures of Asia. The world has become a much smaller place today and Asia's economic and cultural influence has grown. Yet the need for meaningful dialogue and information about this diverse region has never been greater. Over the past seven decades, Tuttle has published thousands of books on subjects ranging from martial arts and paper crafts to language learning and literature—and our talented authors, illustrators, designers and photographers have won many prestigious awards. We welcome you to explore the wealth of information available on Asia at **www.tuttlepublishing.com**.

Published by Tuttle Publishing, an imprint of Periplus Editions (HK) Ltd.

www.tuttlepublishing.com

Copyright © 2020 by Masahiro Tanimori
License for illustrations from JustSystems Corporation using clip art from Ichitaro and Hanako software. Photographs pages 12, 32, 54, 82, 110, 134, 146, 160 Shutterstock.

Library of Congress Catalog-in-Publication Data in progress

ISBN 978-4-8053-1568-2

First edition, 2020

Distributed by

North America, Latin America & Europe
Tuttle Publishing
364 Innovation Drive
North Clarendon,
VT 05759-9436 U.S.A.
Tel: 1 (802) 773-8930; Fax: 1 (802) 773-6993
info@tuttlepublishing.com
www.tuttlepublishing.com

Japan
Tuttle Publishing
Yaekari Building, 3rd Floor,
5-4-12 Osaki, Shinagawa-ku,
Tokyo 141 0032
Tel: (81) 3 5437-017; Fax: (81) 3 5437-0755
sales@tuttle.co.jp
www.tuttle.co.jp

Asia Pacific
Berkeley Books Pte. Ltd.
3 Kallang Sector #04-01
Singapore 349278
Tel: (65) 6741-2178; Fax: (65) 6741-2179
inquiries@periplus.com.sg
www.tuttlepublishing.com

25 24 23 22 21   6 5 4 3 2

Printed in Malaysia   2104VP

TUTTLE PUBLISHING® is a registered trademark of Tuttle Publishing, a division of Periplus Editions (HK) Ltd.

TABLE OF CONTENTS

What's In This Book?

This book contains lessons that will show you how to use key everyday sentence structures and their variations that you need to know in order to be able to communicate easily in Japanese.

Who is this book for?

This book is for students who have already mastered the basics of Japanese at elementary level. You will already know how to conjugate the basic verb tenses using polite forms. You will already know how to construct simple sentences with the correct use of particles. You will have a few-hundred vocabulary words under your belt. Perhaps you've already passed levels N5 and N4 of the Japanese Language Proficiency Test. Or perhaps you just want to improve, revise or perfect your grammar and communication skills.

Whatever your situation, if you are ready to take your language skills to the next level – whether you are studying for level N3 of the Japanese Language Proficiency Test, or simply want to achieve a higher level of fluency in your everyday conversation and writing – this book is for you.

You will see that all model sentences, practice exercises, conversation practice and reading passages are given in Japanese script (using hiragana, katakana and kanji, with spaces between words to aid comprehension), romanized Japanese (romaji) and English. If you are looking to expand your understanding of kanji, this book can help. However, because all key language is given in romaji, you can easily use this book even if you aren't familiar with kanji.

The vocabulary and topics used throughout this book are designed to reflect the trends, culture and language use of contemporary Japanese society, making this an ideal book for young adults or anyone interested in up-to-the minute language and the latest social issues.

How is this book organized?

Each chapter follows the following pattern:

- **Introduction.** A brief outline of the chapter contents.
- **Key Sentence Patterns.** A list of the sentence patterns covered in the chapter.
- **Formation.** A chart showing the formation of the grammatical structures covered in the chapter.
- **Grammar and Usage Notes.** Clear explanations of key sentence patterns and their structures, along with plentiful model sentences, so that each structure may be understood at a glance.
- **Exercises.** Practice exercises to help you master the sentence patterns. These range from translating sentences and constructing sentences from given prompts, to free-practice exercises where you are encouraged to use your creativity to make your own sentences using the target structures.
- **Conversation Practice.** A conversation script of natural interaction between young people that shows the chapter's sentence patterns in action. You can practice alone, using the on-line audio files that go with this book (see URL on the facing page), or in a classroom with fellow students and a teacher.
- **Reading Practice.** Each chapter ends with a reading comprehension passage on a socially or culturally relevant topic, to reinforce and consolidate the grammar that has been introduced and expand your vocabulary.

In addition to the main chapters this book also contains:

- **Glossary of Grammatical Terms.** This gives a clear explanation of all the grammatical terms that are frequently used in this book.
- **Japanese–English and English–Japanese Glossaries.** Alphabetized glossaries allow you to check the meaning of key vocabulary used in the book at a glance.
- **Answer Key.** Contains answers to all the exercises in the book.
- **Online Audio Files.** Contains recordings by Japanese native speakers of all sentence patterns, conversations and reading passages (see URL below).
- **Online Supplementary Materials.** Online supplementary materials include a range of more complex answers to the exercises in the book, if you want to challenge yourself further!

How can this book be used?

This book is suitable for self-study, with a comprehensive answer key and online audio files (see URL below). It is also suitable for classroom use with a teacher. An "at-a-glance" table of contents allows teachers to select the grammar points they wish to cover with their students.

The 12 main chapters of the book progress logically from simple structures to more complex ones, so the self-study student is advised to work through the book in order, referring to the online audio for pronunciation guidance, as well as to the answer key, the glossaries, and the supplementary online materials.

All students are strongly advised to start with the Preliminary Review chapter on page 13 to review key basic verb forms that are an essential foundation for the structures you will go on to meet in the rest of the book.

This book contains numerous practice exercises in every chapter where you will have the opportunity to practice writing sentences using the new grammar you have learned. You can write the answers in romaji, or in kana and kanji, depending on your ability and interest. A prior knowledge of how to write kana and kanji is not a requirement for this book. If you are interested in learning how to write hiragana, katakana or kanji, you'll find a wide range of great books at www.tuttlepublishing.com

I hope that through the activities in this book you can enjoy taking your Japanese language skills to the next level while learning about contemporary Japanese culture and society.

Masahiro Tanimori
Konan University, Kobe

To Download or Stream Online Audio and Supplementary Materials

1. You must have an internet connection.
2. Type the URL below into your web browser.

   http://www.tuttlepublishing.com/japanese-grammar-a-workbook-for-self-study

For support, you can email us at info@tuttlepublishing.com.

Glossary of Grammatical Terms

This glossary defines the grammatical terms used in this book. The term at the head of each entry is the one used throughout the book; I have also listed other names for this term when they exist, in case you have come across them in your prior Japanese study.

Adjectival nouns

These are nouns that can function as an adjective by adding the particle **na** to the end of the noun such as **suteki(na)** and **genki(na)**. Compare with **-I adjectives**.

Dictionary form

This is the most basic form of a verb, so called because it is the form you will find in a dictionary. For example, if you want to look up the verb **tabemasu** in a dictionary, you will have to look for the dictionary form **taberu**.

Front part of the -MASU form

Many verb endings are made by removing the **-MASU** from the end of the verb and adding a new ending. The "front part" of the **-MASU** form means the part of the verb that is left after **-MASU** is removed. For example, the front part of **tabemasu** is **tabe**.

-I adjectives

These are adjectives ending in **-I** that conjugate like verbs, with negative and past forms; for example, **takai, takakunai, takakatta**. Compare with **Adjectival nouns**.

Intransitive verbs   See **Transitive verbs**

Main clause and subordinate clause

A main clause makes sense on its own ("I saw a dog"). A subordinate clause adds meaning to the main clause, and does not exist on its own ("I saw a dog *that was barking*").

Non-volitional verbs   See **Volitional verbs**

Plain form (also known as the casual form)

The plain form of a verb or adjective has 4 forms: the dictionary form (see above), the **-NAI** form, the **-TA** form and the **-NAKATTA** form. These forms of the verb or adjective are used in casual or informal situations.

Polite form (also known as the formal form)

The polite form of the verb has 4 forms: the **-MASU** or **-MASEN** form and the **-MASHITA/-MASEN DESHITA** form. Use these forms in polite or formal situations.

Potential form

This is the form of the verb that describes one's ability or inability to do something.

-RU verbs (also known as **ichi-dan** verbs, **-RU**-dropping verbs, Group 2 verbs)

Japanese verbs are divided into 3 groups: Group 1 or **-U** verbs have a dictionary form that ends in **-U**; Group 2 or **-RU** verbs have a dictionary form that ends in **-IRU** or **-ERU** (although there are some verbs ending in **-IRU** or **-ERU** that are actually **-U** verbs, such as **hairu** [to enter] and **kaeru** [to go back]); Group 3 consists of the two irregular verbs **suru** and **kuru**. When **-RU** verbs are conjugated, the **-MASU** form is simply dropped and the verb ending added to the verb stem (see page 22).

Subordinate clause   See **Main clause and subordinate clause**

Transitive verbs

Transitive verbs require an object in order to be grammatical. Intransitive verbs do not require an object. Many verbs have both transitive and intransitive usage. For example, "She left her book on the table" (transitive); "After the meeting, she left" (intransitive). The terms transitive and intransitive are sometimes abbreviated in this book to v.t. and v.i. respectively.

-U verbs (also known as **go-dan** verbs, **-U**-dropping verbs, Group 1 verbs)

Japanese verbs are divided into 3 groups: Group 1 or **-U** verbs have a dictionary form that ends in **-U**; Group 2 or **-RU** verbs have a dictionary form that ends in **-IRU** or **-ERU** (although there are some verbs ending in **-IRU** or **-ERU** that are actually **-U** verbs, such as **hairu** [to enter] and **kaeru** [to go back]); Group 3 consists of the two irregular verbs **suru** and **kuru**. **-U** verbs conjugate into 5 different forms, each with a different front part (see page 22).

v.i. See **Transitive verbs**

Volitional verbs

These verbs express intentions and plans and give advice. When a verb is described as "volitional," it means that the action is intended. In a non-volitional verb (such as "understand," "[can] see" or "[can] hear," for example), the action is beyond the control of the speaker.

v.t. See **Transitive verbs**

A note about style

Small capital letters are used to refer to the Japanese grammatical words and phrases in this book; for example, verb endings such as the **-MASU** form, particles such as **WA** and **O** or grammatical phrases such as **KOTO GA DEKIRU**. When a Japanese grammatical word has a dash in front of it (or ∼ in the Japanese script), this means that the word is a suffix, and must be attached to the stem of another word.

I Walked Around Kyoto Wearing a Kimono

私は 着物を 着て 京都を 散歩しました

Reviewing the -TE Form of the Verb

Before introducing the key sentence patterns that make up the main content of this book, let's review the structure and usage of the -TE verb form, which is important to know because it combines with other verb forms to make different verb tenses. The -TE form is also used to connect verbs and adjectives, allowing you to speak fluently in clauses rather than in short, disconnected sentences.

🎧 KEY SENTENCE PATTERNS

1. 私は 着物を 着て 京都を 散歩しました。
   Watashi wa kimono o kite kyōto o sanpo shimashita.   *Attendant circumstances*
   I walked around Kyoto wearing a kimono.

2. 日本の 家は 靴を 脱いで 上がります。
   Nihon no ie wa kutsu o nuide agarimasu.   *A succession of events*
   You take off your shoes before entering a Japanese house.

3. 電車に 間に合って 良かったですね。
   Densha ni maniatte yokatta desu ne.   *Reason*
   It was great that we were in time for the train.

4. 太郎は 掃除を して 花子は 料理をします。
   Taro wa sōji o shite hanako wa ryōri o shimasu.   *Contrasted events*
   Taro does the cleaning while Hanako cooks.

5. 犬は ソファーに すわっています。
   Inu wa sofa ni suwatte imasu.   *To be doing something*
   The dog is sitting on the sofa.

6. あの 着物を 着てみます。草履も 履いてみます。
   Ano kimono o kite mimasu. Zōri mo haite mimasu.   *To try doing something*
   I'll try on that kimono. I'll try on Japanese sandals too.

7. たこ焼きが おいしくて 全部 食べて しまいました。
   Takoyaki ga oishikute zenbu tabete shimaimashita.   *Reason why/have completed*
   I've eaten all the takoyaki because they were delicious.   *something*

Formation of the -TE Form of the Verb

Front Part of the -MASU Verb Form + -TE

For -U Verbs

買い(ます)＋て	→	買って	kai + te = katte
書き(ます)＋て	→	書いて	kaki + te = kaite
泳ぎ(ます)＋て	→	泳いで	oyogi + te = oyoide
待ち(ます)＋て	→	待って	machi + te = matte
死に(ます)＋て	→	死んで	shini + te = shinde
飛び(ます)＋て	→	飛んで	tobi + te = tonde
飲み(ます)＋て	→	飲んで	nomi + te = nonde
切り(ます)＋て	→	切って	kiri + te = kitte

For -RU Verbs and Irregular Verbs

食べ(ます)＋て	→	食べて	tabe + te = tabete
し(ます)＋て	→	して	shi + te = shite
来(ます)＋て	→	来て	ki + te = kite

For Adjectives

高い＋て	→	高くて	takai + te = takakute
おいしい＋て	→	おいしくて	oishī + te = oishikute

For Nouns and Adjectival Nouns

Noun/Adjectival Noun + DE

元気(だ／な)＋て	→	元気で	genki (da/na) + te = genki de
休み(だ／の)＋て	→	休みで	yasumi (da/no) + te = yasumi de

GRAMMAR AND USAGE NOTES

1. How to make the ～て -TE form of the verb

The **-TE** form of the verb is created by removing the **-MASU** verb ending and adding **-TE**.

買い<u>ます</u> (to buy)	買い	買い＋て	買って
kaimasu	**kai**	**kai + te**	**katte**

For **-U** verbs (verbs with a dictionary form ending in "u" [including some ending in "ru," which should not be confused with **-RU** verbs]), the **-TA** past form, and **-TARA** and **-TEMO** conditional forms are created by replacing **-TE** with **-TA**, **-TARA** and **-TEMO** respectively (see also 4.6):

買って	買った (bought)	買ったら (if...buy)	買っても (even if...buy)
katte	**katta**	**kattara**	**kattemo**

The **-TE** form of adjectives ending in **-I** is created by replacing the final **I** of the plain form with **-KUTE**. Negative plain forms of verbs and adjectives end with **-NAI**. The **-TE** form of **-NAI** is **-NAKUTE**.

安い (cheap)	安くて	食べない	食べなくて
yasui	**yasukute**	**tabenai**	**tabenakute**

Note that **-TE** always becomes **-DE** after a noun or an adjectival noun. See the table above.

EXERCISE SET 1

Fill in the blanks in the chart with the **-TE** form of each word. Check your answers on page 200.

Verb, -I adjective, adjectival noun	-TE form
1. 会う **au** (to meet)	
2. 泣く **naku** (to cry)	
3. こぐ **kogu** (to row a boat)	
4. 指す **sasu** (to point)	
5. 立つ **tatsu** (to stand)	
6. 学ぶ **manabu** (to learn)	
7. 込む **komu** (to be crowded)	
8. 走る **hashiru** (to run)	
9. 寝る **neru** (to sleep)	
10. 勉強する **benkyō suru** (to study)	
11. 高い **takai** (high, expensive)	
12. ない **nai** (negative auxiliary)	
13. 食べない **tabenai** (to not eat)	
14. おいしくない **oishiku nai** (not delicious)	
15. 元気だ **genki da** (to be fine, healthy)	

🎧 2. Uses of the ～て -TE form of the verb

The **-TE** form is used in the following situations:

❶ Attendant circumstances

> 父は いつも リュックを 背負って 仕事に 行きます。
> **Chichi wa itsumo ryukku o seotte shigoto ni ikimasu.**
> *My father usually carries a backpack to work.*

> ここの レストランは 安くて おいしいです。
> **Kokono resutoran wa yasukute oishī desu.**
> *This restaurant is cheap and delicious.*

❷ A succession of events

The first event, indicated by the **-TE** form, precedes the second event, which occurs subsequently.

> 毎朝 起きて 散歩に 行きます。
> **Maiasa okite sanpo ni ikimasu.**
> *Every morning after I wake up I go for a walk.*

When the speaker emphasizes the temporal order of two events, **KARA** needs to be attached to **-TE**.

まず 乾杯を してから おしゃべりしましょう。
Mazu kanpai o shite kara oshaberi shimashō.
First, let's make a toast and then let's chat.

Thus, **-TE KARA** cannot be used when the temporal order of two events cannot be reversed.

INCORRECT: 父は ドアを 開けてから 出ていきました。
Chichi wa doa o akete kara deteikimashita.
My father went out after opening the door.

❸ Reason

The **-TE** form of the verb, **-I** adjective, adjectival noun or noun can express a reason for the result that follows.

地震が 起こって 怖かったです。
Jishin ga okotte kowakatta desu.
I was scared because there was an earthquake.

❹ Contrasted events

Two (or more) contrasted events which occur at the same time and at different places, or two (or more) contrasted situations, can be expressed by the **-TE** form. Note the sentence structures below. The **WA**-marked subject (topic) can be put inside the relevant **-TE** form phrase. **GA** can replace **WA** when the speaker wants to stress **GA**-marked subjects.

兄は[or が] 大学を 卒業して，私は[or が] 入学します。
Ani wa [or ga)]daigaku o sotsugyō shite, watashi wa [or ga] nyūgaku shimasu.
I'm starting university as my brother graduates.

寿司は(or が) おいしくて 納豆は(or が) まずいです。
Sushi wa (or ga) oishikute nattō wa (or ga) mazui desu.
Sushi is delicious and natto is awful.

EXERCISE SET 2

Use the prompts to translate the sentences into Japanese using the the **-TE** form. Suggested answers on page 200.

Example
I use my personal computer to write the report.
[USE:] パソコン／使う／レポート／書く。
pasokon / tsukau / repōto / kaku
パソコンを 使って レポートを 書きます。
Pasokon o tsukatte repōto o kakimasu.

❶ Attendant circumstances

I often listen to music while walking.
[USE:] よく／音楽／聞く／歩く
　　　yoku / ongaku / kiku / aruku

❷ A succession of events

He aims at the ball and hits it.
[USE:] ボール／狙う／打つ
  bōru / nerau / utsu

_____

❸ Reason

The exam is difficult and I don't know the answers.
[USE:] 試験／難しい／答え／分かる
  shiken / muzukashī / kotae / wakaru

_____

❹ Contrasted events

I brush my teeth while my sister puts on her makeup.
[USE:] ぼく／歯／磨く／お姉さん／化粧をする
  boku / ha / migaku / onēsan / keshō o suru

_____

🎧 3. Using 〜てみる -TE MIRU to express seeing how something goes

-TE MIRU is made of the **-TE** form of the verb + **MIRU** (to see). This phrase means to do something to see what it is like, how it goes or what result follows. It may mean to try doing something.

やって みます。
Yatte mimasu.
I'll try (doing) it. (i.e., I'll try doing it and see what result will follow.)

京都に 行って みたいです。
Kyōto ni itte mitai desu.
I'd like to visit Kyoto. (i.e., I'd like to go to Kyoto and see what it is like.)

EXERCISE SET 3
Translate the sentences using the prompts and **-TE MIRU**, as illustrated in the following example. Suggested answers are on page 200.

Example

I tried asking on the phone.
[USE:] 電話で／聞く
  denwa de / kiku

電話で 聞いてみました。
Denwa de kīte mimashita.

❶ *I tried working part-time for the first time.*
[USE:] 初めて／アルバイトをする
hajimete / arubaito o suru

_____

❷ *I tried seeing the cells with a microscope.*
[USE:] 顕微鏡／細胞／見る
kenbikyō / saibō / miru

_____

❸ *I tried consulting a doctor.*
[USE:] 医者／相談する
isha / sōdan suru

_____

🎧 4. Using ～てしまう -TE SHIMAU to express keeping or putting an end to something

The verb **shimau** means to put something somewhere in order to keep it, or to put an end to something, as follows:

パスポートを かばんに しまってください。
Pasupōto o kaban ni shimatte kudasai.
Please keep your passport in your bag.

道具を しまって 仕事を 終わりましょう。
Dōgu o shimatte shigoto o owarimashō.
Let's put away the tools and finish the job.

The **-TE** form + **SHIMAU** means that someone has completely done something or that someone has done something by mistake. The nuance of the two meanings depends on the context:

ペットの インコが 死んでしまいました。
Petto no inko ga shinde shimaimashita.
My pet lorikeet finally died.

みんな いなくなって しまいました（行って しまいました）。
Minna inaku natte shimaimashita (itte shimaimashita).
All of them have completely disappeared (have gone away).

うっかり 電車で 財布を 落としてしまいました。
Ukkari densha de saifu o otoshite shimaimashita.
I absent-mindedly dropped my purse in the train.

恋に 落ちて しまいました。
Koi ni ochite shimaimashita.
I fell in love (deeply or carelessly).

EXERCISE SET 4

Use the prompts to translate the sentence using **-TE SHIMAU**, as illustrated in the following example. Suggested answers on page 200.

> **Example**
>
> *My stocks have gone down.*
> [USE:] 株／下がる
> **kabu / sagaru**
>
> 株が下がってしまいました。
> **Kabu ga sagatte shimaimashita.**

❶ *I've got hay fever.*
[USE:] 花粉症／なる
kafunshō / naru

_____

❷ *I carelessly strained my shoulder.*
[USE:] 肩／痛める
kata / itameru

_____

❸ *I got tired and fell asleep.*
[USE:] 疲れる／寝る
tsukareru / neru

_____

けんじの　ある日

けんじは　自転車に　乗って　学校まで　行きます。だいたい 30 分 かかります。とても 遠いです。だから，今日は　遅刻して　しまいました。それに，急いでいて，うっかり 弁当を　忘れて　しまいました。お腹が　空いて，とても　困りました。授業が　終わって から，柔道部の　練習に　行きました。練習試合を　やってみました。お腹が　空いて しまって　負けて　しまいました。

Kenji no aru hi

Kenji wa jitensha ni notte gakkō made ikimasu. Daitai sanjuppun kakarimasu. Totemo tōi desu. Dakara, kyō wa chikoku shite shimaimashita. Sore ni, isoide ite, ukkari bentō o wasurete shimaimashita. Onaka ga suite, totemo komarimashita. Jugyō ga owatte kara, jūdōbu no renshū ni ikimashita. Renshū jiai o yatte mimashita. Onaka ga suite shimatte makete shimaimashita.

Kenji's Day

Kenji rides a bike to school. It takes about thirty minutes. It's very far. So today he ended up being late. Also, he carelessly forgot his bento lunch because he was in a hurry. He was hungry and it was awful. After lessons were over, he went to judo practice. He tried taking part in a practice match. He was hungrier than ever so he ended up losing the game.

QUESTIONS

Answers with their suggested sentence structure can be found on page 200.

1. けんじは　どうやって　学校へ　行きますか。
   Kenji wa dōyatte gakkō e ikimasu ka.

2. けんじは　急いで　いて　どうしましたか。
   Kenji wa isoide ite dō shimashita ka.

3. 柔道部の　練習で　何を　しましたか。また，どう　なりましたか。
   Jūdōbu no renshū de nani o shimashita ka. Mata, dō narimashita ka.

CHAPTER 1

This Is the Mobile Game I Often Play
これは 私が よく する モバゲーです

Using Verbs to Modify Nouns

In Japanese you can modify a noun by simply placing the plain form of the verb directly in front of the noun. In this chapter you'll learn how to modify nouns in present, past, negative and continuous situations. When you've mastered the modifying forms in this chapter, you'll be surprised at how much this allows you to extend your range of expressions.

🎧 KEY SENTENCE PATTERNS

1. これは 私が よく する モバゲーです。
   Kore wa watashi ga yoku suru mobagē desu. *Dictionary form of the verb + NOUN*
   This is the mobile game I often play.

2. 私が 使う タブレットは アンドロイドです。
   Watashi ga tsukau taburetto wa andoroido desu. *Dictionary form of the verb + NOUN*
   The tablet I use has the Android operating system.

3. これは 格安チケット・ショップで 買った 切符です。
   Kore wa kakuyasu chiketto shoppu de katta kippu desu. *-TA form of the verb + NOUN*
   This is the ticket I bought at a discount ticket shop.

4. 今 乗っている 電車は 特急じゃなくて 準急です。
   Ima notteiru densha wa tokkyū ja nakute junkyū desu. *-TE IRU form of the verb + NOUN*
   The train we are riding now is not a limited express but a local express.

Formation of the Modified Noun Phrase

	-MASU Form	→	Dictionary Form + Example Noun			
-U Verbs	読みます **yomimasu**	→	読む **yom<u>u</u>**	+ 本 + **hon**	読む本 **yomu hon**	a book to read
-RU Verbs ①	あげます **agemasu**	→	あげる <u>**ageru**</u>	+ お土産 + **omiyage**	あげるお土産 **ageru omiyage**	a souvenir to give (you)
-RU Verbs ②	見ます **mimasu**	→	見る **m<u>iru</u>**	+ アニメ + **anime**	見るアニメ **miru anime**	an anime to see
Irregular Verbs	します **shimasu**	→	する **suru**	+ こと + **koto**	すること **suru koto**	things to do
	来ます **kimasu**	→	来る **kuru**	+ 時 + **toki**	来る時 **kuru toki**	when (someone) comes

GRAMMAR AND USAGE NOTES

1.1 Verb conjugations

The dictionary form of the verb is used to modify nouns, so let's start this chapter by reviewing the dictionary form and its conjugations. Below, the dictionary form of each type of Japanese verb is given on the left, and the conjugations for this type of verb are given on the right.

❶ -U Verbs

Verbs of this type are also known as **go-dan** verbs (five-step verbs) as they conjugate into five different forms following the pattern below:

書く **kaku** (to write)

1st step **kak<u>a</u>-** (precedes **nai**, **reru**, etc.)
2nd step **kak<u>i</u>-** (precedes **masu**, etc.)
3rd step **kak<u>u</u>** [dictionary form] (precedes noun)
4th step **kak<u>e</u>-** [command form] (precedes **ba**, etc.)
5th step **kak<u>o</u>-** (precedes **o** as in **kakō**, etc.)

❷ -RU Verbs

Verbs of this type are also known as **ichi-dan** verbs (one-step verbs) because the front part (or stem) of the verb does not vary when it is conjugated. These verbs are divided into two categories: verbs ending in **-ERU**, and verbs ending in **-IRU**.

① **-ERU** verbs (the dictionary form ends with **-ERU**.)

あげる **ageru** (to raise, give)

age-(**masu/nai/te/nagara/rareru/yō**, etc.)
age-**ru** [dictionary form] (precedes noun)
age-**re** (precedes **ba**, etc.)
age-**ro** (command form)

② **-IRU** verbs (the dictionary form ends with **-IRU**.)

見る **miru** (to see)

mi-(**masu/nai/te/nagara/rareru/yō**, etc.)
mi-**ru** [dictionary form] (precedes noun)
mi-**re** (precedes **ba**, etc.)
mi-**ro** (command form)

❸ Irregular Verbs

The two main irregular verbs in Japanese are **suru** and **kuru**.

① する **suru** (to do)

- **sa-(reru**, etc.)
- **shi-(masu/ nai/te/nagara/yō**, etc.)
- **suru** [dictionary form] (precedes noun)
- **su<u>re</u>** (precedes **ba**, etc.)
- **shi<u>ro</u>** (command form)

② 来る **kuru** (to come)

- **ko- (nai/zuni**, etc.)
- **ki-(masu/te/nagara**, etc.)
- **kuru** [dictionary form] (precedes noun)
- **ku<u>re</u>** (precedes **ba**, etc.)
- **koi** [command form]
- **koyō** [volitional form]

EXERCISE SET 1

Fill in the blanks in the chart with the dictionary form of the verb. Check your answers on page 200.

-MASU form	Dictionary form
1. 旅行 します **ryokō shimasu** (to travel)	
2. 読みます **yomimasu** (to read)	
3. 走ります **hashirimasu** (to run)	
4. 起きます **okimasu** (to get up)	
5. 寝ます **nemasu** (to sleep)	
6. 食べます **tabemasu** (to eat)	
7. 作ります **tsukurimasu** (to make)	
8. 買います **kaimasu** (to buy)	
9. 飲みます **nomimasu** (to drink)	
10. 予約します **yoyaku shimasu** (to reserve)	

1.2   Using the dictionary form to modify a noun

The square-bracketed phrase ending with the dictionary form modifies the noun that follows.

〜ます。 → [dictionary form] + NOUN
sentence with a period   modified noun phrase

よく ゲームを します。 → ［よく する］ゲーム
yoku gēmu o shimasu   **[yoku suru] gēmu**
I often play games.   *the games [that I often play]*

The polite **-MASU** form usually does not modify the noun that follows.

INCORRECT: [よく　します] ゲーム
[yoku shimasu] gēmu

The noun phrase containing the modified noun behaves as an element (the subject, the object, etc.) of the sentence.

[友だちと　よく　する　ゲーム]　　は　将棋　です。
[Tomodachi to yoku suru gēmu]　　wa shōgi desu.
[The game I often play with my friends] is shogi.
　　　(= the subject)

私も　　　　[あなたが　買った　タブレット]　を　買います。
Watashi mo　[anata ga katta taburetto]　　o　kaimasu.
I will also buy [the tablet you bought].
　　　　　　(= the object)

EXERCISE SET 2

Rephrase the following sentences so that the verb modifies the noun, as illustrated in the example. See suggested answers on page 200.

Example: ここに　荷物を　置きます。→　　　ここに　置く　荷物　は　スーツケース　です。
Koko ni nimotsu o okimasu. (sūtsu kēsu) → Koko ni oku nimotsu wa sūtsu kēsu desu.
　　　　　　　　　　　　　　　　　　　　　The bag you put here is a suitcase.

❶ 友だちと　毎週　スポーツを　します。（テニス）
Tomodachi to maishū supōtsu o shimasu. (tenisu)

_____ は _____ 。

❷ 夜中に　ネットで　音楽を　聞きます。（ジャズ）
Yonaka ni netto de ongaku o kikimasu. (jazu)

_____ は _____ 。

❸ 彼女に　おみやげを　あげます。（チョコレート）
Kanojo ni omiyage o agemasu. (chokorēto)

_____ は _____ 。

❹ よく　マンガを　読みます。（ドラゴンボール）
Yoku manga o yomimasu. (doragonbōru)

_____ は _____ 。

❺ ときどき　和食を　食べます。（すし）
Tokidoki washoku o tabemasu. (sushi)

_____ は _____ 。

🎧 1.3 Other verb and adjective forms used to modify nouns

The other plain forms of the verb/adjective can also modify the noun that follows.

❶ In the case of verbs

Plain Form of Verb	Modifying Form
	-U /-RU form (present form)
	-TA form (past form)
	-NAI form (negative form)
	-TE IRU form (progressive form)

NOTE: IRU of the **-TE IRU** progressive form of the verb is in fact the dictionary form. In the same way, you can consider **-TE ITA** and **-TE INAI** to be the **-TA** form and **-NAI** form respectively.

Example: 私が している ゲーム は RPG* です。 *The game I am playing is an RPG.*
Watashi ga shite iru gēmu wa āru pī jī desu.   *RPG = role-playing game

❷ In the case of adjectives

Plain Form of Adjective	Modifying Form
	-I (present form)
	-KATTA form (past form)
	-KUNAI form (negative form)

Example: 重くない スーツケースが いいです。 *The suitcase that is not heavy is better.*
Omokunai sūtsu kēsu ga ī desu.

❸ In the case of adjectival nouns

Plain Form of Adjectival Noun	Modifying Form
	adjectival noun + **NA**/ noun + **NO**
	-DATTA form (past form)
	-JA NAI form (negative form)

Example: 病気だった 父が 今は元気です。 *My father, who was sick, is now okay.*
Byōki datta chichi ga ima wa genki desu.

🎧 1.4 Example verb forms used in modified sentences

In each sentence, the bracketed phrase containing the plain form of the verb (**-TA** form, **-NAI** form, etc.) modifies the noun that follows. Note that the modified noun is not always the object of the action expressed by the verb, as shown in examples ❷-❽.

❶ **-TA** form + NOUN:
      [私が きのう 見た お寺] は 清水寺です。
      [Watashi ga kinō mita otera] wa kiyomizudera desu.
      The temple I saw yesterday was Kiyomizudera.

❷ **-TA** form + NOUN:

［私が <u>きのう 着いた 空港</u>］ は 関空です。

[Watashi ga <u>kinō tsuita kūkō</u>] wa kankū desu.

The airport I arrived at yesterday was Kanku.

❸ **TE-IRU** form + NOUN:

［猫が <u>寝ている テーブル</u>］ は 「こたつ」と 言います。

[Neko ga <u>nete iru tēburu</u>] wa "kotatsu" to īmasu.

The table where cats sleep is called a kotatsu.

❹ **TE-IRU** form + NOUN:

［コンビニで <u>アルバイトをしている 学生</u>］は リーさんです。

[Konbini de <u>arubaito o shite iru gakusei</u>] wa rī san desu.

The student who is working part-time in a convenience store is Lee.

❺ **-TE ITA** form + NOUN:

［<u>ホームステイを していた 町</u>］は 神戸です。

[<u>Hōmusutei o shite ita machi</u>] wa kōbe desu.

The city where I did a homestay was Kobe.

❻ **-NAI** form + NOUN:

［日本で 雨が <u>あまり 降らない 季節</u>］は いつですか。

[Nihon de ame ga <u>amari furanai kisetsu</u>] wa itsu desu ka.

What is <u>the season when it hardly ever rains</u> in Japan?

❼ DICTIONARY form + NOUN:

［<u>たこ焼きを 食べる 爪楊枝</u>］は ありますか。

[<u>Takoyaki o taberu tsumayōji</u>] wa arimasu ka.

Do you have <u>a toothpick to eat takoyaki with</u>?

❽ **-NAKATTA** form (the past negative form) + NOUN:

今度また ［<u>今回 写真を 撮らなかった 神社</u>］に 行きます。

Kondo mata [<u>konkai shashin o toranakatta jinja</u>] ni ikimasu.

Next time I'll go back to <u>the shrines whose photos I didn't take</u> this time.

NOTE: The following phrase "the way to the station" is frequently and commonly used.

［<u>駅へ 行く 道</u>］を 教えてください。

[<u>Eki e iku michi</u>] o oshiete kudasai.

Please tell me <u>the way to the station</u>.

EXERCISE SET 3

Match each structure in the sentences ❶-❽ above with a sentence that has the same structure from the list （ア）–（ク）on the facing page. Answers on page 200.

❶	❷	❸	❹	❺	❻	❼	❽

（ア） 味噌汁を 飲む スプーンが ほしいです。
Misoshiru o nomu supūn ga hoshī desu.
I want a spoon to eat miso soup with.

（イ） よく 聞く 音楽は J-Pop です。
Yoku kiku ongaku wa jei poppu desu.
The music I often listen to is J-Pop.

（ウ） いつも 買い物に行く デパートは 三越です。
Itsumo kaimono ni iku depāto wa mitsukoshi desu.
The department store I usually go to is Mitsukoshi.

（エ） 祖母が 生まれた年は 明治 20 年です。
Sobo ga umareta toshi wa meiji ni jū nen desu.
The year my grandmother was born is Meiji 20.

（オ） よく コーヒーを 飲む 店は スターバックスです。
Yoku kōhī o nomu mise wa sutābakkusu desu.
The shop where I often drink coffee is Starbucks.

（カ） 財布を なくした 学生は だれですか。
Saifu o nakushita gakusei wa dare desu ka.
Who is the student who lost their wallet?

（キ） 私が 電話番号を 知っている 日本人学生は まゆみです。
Watashi ga denwa bangō o shitte iru nihonjin gakusei wa mayumi desu.
The Japanese student whose telephone number I know is Mayumi.

（ク） 電車の 中で 荷物を 置く 棚は 「網棚」 と 言います。
Densha no naka de nimotsu o oku tana wa "amidana" to īmasu.
The rack where you put your luggage on the train is called an amidana.

EXERCISE SET 4

Use the prompts to create sentences where the noun is modified with the **-TA** form of the verb, as illustrated in the following example. See suggested answers on page 200.

> **Example**
>
> [USE:] 私/テレビ/ 買う/有機 EL
> **Watashi / terebi / kau / yūki īeru**
>
> 私が買ったテレビは有機 ELです。
> **Watashi ga katta terebi wa yūki īeru desu.**
> *The TV that I bought is an OLED one.*

❶ [USE:] 父／パソコン／買う／ウィンドウズテン
chichi /pasokon / kau / windōzu 10

_____ は _____ です。

❷ [USE:] 彼ら／毎日／スポーツ／練習する／剣道
karera / mainichi / supōtsu / renshū suru / kendō

_____ は _____ です。

❸ [USE:] けんじ／写真／取る／電車／新幹線
kenji / shashin / toru / densha / shinkansen

_____ は _____ です。

❹ [USE:] 東京／私たち／お寺／訪れる／浅草寺
tōkyō / watashitachi / otera / otozureru / sensōji

_____ は _____ です。

❺ [USE:] 毎日／食べる／うどん／きつねうどん
mainichi / taberu / udon / kitsune udon

_____ は _____ です。

🎧 1.5 Example adjective and adjectival noun forms used in modified sentences

The square-bracketed phrases below containing the plain form of the adjective (dictionary form, **-TA** form, **-NAI** form, etc.) modify the noun that follows. Note that the modified noun is not always the subject of the state expressed by the adjective, as in ❷ and ❸.

❶ DICTIONARY form + NOUN:
[駅に 近いアパート] は いいです。
[Eki ni <u>chikai</u> apāto]   wa ī desu.
The apartment block that is near the station is good.

❷ **-TA** form + NOUN:
[サービスが よかった店] には また 行きます。
[Sābisu ga <u>yokatta</u> mise]   ni wa mata ikimasu.
I will go back to the shop where the service was good.

❸ **-NAI** form + NOUN:
[値段が あまり 高くない レストラン]に 行きましょう。
[Nedan ga amari takaku<u>nai</u> resutoran]   ni ikimashō.
Let's go to the restaurant where the prices are not so high.

❹ **NA** form + NOUN:
[おいしい ビーフで 有名な 町] は 神戸です。
[Oishī bīfu de yūmei <u>na</u> machi]   wa kōbe desu.
The city that is famous for delicious beef is Kobe.

EXERCISE SET 5

Translate the sentences using "... **GA** + adjective/(adjectival) noun + noun," and the key words indicated, as in the following example. See suggested answers on page 200.

I bought a TV with a large screen.
画面／大きい／テレビ／買う
gamen / ōkī / terebi / kau

画面が 大きい テレビを 買いました。
Gamen ga ōkī terebi o kaimashita.

❶ *I ate takoyaki that had big pieces of octopus.*
[USE:] たこ／とても／大きい／たこ焼き／食べる
    tako / totemo / ōkī / takoyaki / taberu

_____

❷ *We went to a park where the cherry blossoms are beautiful.*
[USE:] 私たち／桜／きれい／公園／行く
    watashitachi / sakura / kirei / kōen / iku

_____

🎧 CONVERSATION PRACTICE

ビールのブランド

けんじ： いつも よく 飲む ビールのブランド は 何ですか。
マイク： 僕が よく 飲む ブランドは キリンですね。
けんじ： 僕が いつも 買う ビールは アサヒです。
よう子： 私は ブランドは 気にしません。みんな おいしいです。
         サッポロも 飲みます。
マイク： 発泡酒は 安いですね。味も ビールと 同じぐらい おいしいですね。
よう子： 最近は 第三のビールが 格安です。みんな おいしくて，私は 種類を
         気にしません。(笑)
けんじ： 僕は やっぱり ビールが いいです。

Bīru no burando

Kenji: **Itsumo yoku nomu bīru no burando wa nan desu ka.**
Mike: **Boku ga yoku nomu burando wa kirin desu ne.**
Kenji: **Boku ga itsumo kau bīru wa asahi desu.**
Yoko: **Watashi wa burando wa ki ni shimasen. Minna oishī desu. Sapporo mo nomimasu.**
Mike: **Happōshu wa yasui desu ne. Aji mo bīru to onaji gurai oishī desu ne.**
Yoko: **Saikin wa daisan no bīru ga kakuyasu desu. Minna oishikute, watashi wa shurui o ki ni shimasen. (wara)**
Kenji: **Boku wa yappari bīru ga ī desu.**

Beer Brands

Kenji: What brand of beer do you always drink?

Mike: A brand I often drink is Kirin.

Kenji: The beer I always buy is Asahi.

Yoko: I don't care about the brand. Any brand is delicious. I also drink Sapporo.

Mike: Low-malt beer is cheap, isn't it? It tastes as good as beer.

Yoko: Daisan beer [*a beer-flavored beverage*] is cheap these days. They're all delicious and I don't care which kind. (LOL)

Kenji: After all that, a beer might be good!

TASK

Create a dialogue with "plain form + noun" as illustrated in the example and practice it.

五郎：　さっき 聞いていた 音楽は 何ですか。

よう子：あ，スピッツの 「ロビンソン」 です。軽快な リズムの いい曲ですよ。

Goro: **Sakki kīte ita ongaku wa nan desu ka.**

Yoko: **A, supittsu no "robinson" desu. Keikai na rizumu no ī kyoku desu yo.**

_____ : _____ は 何ですか。

_____ : _____ です。 _____。

🎧 READING PRACTICE

格安チケット

私は 先週 羽田空港に 着きました。羽田空港は 東京に 近くて，すぐに 着きました。京急線で 品川駅まで 10分ちょっとで，便利です。

銀座は 東京駅から 近いです。そこへ 歩いて 買い物に 行きました。20分ぐらいで 着きました。途中で いろいろな店を 見て，ウインドー・ショッピングを 楽しみました。それから，また 東京駅に 戻って，新幹線で 大阪まで 来ました。その時 私が 乗った新幹線は 「のぞみ」 でした。ジャパン・レール・パスは ジェイ・アール (JR) の 電車

に 乗り放題の 切符です。でも「のぞみ」は だめです。それに、ジャパン・レール・パスは 観光客が買う切符です。私は 留学生で、買いませんでした。

格安チケット売り場で 少し安く 切符を売っています。だから、駅の窓口では 買いませんでした。

Kakuyasu chiketto

Watashi wa senshū haneda kūkō ni tsukimashita. Haneda kūkō wa tōkyō ni chikakute, sugu ni tsukimashita. Keikyū sen de shinagawa eki made juppun chotto de, benri desu.

Ginza wa tōkyō eki kara chikai desu. Soko e aruite kaimono ni ikimashita. Ni juppun gurai de tsukimashita. Tochū de iroiro na mise o mite, uindō shoppingu o tanoshimimashita.

Sorekara, mata tōkyō eki ni modotte, shinkansen de ōsaka made kimashita. Sono toki, watashi ga notta shinkansen wa "nozomi" deshita. Japan rēru pasu wa jeiāru no densha ni norihōdai no kippu desu. Demo, "nozomi" wa dame desu. Soreni, japan rēru pasu wa kankōkyaku ga kau kippu desu. Watashi wa ryūgakusei de, kaimasen deshita.

Kakuyasu chiketto uriba de sukoshi yasuku kippu o utte imasu. Dakara, eki no madoguchi de wa kaimasen deshita.

Cheap Tickets

I arrived at Haneda Airport last week. Haneda Airport is close to Tokyo, so I got there quickly. It is a little over 10 minutes to Shinagawa Station on the Keikyu line, so it is convenient.

Ginza is near Tokyo Station. I walked there to go shopping. I got there in about 20 minutes. I saw various stores on the way and enjoyed window-shopping.

After that, I returned to Tokyo Station and came to Osaka by bullet train. The bullet train I took was the "Nozomi." A Japan Rail Pass is an unlimited-ride ticket for JR trains. But you can't ride on the "Nozomi." And only tourists can buy this pass. I am a foreign student, so I didn't buy it.

There are cheap ticket counters where you can buy low-price tickets. So I didn't buy my ticket at the station ticket office.

QUESTIONS

Answers with their suggested sentence structure can be found on page 200.

1. この人は 何空港に 来ましたか。また、なぜ その空港へ 来ましたか。
   Kono hito wa nani kūkō ni kimashita ka. Mata, naze sono kūkō e kimashita ka.

2. この人は どこで 何をして 楽しみましたか。
   Kono hito wa doko de nani o shite tanoshimimashita ka.

3. 乗り放題の 切符は どんな切符ですか。
   Norihōdai no kippu wa donna kippu desu ka.

4. この人が 買った切符は どんな切符ですか。
   Kono hito ga katta kippu wa donna kippu desu ka.

CHAPTER 2

I Can Write About 100 Kanji

私は 漢字が 百字ぐらい 書けます

Using the Potential Form of the Verb

A "potential" verb conveys one's ability (or inability) to do something. In this chapter you'll learn how to talk about what can and can't be done using a variety of constructions: the **-ARERU** verb form; the potential idiom **KOTO GA DEKIRU**; the verbs **MIERU** (to be visible) and **KIKOERU** (to be audible); and the verbs of saying and thinking, **TO IERU**, **TO KANGAERARERU** and **TO OMOWARERU**. You'll also learn how to ask politely if you can do something.

勉強　大学

🎧 KEY SENTENCE PATTERNS

1. 私は 漢字が 百字ぐらい 書けます。
   Watashi wa kanji ga hyakuji gurai kakemasu.　　Potential form of the **-U** verb
   I can write about 100 kanji.

2. 私は 刺身は 食べられません。納豆は 大丈夫です。
   Watashi wa sashimi wa taberaremasen. Nattō wa daijōbu desu.　　Potential form of the **-RU** verb
   I cannot eat sashimi. Natto is ok.

3. 私は マニュアル・ミッションの車が 運転できます。
   Watashi wa manyuaru misshon no kuruma ga unten dekimasu.　　Potential form of **SURU**
   I can drive a car with a manual transmission.

4. このホテルは ネットで 予約する ことができます。
   Kono hoteru wa netto de yoyaku suru koto ga dekimasu.　　The potential idiom
   You can reserve this hotel on the Internet.

Formation of the Potential Form

		Potential Forms	
-U Verbs	書きます／書く	→ 書けます／書ける	
	kakimasu / kaku	**kakemasu / kakeru**	
-RU Verbs ①	見ます／見る	→ 見られます／見られる	
	mimasu / miru	**miraremasu / mirareru**	insert **-rare**
-RU Verbs ②	寝ます／寝る	→ 寝られます／寝られる	
	nemasu / neru	**neraremasu / nerareru**	insert **-rare**
Irregular Verbs	します／する	→ できます／できる	
	shimasu / suru	**dekimasu / dekiru**	
	来ます／来る	→ 来られます／来られる	
	kimasu / kuru	**koraremasu / korareru**	

GRAMMAR AND USAGE NOTES

2.1 The potential form using -ARERU

The verb ending **-ARERU** is used with **-U** verbs and **-RU** verbs to express potential. In principle, **-ARERU** follows the front part of the dictionary form without the **U**.

❶ **-U** Verbs

書く **kaku** (to write)
kak- + **areru** → ***kakareru** → **kakeru** (can write)
Replace the last letter of the dictionary form with **e** and add **ru**. It becomes an **-RU** verb.
*Kakareru has become **kakeru** in modern Japanese.

❷ **-RU** Verbs

見る **miru** (to see)
mir- + **areru** → **mirareru** → ***mireru** (can see)
*This type of potential form is slang, but widely used by young people.

❸ Irregular verbs

① する **suru** → できる **dekiru** (can do; can perform; can play; can accomplish, etc.)
In many cases **dekiru** takes the **ga**-marked object rather than the **o**-marked object:

柔道が できますか。 **Jūdō ga dekimasuka.** *Can you do judo?*

② 来る **kuru** → 来られる **korareru** → *来れる **koreru** (can come)
*Koreru is slang but is more widely used than **mireru** above, by older people too.

時間通りに 来れますか。 **Jikan dōri ni koremasuka.** *Can you come on time?*

NOTE: GA is used rather than **O** as the object marker before the potential form of the verb.

POSSIBLE:	日本語を 少し 話せます。	**Nihongo o sukoshi hanasemasu.**
BETTER:	日本語が 少し 話せます。	**Nihongo ga sukoshi hanasemasu.**
		I can speak Japanese a little.

EXERCISE SET 1

Fill in the blanks with the potential form of the verb. Check your answers on page 201.

-MASU form	Potential form
1. 読みます **yomimasu** (to read)	
2. 走ります **hashirimasu** (to run)	
3. 起きます **okimasu** (to get up)	
4. 行きます **ikimasu** (to go)	
5. 買います **kaimasu** (to buy)	
6. 出ます **demasu** (to go out)	
7. 入ります **hairimasu** (to enter)	
8. 歩きます **arukimasu** (to walk)	
9. 持ちます **mochimasu** (to have)	
10. 予約します **yoyaku shimasu** (to reserve)	

🎧 2.2 The potential idiom ことが できる KOTO GA DEKIRU

The phrase **KOTO GA DEKIRU** is another way of expressing potential. It is used in slightly more formal situations. The object is not marked by **GA** but by **O**. The structure is as follows:

O + dictionary form of the verb + **KOTO GA DEKIRU**

私は 上手に アニメのキャラクターを 描く ことが できます。
Watashi wa jōzu ni anime no kyarakutā o kaku koto ga dekimasu.
I can draw anime characters well.

Note that the above sentence is a more formal version of **anime no kyarakutā ga kakemasu.**

In many cases **KOTO GA DEKIRU** can be used by the speaker to ask for permission.

仏像の 写真を 撮る ことが できますか。
Butsuzō no shashin o toru koto ga dekimasu ka.   *May I take a photo of the Buddhist statue?*

For more personal types of permission involving the consent of another, **-TEMO Ī DESU KA** is better.

CORRECT:　（あなたの）写真を 撮っても いいですか。
　　　　　　(Anata no) shashin o tottemo ī desu ka. *May I take a photo of you?*
INCORRECT: （あなたの）写真を 撮る ことが できますか。
　　　　　　(Anata no) shashin o toru koto ga dekimasu ka.

A negative sentence using **KOTO GA DEKIMASEN** occasionally expresses prohibition, especially when the subject is "we," "you," or "they."

路上で たばこを 吸うことが できません。
Rojō de tabako o sū koto ga dekimasen. *You must not smoke on the street.*

EXERCISE SET 2

Fill in the blanks with the **KOTO GA DEKIRU** form of the verb. Check your answers on page 201.

-MASU form	-KOTO GA DEKIRU form
1. 出発します **shuppatsu shimasu** (to depart)	
2. 読みます **yomimasu** (to read)	
3. 起きます **okimasu** (to get up)	
4. 行きます **ikimasu** (to go)	
5. 出ます **demasu** (to go out)	
6. 持ちます **mochimasu** (to have)	
7. 予約します **yoyaku shimasu** (to reserve)	

EXERCISE SET 3

Use the pictures and the prompts to create sentences with (a) the potential form and (b) the potential idiom **KOTO GA DEKIRU.** See suggested answers on page 201.

❶ ユキさん／なわとび/100回連続
Yuki san / nawatobi / 100 kai renzoku

(a) _____

(b) _____

❷ 私／ うまく／グラフを かく
watashi / umaku / gurafu o kaku

(a) _____

(b) _____

❸ けんじ／ シングルスの試合／太郎／勝つ
Kenji / shingurusu no shiai / Taro / katsu

(a) _____

(b) _____

EXERCISE SET 4

Translate the dialogues as illustrated in the following example.
Use **KOTO GA DEKIMASU/DEKIMASEN.** See suggested answers on page 201.

Example

May I smoke here?
ここで たばこを 吸うことが できますか。
Koko de tabako o sū koto ga dekimasu ka.

No, you may not smoke here.
いいえ、 ここで<u>は</u> たばこを 吸うことが できません。
Īe, koko de <u>wa</u> tabako o sū koto ga dekimasen.

NOTE: The above は **wa** performs the function of a contrast marker,
implying that you can smoke somewhere else.

---

❶ *Can I use my phone in the train? No, you can't.*

_____

_____

❷ *Can I photograph the display items in the art gallery? No, you can't.*

_____

_____

❸ *Can I throw the plastic bottle in that bin? No you can't.*

_____

_____

🎧 2.3 The potential verbs 見える MIERU and 聞こえる KIKOERU

Note that there are two special potential verbs 見える **MIERU** and 聞こえる **KIKOERU** that are
distinct from the potential forms 見られる **MIRARERU** and 聞ける **KIKERU.**

❶ 見える　　**MIERU**　to be visible
MIERU implies that an object comes into your vision regardless of your will to see it. That is
why the object takes the particle **GA**, which is used to mark things that are being mentioned
for the first time. If you intentionally make an effort to see something or if you can see it
because of your good eyesight, **MIRARERU** is more suitable.

新幹線のＥ席からは 富士山が よく見えます。
Shinkansen no ī seki kara wa fujisan ga yoku miemasu.
Mount Fuji can be seen well from seat E in the bullet train.

人ごみで 祭りの ぎゅうしゃが 見えません。
Hito gomi de matsuri no gyūsha ga miemasen.
I can't see the festival oxcart because of the crowd.

❷ 聞こえる　**KIKOERU**　to be audible
KIKOERU implies that the sound of something comes into your ears regardless of your will to hear it. The thing that is being heard is marked by the particle **GA**. If you can hear something after trying to hear it or because of your good hearing, **KIKERU** is more suitable.

虫の声が 聞こえますか。
Mushi no koe ga kikoemasu ka.
Can you hear the sound of the insects?

Compare the following forms of **MIERU/MIRARERU** and **KIKERU/KIKOERU**:

見えますか。	**Miemasu ka.**	*Can you see it?/Is it visible to you?*
見られますか。	**Miraremasu ka.**	*Can you see it?/May I see it?* (asking about chance or possibility) *Will you see it?* (asking respectfully)
見ることが できますか。	**Miru koto ga dekimasu ka.**	*May I see it?* (asking for permission) *Can you see it?*
見ても いいですか。	**Mitemo ī desu ka.**	*May I see it?* (asking for permission)
聞こえますか。	**Kikoemasu ka.**	*Can you hear it/me?/Is it audible (to you)?*
聞けますか。	**Kikemasu ka.**	*Can I listen to it?* (asking about chance or possibility)
聞くことが できますか。	**Kiku koto ga dekimasu ka.**	*May I hear it?* (asking for permission) *Can you hear it?*
聞いても いいですか。	**Kitemo ī desu ka.**	*May I listen to it?* (asking for permission)

EXERCISE SET 5
Look at the pictures and create sentences using **MIERU** or **KIKOERU**. Suggested answers on page 201.

❶ [USE:] きれいな／満月
kirei na / mangetsu

_____

❷ [USE:] チェロ／美しい／音色／部屋から
chero / utsukushī / neiro / heya kara

_____

🎧 2.4 The potential verbs と 言える TO IERU, と 考えられる TO KANGAERARERU and と 思われる TO OMOWARERU

The above three verb phrases are the potential forms of saying, thinking and guessing in formal written style.

❶ と 言える **TO IERU** *It can be said that.../We can say that.../It is considered that...*

> 最近は 結婚をしたくない 若い人が 増えている と言える。
> **Saikin wa kekkon o shitakunai wakai hito ga fuete iru to ieru.**
> *It can be said that the number of young people who do not want to marry is increasing.*

❷ と 考えられる **TO KANGAERARERU** *It can be thought that...* (**kangaeru** means to think, consider)

> 洪水の原因は 地球温暖化だと 考えられる。
> **Kōzui no gen'in wa chikyū ondanka da to kangaerareru.**
> *It can be thought that the cause of the flood is global warming.*

❸ と 思われる **TO OMOWARERU** *It can be thought that...* (**omou** means to think, to predict)

> 戦争が 起こるとは 思われない。
> **Sensō ga okoru to wa omowarenai.**
> *It is unthinkable that a war may occur.*

EXERCISE SET 6
Use one of the phrases **TO IERU**, **TO KANGAERARERU** or **TO OMOWARERU** and create your own sentence.   Compare your sentence with the examples given on page 201.

🎧 CONVERSATION PRACTICE

温泉

けんじ： マイクさん、温泉に 入れますか。
マイク： はい、入れると 思います。
けんじ： みんなと 一緒に 裸で 入れますか。
マイク： みんなと 裸で 入ったことが ありません。でも、大丈夫
　　　　 でしょう。
けんじ： じゃ、今から 入りましょう。
マイク： こうやって 入りますね。
けんじ： あ、ダメですね。タオルを 浸けて 入ることが できません。
マイク： え、なぜですか。
けんじ： お風呂の お湯が 汚れますね。湯船は 暖まるところです。
マイク： じゃ、どこで 洗えますか。
けんじ： 湯船の 外で 洗えます。湯船の 中で 洗うことが できません。
マイク： そうですか。タオルは どうしたら いいですか。
けんじ： タオルは 頭の上に 乗せて 入ることができますよ。

Onsen

Kenji: Maiku san, onsen ni hairemasu ka.
Mike: Hai, haireru to omoimasu.
Kenji: Minna to isshoni hadaka de hairemasu ka.
Mike: Minna to hadaka de haitta koto ga arimasen. Demo daijōbu deshō.
Kenji: Ja, ima kara hairimashō.
Mike: Kō yatte hairimasu ne.
Kenji: A, dame desu ne. Taoru o tsukete hairu koto ga dekimasen.
Mike: E, naze desu ka.
Kenji: Ofuro no oyu ga yogoremasu ne. Yubune wa atatamaru tokoro desu.
Mike: Ja, doko de araemasu ka.
Kenji: Yubune no soto de araemasu. Yubune no naka de arau koto ga dekimasen.
Mike: Sō desu ka. Taoru wa dō shitara ī desu ka.
Kenji: Taoru wa atama no ue ni nosete hairu koto ga dekimasu yo.

A Hot-Spring Bath

Kenji: Can you get into a hot-spring bath, Mike?
Mike: Yes, I think so.
Kenji: Can you go in naked with us?
Mike: I haven't been in one naked with other people. But it will probably be OK.
Kenji: Then let's get in right now.
Mike: I can go in like this, right?
Kenji: Oh, that's not right. You can't get in wearing a towel.
Mike: What? Why?
Kenji: It will make the bath water dirty. The bathtub is just for warming yourself.
Mike: Then where can I wash myself?
Kenji: You can wash yourself outside the bathtub. You cannot wash in the bathtub.
Mike: Really? What should I do with my towel?
Kenji: You can get in the bath with your towel on your head.

TASK

Create a dialogue with the potential form and practice it.

_____ : _____

_____ : _____

🎧 READING PRACTICE

漢字とオノマトペ

日本語の新聞には むずかしい漢字が 本当に たくさん あります。だから まだ 私は 日本語の新聞が 読めません。もっと 漢字を 覚えなければなりません。今は 1日に 漢字を 3つ 覚えられます。まだ新聞を 読んだり、レポートを 書いたりできません。

でも 新聞が 読めなくても いいです。実は 今 マンガを 読んでいます。私でも マンガは 読むことができます。マンガの絵を 見て、話を 理解することが できます。

マンガの中に 理解できない言葉が たくさん あります。それは 人間の 気持ちや 様子や 音を 表す言葉です。これは 「オノマトペ」と 言います。音を 表す 言葉は 少し 分かります。

例えば、銃を 撃つ 音は 「ズドーン」で、感じがつかめます。でも、気持ちや 様子を 表す 言葉は むずかしいです。例えば、「ドキドキ」や「ざわざわ」 などです。マンガを 読むとき オノマトペの 意味は 絵で つかめます。マンガは 日本語の オノマトペの 教科書と 言えます。

Kanji to onomatope

Nihongo no shinbun ni wa muzukashī kanji ga hontō ni takusan arimasu. Dakara, mada watashi wa nihongo no shinbun ga yomemasen. Motto kanji o oboenakereba narimasen. Ima wa ichi nichi ni kanji o mittsu oboeraremasu. Mada shinbun o yondari, repōto o kaitari dekimasen.

Demo shinbun ga yomenakutemo ī desu. Jitsu wa ima manga o yonde imasu. Watashi demo manga wa yomu koto ga dekimasu. Manga no e o mite, hanashi o rikai suru koto ga dekimasu.

Manga no naka ni rikai dekinai kotoba ga takusan arimasu. Sore wa ningen no kimochi ya yōsu ya oto o arawasu kotoba desu. Kore wa "onomatope" to īmasu. Oto o arawasu kotoba wa sukoshi wakarimasu.

Tatoeba, jū o utsu oto wa "zudōn" de, kanji ga tsukamemasu. Demo, kimochi ya yōsu o arawasu kotoba wa muzukashī desu. Tatoeba, "dokidoki" ya "zawazawa" nado desu. Manga o yomu toki onomatope no imi wa e de tsukamemasu. Manga wa nihongo no onomatope no kyōkasho to iemasu.

Kanji and Onomatopoeia

There really are many difficult kanji characters in Japanese newspapers. So I cannot read a Japanese newspaper yet. I have to memorize more kanji characters. Now I memorize three kanji every day. I cannot read a newspaper or write a report yet.

But it's OK that I cannot read a newspaper. To tell the truth, I read manga now. Even I can read manga. I can understand the story in the manga by looking at the pictures.

In comics, a lot of words that I don't understand are used. These are the words that express human feelings and appearance, or sounds. We call these words "onomatopoeia." I understand a few of the words expressing sounds.

For example, the sound of a gun is **zudōn** and I can grasp the feeling. But words that express a feeling or a situation are difficult; for example, **dokidoki**, (excitedly), **zawazawa** (rustling), etc. When I read manga, the pictures help me grasp the meaning of onomatopoeia. Manga can be said to be the textbooks of Japanese onomatopoeia.

QUESTIONS
Answers with their suggested sentence structure can be found on page 201.

1. この人は 漢字を どれぐらい 覚えられますか。
   Kono hito wa kanji o dore gurai oboeraremasu ka.

2. この人は 日本語の 新聞を 読めなければいけませんか。
   Kono hito wa nihongo no shinbun o yomenakereba ikemasen ka.

3. どんな 言葉が むずかしいですか。
   Donna kotoba ga muzukashī desu ka.

CHAPTER 3

Please Don't Use Your Smartphone While Walking
歩きながら スマホを しないで下さい

Doing Two Things at Once

In this chapter you'll enrich your everyday conversation by learning how to use the forms **-NAGARA**, **-NAIDE** and **-ZUNI** to talk about situations where two things are happening simultaneously. We will also look at the uses of **DAKE** and **SHIKA** to express limitation. Mastering the use of **SHIKA** can add depth to your daily interactions with others by helping you express emotions such as disappointment and dissatisfaction.

🎧 KEY SENTENCE PATTERNS

1. 歩きながら スマホを しないで下さい。
   Arukinagara sumaho o shinaide kudasai.   *Simultaneous actions*
   Please don't use your smartphone while walking.

2. スマホを 見ないで 勉強しましょう。
   Sumaho o minaide benkyō shimashō.   *Non-simultaneous actions*
   Let's study without using our smartphones.

3. 予約しないで 旅行しない方が いいです。
   Yoyaku shinaide ryokō shinai hō ga ī desu.   *Negative precondition*
   If you haven't made reservations, it's better not to travel.

4. アポを 取らずに 会うことは できません。
   Apo o torazuni au koto wa dekimasen.   *Negative precondition*
   You cannot meet him without making an appointment.

5. 1万円しか 持っていません。だから 5千円だけ 貸せます。
   Ichiman en shika motte imasen. Dakara gosen en dake kasemasu.   *Limitation*
   I only have 10,000 yen. So I can only lend you 5,000 yen.

Formation of the -NAGARA Form of the Verb

	-MASU Form		-NAGARA Form
-U Verbs	歩きます	→	歩きながら
	arukimasu		**arukinagara**
-RU Verbs ①	見ます	→	見ながら
	mimasu		**minagara**
-RU Verbs ②	寝ます	→	寝ながら
	nemasu		**nenagara**
Irregular Verbs	します	→	しながら
	shimasu		**shinagara**
	来ます	→	来ながら
	kimasu		**kinagara**

EXERCISE SET 1

Fill in the blanks with the **-NAGARA** form of the verb. Check your answers on page 201.

-MASU form	-NAGARA form
1. 読みます **yomimasu** (to read)	
2. 走ります **hashirimsu** (to run)	
3. 行きます **ikimasu** (to go)	
4. 入ります **hairimasu** (to enter)	
5. 持ちます **mochimasu** (to have)	
6. 食べます **tabemasu** (to eat)	
7. 見ます **mimasu** (to see)	
8. 練習します **renshū shimasu** (to practice)	

GRAMMAR AND USAGE NOTES

🎧 3.1 Using the ～ながら -NAGARA form of the verb

The verb ending in **-NAGARA** expresses a sub-action that is going on at the same time as a main action. The verb at the end of the sentence expresses the main action.

音楽を 聞きながら 勉強します。
Ongaku o kikinagara benkyō shimasu.
I study while listening to music.

勉強しながら 音楽を 聞きます。
Benkyō shinagara ongaku o kikimasu.
I listen to music while I study.

EXERCISE SET 2

Look at the pictures and create sentences with **-NAGARA**. Use the sentences structure at the bottom of page 44 as a model. See suggested answers on page 201.

❶ [USE:] スキーをする／ジャンプをする
suki o suru / janpu o suru

_____

❷ [USE:] 歌う／踊る
utau / odoru

_____

❸ [USE:] 選手／ボール／蹴る
senshu / bōru / keru

_____

🎧 3.2 The 〜ながら -NAGARA form and the 〜て -TE form

The subject of the two verbs in the sentence with **-NAGARA** must be the same person.

INCORRECT: 友だちが　カーナビを　見ながら　私が　車を　運転します。
Tomodachi ga kānabi o minagara watashi ga kuruma o unten shimasu.
I drive the car while my friend looks at the GPS.

CORRECT: 私は　カーナビを　見ながら　車を　運転します。
Watashi wa kānabi o minagara kuruma o unten shimasu.
I drive the car while looking at the GPS.

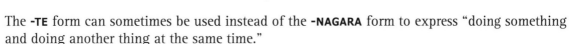

The **-TE** form can sometimes be used instead of the **-NAGARA** form to express "doing something <u>and</u> doing another thing at the same time."

J-Pop を 聞きながら 勉強します。
Jei poppu o kikinagara benkyō shimasu.
I study while listening to J-Pop.

J-Pop を 聞いて 勉強します。
Jei poppu o kīte benkyō shimasu.
I listen to J-Pop <u>and</u> study.

タブレットで 新聞を 見ながら 通勤します。／タブレットで 新聞を 見て 通勤します。
Taburetto de shinbun o minagara tsūkin shimasu. / Taburetto de shinbun o mite tsūkin shimasu.
I read a newspaper on my tablet on my way to work.

For actions in succession, **-NAGARA** is not suitable. The **-TE** form should be used instead:

INCORRECT: シャワーを　浴びながら　寝ます。
Shawā o abinagara nemasu.

CORRECT: シャワーを　浴びて　寝ます。
Shawā o abite nemasu.
I take a shower and then go to bed.
[Showering and sleeping cannot be done at the same time.]

EXERCISE SET 3

Rephrase the sentences, replacing the **-NAGARA** form with the **-TE** form. See suggested answers on page 201.

❶ タバコを 吸いながら 道路を 歩かないで下さい。
Tabako o suinagara dōro o arukanaide kudasai.

---

❷ 電車の中で 大きな 声を 出しながら 電話しない方が いいです。
Densha no naka de ōkina koe o dashinagara denwa shinai hō ga ī desu.

---

❸ アルバイトを しながら 留学を 続けています。
Arubaito o shinagara ryūgaku o tsuzukete imasu.

🎧 3.3 Using the ～ないで -NAIDE and ～ずに -ZUNI forms of the verb

Verb + **-NAIDE/-ZUNI** means "without doing/instead of doing something." This structure is the opposite of **-NAGARA**. **-NAIDE** is the negative of the **-TE** form and -**ZUNI** is its classical version, which is still used in modern Japanese. However, unlike **-NAIDE**, -**ZUNI** cannot be used before **kudasai**.

CORRECT:朝ご飯を 食べないで 行きます。   CORRECT: 朝ご飯を 食べずに 行きます。
    Asa gohan o tabenaide ikimasu.   **Asagohan o tabezuni ikimasu.**
    (I'll) go without eating breakfast.   *(I'll) go without eating breakfast.*

CORRECT:行かないで 下さい。   INCORRECT:行かずに 下さい。
    Ikanaide kudasai.   **Ikazuni kudasai.**
    Please don't go.

Formation of the -NAIDE and -ZUNI Forms of the Verb

	-MASU form	→ -NAI form	→ -NAIDE form/-ZUNI form
-U Verbs	歩きます	→ 歩かない	→ 歩かないで／歩かずに
	arukimasu	**aruka**nai	**arukanaide** / **arukazuni**
-RU Verbs ①	見ます	→ 見ない	→ 見ないで／見ずに
	mimasu	**mi**nai	**minaide** / **mizuni**
-RU Verbs ②	寝ます	→ 寝ない	→ 寝ないで／寝ずに
	nemasu	**ne**nai	**nenaide** / **nezuni**
Irregular Verbs	します	→ しない	→ しないで／せずに
	shimasu	**shi**nai	**shinaide** / **sezuni**
	来ます	→ 来ない	→ 来ないで／来ずに
	kimasu	**ko**nai	**konaide** / **kozuni**

EXERCISE SET 4

Fill in the blanks with the **-NAIDE** and **-ZUNI** forms of the verb. Check your answers on page 201.

-MASU form	-NAIDE form/-ZUNI form
1. 読みます **yomimasu** (to read)	
2. 走ります **hashirimasu** (to run)	
3. 待ちます **machimasu** (to wait)	
4. 持ちます **mochimasu** (to have)	
5. 食べます **tabemasu** (to eat)	
6. 見ます **mimasu** (to see)	
7. 練習します **renshū shimasu** (to practice)	

EXERCISE SET 5

Look at the pictures and create sentences with **-NAIDE** or **-ZUNI**, as illustrated in the following example. See suggested answers on page 202.

> **Example**
>
> *Let's take the Yamanote line instead of going by taxi.*
> タクシーに 乗らないで 山手線で 行きましょう。
> **Takushī ni noranaide yamanotesen de ikimashō.**

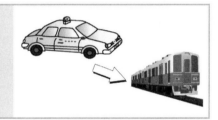

❶ [USE:] お菓子／やさい
     okashi / yasai

_____

❷ [USE:] タバコを吸う／コーヒーを飲む
     tabako o sū / kōhī o nomu

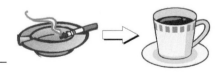

_____

❸ [USE:] エアコンを付ける／扇風機を使う
     eakon o tsuku / senpūki o tsukau

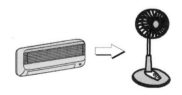

_____

④ [USE:] テレビ／本
　　　terebi / hon

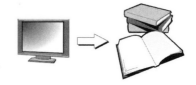

_____

🎧 3.4　Expressing limitation using だけ DAKE and しか SHIKA

To express the meaning "only," the particle **DAKE** or **SHIKA** follows the number (and counter) that comes after the subject or object.

❶ [subject + **WA/GA**] + [number + counter] + **DAKE/SHIKA (...NAI)**

空き部屋が あと 2部屋だけ あります。
Akibeya ga ato ni heya <u>dake</u> arimasu.
They have two more rooms available. (There are only two rooms available.)

❷ [the object + **O**] + [number + counter] + **DAKE/SHIKA (...NAI)**

私は ビールを　グラス 1杯しか 飲めません。
Watashi wa bīru <u>o</u> gurasu ippai <u>shika</u> nomemasen.
I can drink no more than one glass of beer.

DAKE or **SHIKA** can also be used directly after a noun.

女性専用車両は 女性しか 乗れません。
Josei sen'yō sharyō wa josei <u>shika</u> noremasen.
The women-only train car is exclusively for women's use.
(Only women can ride the women-only train car.)

The particle **DAKE** objectively expresses "only a certain quantity." **SHIKA ...-NAI** emotively implies that the quantity stated is unsatisfactory for the speaker, or emphasizes the limited quantity.

千円 だけ あります。
Sen yen <u>dake</u> arimasu.
Now I have just one thousand yen. (Simply stating the amount of money.)

千円 しか ありません。
Sen yen <u>shika</u> arimasen.
I have no more than one thousand yen. (I don't have enough money.)

空き部屋が あと 2部屋しか ありません。
Akibeya ga ato ni heya <u>shika</u> arimasen.
They have no more than two rooms available. (We should hurry with our booking.)

親友は 1人 しか いません。
Shinyū wa hitori <u>shika</u> imasen.
I have only one close friend. (Emphasizing the word one.)

EXERCISE SET 6

Use the prompts to create sentences with **SHIKA**. See suggested answers on page 202.

> **Examples**
>
> *There is only one chair.*
> いすが 1つしか ありません。
> **Isu ga hitotsu shika arimasen.**
>
> *Only one person can sit down.*
> 1人しか 座れません。
> **Hitori shika suwaremasen.**

❶ [USE:] 三味線 ／ 弦 ／三本
    shamisen / gen (strings) **/ sanbon**
(*gen = strings; **bon** is the counter for strings)

_____

❷ [USE:] かご／一人／乗れる
    kago / hitori / noreru (*kago = palanquin)

_____

🎧 3.5 More uses of だけ DAKE and しか SHIKA

TATTA (たった) and its formal version **WAZUKA** (わずか) may be put before the number + counter followed by **SHIKA** (しか) to emphasize the limited quantity:

このパソコンは 厚さが <u>たった</u> 9mmしか ありません。
Kono pasokon wa atsusa ga <u>tatta</u> kyū miri shika arimasen.
This personal computer is only 9 millimeters thick.

SHIKA may follow a particle:

今月の アルバイト代は たった2万円に しか なりません。
Kongetsu no arubaito dai wa tatta ni man yen <u>ni shika</u> narimasen.
This month's part-time pay is no more than twenty thousand yen.

84円の 切手では 手紙を 25グラムまで しか 送れません。
Hachi jū yo en no kitte de wa tegami o ni jū go guramu <u>made shika</u> okuremasen.
You can send a letter of no more than 25 grams with an 84-yen stamp.

DAKE may follow or precede a particle:

あなたに だけ／あなただけに 話します。
Anata <u>ni dake</u>/Anata <u>dake ni</u> hanashimasu.
I will only speak to you.

DAKE may precede **SHIKA** to emphasize the meaning:

あなた だけ しか 愛せません。
Anata <u>dake</u> <u>shika</u> aisemasen.
I can love nobody but you.

DAKE may follow a verb:

店員：何か お探し ですか。
Ten'in: Nanika osagashi desu ka.
Shop assistant: Are you looking for something? (May I help you?)

客：いえ、ちょっと 見ているだけ です。
Kyaku: Ie, chotto <u>mite iru dake</u> desu.
Customer: No, nothing special. I'm just looking.

🎧 CONVERSATION PRACTICE

歩きスマホ

歩きスマホは
！
やめましょう。

けんじ： マイクさん、歩きスマホを しないで 下さい。危ないですよ。
マイク： え？歩きスマホって？
けんじ： 歩きながら する スマホですよ。
マイク： へえ、「歩きながら スマホ」って 言わないですか。
よう子： 「ながら」を 取って、短く 「歩きスマホ」って 言います。
けんじ： 歩きスマホを しながら 歩いていて、事故に 遭う 人も います。
マイク： たしかに、危ないですね。スマホを しないで、前を見ながら
　　　　 歩きましょう。
よう子： それから、歩きタバコも ダメですよ。
マイク： あ、それは 歩きながら 吸うたばこですね。僕は タバコを 吸いません。
よう子： けんじさんは タバコを 吸いますね。体に 悪いですよ。
けんじ： ええ、でも 1日に タバコを 3本しか 吸いませんよ。
マイク： 3本でも 体に 悪いでしょう。
けんじ： そうですか。じゃ、今日から 1本だけ 吸います。
よう子： 1本も 3本も 同じですよ。タバコを 吸わずに、新鮮な 空気を 吸いながら 歩いて
　　　　 下さいね。

Aruki sumaho

Kenji: Maiku san, aruki sumaho o shinaide kudasai. Abunai desu yo.

Mike: E? Aruki sumaho tte?

Kenji: Arukinagara suru sumaho desu yo.

Mike: Hē, "arukinagara sumaho" tte iwanai desu ka.

Yoko: "Nagara" o totte, mijikaku "aruki sumaho" tte īmasu.

Kenji: Aruki sumaho o shinagara aruite ite, jiko ni au hito mo imasu.

Mike: Tashika ni, abunai desu ne. Sumaho o shinaide, mae o minagara arukimashō.

Yoko: Sorekara, aruki tabako mo dame desu yo.

Mike: A, sore wa arukinagara sū tabako desu ne. Boku wa tabako o suimasen.

Yoko: Kenji san wa tabako o suimasu ne. Karada ni warui desu yo.

Kenji; Ē, demo ichi nichi ni tabako o sanbon shika suimasen yo.

Mike: Sanbon demo karada ni warui deshō.

Kenji: Sō desu ka. Ja, kyō kara ippon dake suimasu.

Yoko: Ippon mo sanbon mo onaji desu yo. Tabako o suwazuni, shinsen na kūki o suinagara aruite kudasai ne.

Smartphone Use While Walking

Kenji: Mike, please don't do "aruki sumaho." It is dangerous.

Mike: What? "Aruki sumaho?"

Kenji: It means using a smartphone while walking.

Mike: Don't you say "arukinagara sumaho?"

Yoko: We take away "nagara" to shorten it, and we say "aruki sumaho."

Kenji: Some people who use their phones while walking cause accidents.

Mike: It's dangerous, for sure. Let's walk looking ahead and not at our smartphone.

Yoko: And "aruki tabako" is also bad.

Mike: Oh, you mean smoking while walking? I don't smoke.

Yoko: You smoke, Kenji, don't you? It's bad for you.

Kenji: Yes, but I don't smoke more than three cigarettes a day.

Mike: Even three is bad for you.

Kenji: Is it? Then, from today I will smoke only one.

Yoko: One and three are the same. Please walk without smoking, breathing in the fresh air.

TASK

Create a dialogue with **-NAGARA** and **-NAIDE/-ZUNI** and practice it.

_____: _____

_____: _____

ながら族

ラジオや 音楽を 聞いて 勉強する人を 「ながら族」と 言います。そうする 勉強は 「ながら勉強」とも 言います。ラジオや 音楽を 聞かないで 静かに 勉強する人は、勉強だけに 集中します。ながら族 は、音楽を 聞きながら、リラックスして 勉強に 集中できる人です。

最近は 音楽も スマホで 聞けます。だから 「歩きスマホ」を する人を、「スマホながら 族」と 言うことも できます。しかし、スマホながら族は、スマホを しながら 歩いたり 自転車を 運転したり します。とても 危なくて、事故を 起こしたり します。

駅のホームで 歩きスマホを していて、電車に ぶつかった人も います。危ない ところ では スマホを 見ないで 行動しましょう。本屋で 立ちながら 本を 読む人が 多いです。 これは 「立ち読み」と 言います。本を 買わないで、ただで 本を 読むだけでしょう。

立ちながら うどんや そばを 食べる店も 多いです。これは 「立ち食い」と 言います。 「食う」は 食べる意味で、ちょっと きたない 言葉です。だから 男の人しか 使いませ ん。女の人は 「ご飯を 食う」などと 言わないです。でも、「立ち食べ」と 言うことが できません。だから 女の人も 「立ち食い」は 大丈夫です。

Nagara zoku

Rajio ya ongaku o kīte benkyō suru hito o "nagara zoku" to īmasu. Sō suru benkyō wa "nagara benkyō" to mo īmasu. Rajio ya ongaku o kikanaide shizuka ni benkyō suru hito wa, benkyō dake ni shūchū shimasu. Nagara zoku wa, ongaku o kikinagara, rirakkusu shite benkyō ni shūchū dekiru hito desu.

Saikin wa ongaku mo sumaho de kikemasu. Dakara "aruki sumaho" o suru hito o, "sumaho nagara zoku" to iu koto mo dekimasu. Shikashi, sumaho nagara zoku wa, sumaho o shinagara aruitari jitensha o unten shitari shimasu. Totemo abunakute, jiko o okoshitari shimasu.

Eki no hōmu de aruki sumaho o shite ite, densha ni butsukatta hito mo imasu. Abunai tokoro de wa sumaho o minaide kōdō shimashō. Hon'ya de tachinagara hon o yomu hito ga ōi desu. Kore wa "tachiyomi" to īmasu. Hon o kawanaide, tada de hon o yomu dake deshō.

Tachinagara udon ya soba o taberu mise mo ōi desu. Kore wa "tachigui" to īmasu. "Kū " wa taberu imi de, chotto kitanai kotoba desu. Dakara, otoko no hito shika tsukaimasen. Onna no hito wa "gohan o kū" nado to iwanai desu. Demo, "tachitabe" to iu koto ga dekimasen. Dakara, onna no hito mo "tachigui" wa daijōbu desu.

People Who Do Two Things at the Same Time

Those who study while listening to the radio or music are called **nagara zoku** (people who do two things at the same time). Studying like this is also called **nagara benkyō**. Those who study quietly without listening to the radio or music concentrate only on their study. **Nagara zoku** are those who can relax and concentrate on their study while listening to music.

We can also listen to music on smartphones these days. Therefore, those who do **aruki sumaho** can also be said to be **sumaho nagara zoku**. However, **sumaho nagara zoku** walk or ride a bicycle while using a smartphone. This is very dangerous and may cause an accident.

Some people use their smartphones while walking on a station platform and collide with a train. You shouldn't look at your phone while doing something else when you are in a dangerous place. There are many people who read a book while standing in a bookstore. This is called **tachiyomi**. They may be just reading a book for free without buying it.

There are also many stores where you eat udon or soba noodles while standing. This is called **tachigui**. The word **kū** means to eat and is slightly coarse. So only men use it. Women do not say **gohan o kū**. But you can't say **tachitabe**. So it's all right for a woman to say **tachigui**.*

QUESTIONS
Answers with their suggested sentence structure can be found on page 202.

1. 「ながら族」の方が よく 勉強ができますか。
   "Nagara zoku" no hō ga yoku benkyō dekimasu ka.

2. 「スマホながら族」は どんなことを しますか。
   "Sumaho nagara zoku" wa donna koto o shimasu ka.

3. 立ち読みは どんなことですか。
   Tachiyomi wa donna koto desu ka.

*Note that the **gu** of **tachigui** is the word **kū**.

CHAPTER 4

It's Cheap, Delicious and Quick, So Let's Have a Beef Rice Bowl

安いし おいしいし 早いし、牛丼に しましょう

Expressing Consequence and Giving Reasons

In this chapter you'll learn how to construct and use sentences using **GA**, **KEREDOMO**, **NO NI**, **SHI** and **-TEMO/DEMO** to express consequence and to give reasons for something. Mastering constructions that use these words will allow you to build multiclause sentences that connect a sequence of ideas, which is an important step toward everyday fluency.

🎧 KEY SENTENCE PATTERNS

1. 空気清浄機は 少し 高いですが、やっぱり 買います。
   Kūki seijōki wa sukoshi takai desu ga, yappari kaimasu.   *Though...*
   The air purifier is a little expensive but I'll buy it anyway.

2. せっかく 急いで 来たのに、電車が 遅れています。
   Sekkaku isoide kita no ni, densha ga okurete imasu.   *Although/despite...*
   Although we took the trouble to arrive early, the train is late.

3. 雨が 降っているし、疲れたし、タクシーに しよう。
   Ame ga futte iru shi, tsukareta shi, takushī ni shiyō.   *And (so)...*
   It is raining and I'm tired, so let's take a taxi.

4. 安いし おいしいし 早いし、牛丼に しましょう。
   Yasui shi, oishī shi, hayai shi, gyūdon ni shimashō.   *And (so)...*
   It's cheap, delicious and quick, so let's have a beef rice bowl.

5. 安くても おいしくなかったら 食べたくないです。
   Yasukutemo oishiku nakattara tabetakunai desu.   *Even if.../even though...*
   Even if it's cheap, I don't want to eat it if it doesn't taste good.

Formation of Sentences Expressing Consequence

❶ Clause 1 + **GA/KEREDOMO**, Clause 2.
[Though + Clause 1], Clause 2.
❷ Clause 1 (dict. form/adjectival noun + **NA**) + **NO NI**, Clause 2.
[Although/despite + Clause 1], Clause 2.
❸ Clause 1 + **SHI**、 Clause 2 + **SHI**, ...
[Clause 1], [Clause 2], **and so** [conclusion].
❹ Clause 1 + **DEMO**, Clause 2.
[Even if/even though + Clause 1], Clause 2.

GRAMMAR AND USAGE NOTES

🎧 4.1 Using が GA to express "though"

When **GA** is used as a conjunction meaning "though," it directly follows the plain form or polite form of the verb, **-I** adjective, or adjectival noun + linking verb **DA/DESU.**

GA table	
確認する が／確認します が **Kakunin suru ga / kakunin shimasu ga**	Though I confirm it,
確認した が／確認しました が **Kakunin shita ga / kakunin shimashita ga**	Though I confirmed it,
確認しなかった が／確認しませんでした が **Kakunin shinakatta ga / kakunin shimasen deshita ga**	Though I did not confirm it,
正しい が／正しいです が **Tadashī ga / tadashī desu ga**	Though it is correct,
正しくない が／正しくありません が **Tadashiku nai ga / tadashiku arimasen ga**	Though it is not correct,
正しかった が／正しかったです が **Tadashikatta ga / tadashikatta desu ga**	Though it was correct,
賢明だ が／賢明です が **Kenmei da ga / kenmei desu ga**	Though it is sensible,
賢明だった が／賢明でした が **Kenmei datta ga / kenmei deshita ga**	Though it was sensible,
つまらない物だ が／つまらない物 です が **Tsumaranai mono da ga / tsumaranai mono desu ga**	Though it is a trifling thing,
つまらない物だった が／つまらない物でした が **Tsumaranai mono datta ga / tsumaranai mono deshita ga**	Though it was a trifling thing,
大変だろう が／大変でしょう が **Taihen darō ga / taihen deshō ga**	Though it will be hard,

EXERCISE SET 1

Referring to the **GA** table on the facing page, translate each phrase using the plain form and polite form of the verb + **GA**. Answers on page 202.

	GA + plain form / GA + polite form
1. Though the war is over, ...	/
2. Though it is raining, ...	/
3. Though it was cheap, ...	/
4. Though it is important, ...	/

In principle, **GA** follows the plain form in formal writing. In speech, the polite form + **GA** sounds formal. Both clauses in a sentence should use the same form of the verb (plain or polite).

事件を 調査<u>した</u>が、原因が 分から<u>なかった</u>。
Jiken o chōsa <u>shita</u> ga, gen'in ga wakara<u>nakatta</u>.
Though we investigated the incident, its cause did not become clear.

伺い<u>ました</u>が、お留守 <u>でした</u>。
Ukagai<u>mashita</u> ga, orusu <u>deshita</u>.
Though I visited you, you were away.

INCORRECT: 伺<u>った</u> が、お留守<u>でした</u>。
        Ukaga<u>tta</u> ga, orusu <u>deshita</u>.

EXERCISE SET 2

Use the prompts to create sentences with **GA**. See suggested answers on page 202.

> **Examples**
>
> *sign language = 手話 **(shuwa)**
>
> *I learned sign language but I can't communicate well yet.*
> 手話を 覚えましたが、まだ うまく できません。
> **Shuwa o oboemashita ga, mada umaku dekimasen.**
>
> *I spoke in sign language but they didn't understand.*
> 手話で 話しましたが、 分かりませんでした。
> **Shuwa de hanashimashita ga, wakarimasen deshita.**

❶ [USE:] 手／洗う／まだ／かゆい
     te / arau / mada / kayui

_____

❷ [USE:] 急 ぐ／電車 に 間 に 合 う
   isogu / densha ni maniau

❸ [USE:] 早 く／帰 りたい／会 議／とても 長 い
   hakayu / kaeritai / kaigi / totemo nagai

🎧 4.2 Using が GA to express "and"

The conjunction **GA** may also be used to mean "and."

> 電動 カート を 買 いました<u>が</u>、とても 楽 です。
> **Dendō kāto o kaimashita <u>ga</u>, totemo raku desu.**
> *I bought an electric cart and it is very comfortable.*

EXERCISE SET 3
Use the prompts to create sentences with **GA**. See suggested answers on page 202.

❶ [USE:] 彼女／メッセージ／もらう／懐 かしい
   kanojo / messēji / morau / natsukashī

❷ [USE:] マラソン／出 る／優勝 する
   marason / deru / yūshō suru

4.3 Using けれども KEREDOMO to express "though"

The conjunction **KEREDOMO** is an informal version of **GA,** with three different forms that vary in informality as shown below. **KEREDOMO** and its variants nearly always follow the plain form.

けれども	けれど	けど
keredomo	**keredo**	**kedo**
informal	casual	very casual

EXERCISE SET 4

Translate the phrases using **KEREDOMO.** Check your answers on page 202.

	Plain form + KEREDOMO
1. Though I bought it, ...	
2. Though the weather is bad, ...	
3. Though he is kind, ...	

EXERCISE SET 5

Use **KEREDOMO, KEREDO** or **KEDO** to rephrase the following sentences. Suggested answers on page 202.

❶ *I got married but I'm not so happy.*
結婚 しましたが、 あまり 幸せでは ありません。
Kekkon shimashita ga, amari shiawase de wa arimasen.

_____

❷ *I bought a washing machine last year but it is broken now.*
去年 洗濯機を 買いましたが、 今は 壊れています。
Kyonen sentakuki o kaimashita ga, ima wa kowarete imasu.

_____

🎧 4.4 Using の に NO NI to express "though"

NO NI is similar in meaning and form to **KEREDOMO.** However, **NO NI** implies that the speaker is dissatisfied with, regretful about, or anxious about the consequence. The plain form usually precedes **NO NI** even when the final verb of the sentence is in the polite form.

一生懸命 頑張ったのに、 ダメでした。
Isshōkenmei <u>ganbatta</u> no ni, dame <u>deshita</u>.
Though I tried hard, I failed.

When used after an adjectival noun or noun, **NO NI** is always preceded by **NA.**

このゲームのルールは 簡単<u>な</u>のに、 プレーするのは むずかしいですね。
Kono gēmu no rūru wa kantan <u>na</u> no ni, purē suru no wa muzukashī desu ne.
Although the rules of this game are simple, it's difficult to play, isn't it?

雨<u>な</u>のに ゴルフを しに 行きますか。
Ame <u>na</u> no ni gorufu o shini ikimasu ka.
Are you going to play golf in spite of the rain?

太郎さんは イケメン<u>な</u>のに、 あまり 女性に 持てないです。
Tarō san wa ikemen <u>na</u> no ni, amari josei ni motenai desu.
Although Taro is a good-looking guy, he is not very attractive to women.

EXERCISE SET 6
Use the prompts to create sentences with **NO NI**. See suggested answers on page 202.

❶ [USE:] 新車／買う／ひどい／事故／会う
　　　 shinsha / kau / hidoi / jiko / au

_____

❷ [USE:] 空／きれい／汚い／煙
　　　 sora / kirei / kitanai / kemuri

_____

🎧 4.5   Using し **SHI** to give a list of of reasons

Phrases ending with the conjunction **SHI** may be used in succession in one sentence, to express a list of reasons. **SHI** is a casual expression that usually follows the plain form. It is sometimes colloquially used only once in a sentence, as in the second example.

> ちょっと 用事が ある<u>し</u>、時間が ない<u>し</u>、すみません。
> **Chotto yōji ga aru <u>shi</u>, jikan ga nai <u>shi</u>, sumimasen.**
> _I have things to do, and I don't have time, so I'm sorry (to decline your offer)._

> 仕事が 終わった<u>し</u>、もう 帰ります。
> **Shigoto ga owatta <u>shi</u>, mō kaerimasu.**
> _As I've finished my work, I'll go home now._

EXERCISE SET 7
Translate the phrases using the plain form of the verb + **SHI**. Check your answers on page 202.

❶ It's raining and there's no bus, so ...

_____

❷ I'm tired and sleepy, so ...

_____

❸ I'm thirsty and have a headache, so ...

_____

❹ It's hot and I don't want to go, so ...

_____

❺ I've eaten and have no money, so ...

_____

EXERCISE SET 8

Use each prompt to create a sentence that uses **SHI** twice. See suggested answers on page 202.

> **Examples**
>
> *Karaoke is fun and I want to listen to songs, so let's go there.*
> カラオケは楽しいし、歌が 聞きたいし、行こうよ。
> **Karaoke wa tanoshī shi, uta ga kikitai shi, ikō yo.**
>
> *That old guy is bad at singing and never stops, so don't you want to go home now?*
> おじさんは 歌が 下手だし、歌を やめないし、もう 帰りたいね。
> **Ojisan wa uta ga heta da shi, uta o yamenai shi, mō kaeritai ne.**

❶ [USE:] 今日／祭り／面白い／行く
    kyō / matsuri / omoshiroi / iku

_____

❷ [USE:] 二十歳／なる／お酒／飲める／居酒屋／行く
    hatachi / naru / osake / nomeru / izakaya / iku

_____

❸ [USE:] 暑い／疲れた／帰りたいよ
    atsui / tsukareta / kaeritai yo

_____

❹ [USE:] 天気／悪い／道／狭い／大変
    tenki / warui / michi /semai / taihen

_____

🎧 4.6 Using 〜ても／でも -TEMO/DEMO to express "even if"

To express "even if," add **-MO** to the **-TE** form of the verb or **-I** adjective. Nouns and adjectival nouns, which do not have a **-TE** form, are always directly followed by **DEMO** without the linking verb.

EXERCISE SET 9

Translate the phrases to end in **-TEMO/DEMO**. Check your answers on page 202.

	-TEMO/DEMO
1. Even if (I/you) go, ...	
2. Even if (I/you) drink, ...	
3. Even if (I/you) do, ...	
4. Even if (it is) expensive, ...	
5. Even if (it is) not good, ...	
6. Even if (it is) inconvenient, ...	

For a sentence in the the past tense, don't use the past tense in the clause that ends with **-TEMO/DEMO**.

東京ディズニーシーへ <u>行っても</u>、 ジェットコースターに <u>乗れない</u>よ。
Tōkyō dizunīshī e <u>ittemo</u>, jetto kōsutā ni <u>norenai</u> yo.
Even if you go to Tokyo DisneySea, you won't be able to ride the roller coaster.

東京ディズニーシーへ <u>行っても</u>、 ジェットコースターに <u>乗れなかった</u>よ。
Tōkyō dizunīshī e <u>ittemo</u>, jetto kōsutā ni <u>norenakatta</u> yo.
Even though I went to Tokyo DisneySea, I couldn't ride the roller coaster.

Sentences using whatever/whoever, etc., + verb/**-I** adjective/(adjectival) noun + **-TEMO/DEMO** are structured as follows:

何〜ても／でも
nani...temo/demo   *whatever/no matter what ... may ...*
だれ〜も／でも
dare...temo/demo   *whoever/no matter who ... may ...*
どこ〜ても／でも
doko...temo/demo   *wherever/no matter where ... may ...*
いつ〜ても／でも
itsu...temo/demo   *whenever/no matter when ... may ...*
どのように〜ても／でも
dono yō ni...temo/demo   *however/no matter how ... may ...*
いくら〜ても／でも
ikura...temo/demo   *however/no matter how (hard, fast, long, etc) ... may .../ no matter how many times ... may ...*

何／どんな 〜ても／でも
nan / donna...temo/demo   *whatever/no matter what ... may ...*

どこへ行っても コンビニが あるから 便利です。
Doko e ittemo konbini ga aru kara benri desu.
Wherever we may go, there are convenience stores, so that's handy.

いくら やっても オセロで パソコンに 勝てないよ。
Ikura yattemo osero de pasokon ni katenai yo.
No matter how many times I play, I can't beat my computer at Othello.

EXERCISE SET 10

Use the prompts to create sentences with **-TEMO/DEMO**. See suggested answers on page 202.

❶ [USE:] いくら／忙しい／メール／チェックする
ikura / isogashī / mēru / chekku suru

_____

❷ [USE:] いくら／大変な／仕事／任せる ／ください
ikura / taihen na / shigoto / makaseru / kudasai

_____

❸ [USE:] いくら／教える／わかる
ikura / oshieru / wakaru

_____

❹ [USE:] いくら／考える／うまく／かける
ikura / kangaeru / umaku / kakeru

_____

🎧 CONVERSATION PRACTICE

ゴミは 朝 出します

マイク： ちゃんと ゴミを 分けて 出しましたが、すごい ことに なっています。

けんじ： どう なってるの？

マイク： せっかく ゴミを 出したのに 袋が 破れて、ゴミが 袋から 出ています。

よう子： だれか いたずらしたのかしら。

けんじ： もしかしたら カラスじゃない？カラスは かしこいし 人間をよく 見てるし...

マイク： カラスって？

けんじ： 鳥だよ。黒い 大きな 鳥。カアカアって 鳴くよ。

マイク： ああ、日本では どこへ 行っても たくさん 見ますね。
　　　　 ゴミを 食べるために 破りましたか。
よう子： せっかく ゴミを 出しても 汚くなったら 困りますよね。
けんじ： いつ ゴミを 出したの？
マイク： ゆうべですが。
よう子： あ、それは だめですね。ゴミは せっかく 分別しても、朝 出して
　　　　 くださいね。

Gomi wa asa dashimasu

Mike: **Chanto gomi o wakete dashimashita ga, sugoi koto ni natte imasu.**
Kenji: **Dō natteru no?**
Mike: **Sekkaku gomi o dashita no ni fukuro ga yaburete, gomi ga fukuro kara dete imasu.**
Yoko: **Dareka itazura shita no kashira.**
Kenji: **Moshikashitara karasu ja nai? Karasu wa kashikoi shi ningen o yoku miteru shi...**
Mike: **Karasu tte?**
Kenji: **Tori da yo. Kuroi ōkina tori. Kākā tte naku yo.**
Mike: **Ā, nihon de wa doko e ittemo takusan mimasu ne. Gomi o taberu tame ni yaburimashita ka.**
Yoko: **Sekkaku gomi o dashitemo kitanaku nattara komarimasu yo ne.**
Kenji: **Itsu gomi o dashita no?**
Mike: **Yūbe desu ga.**
Yoko: **A, sore wa dame desu ne. Gomi wa sekkaku bunbetsu shitemo, asa dashite kudasai ne.**

We Take Out the Garbage in the Morning

Mike: I separated the garbage properly and took it out, but look at the state of it.
Kenji: What happened?
Mike: Even though I put it out in the correct way, the bag is torn and the garbage is coming out.
Yoko: I wonder if somebody did it as a prank.
Kenji: Couldn't a karasu have done it? Karasu are wise and they often watch people ...
Mike: Karasu?
Kenji: It's a bird. A big black bird. It goes *kaa kaa*.
Mike: Oh, wherever I go in Japan, I see a lot of them. Did they rip open the bag so they could eat the garbage?
Yoko: It's a nuisance when the garbage ends up in this mess even though you've made the effort to put it out properly.
Kenji: When did you take the garbage out?
Mike: Last night, but why?
Yoko: Oh, you shouldn't do that. Even if you've gone to the trouble of separating the garbage, please take it out in the morning.

TASK
Create a dialogue with **SEKKAKU...NO NI...** and **-TEMO/DEMO** and practice it.

_____ : _____

_____ : _____

ゴミの分別

日本で ゴミを うまく 捨てられますか。まず、燃えるゴミと 燃えないゴミを 分ける ことは ちょっと むずかしいですが、例えば、古紙類しか 出せない 曜日が あるし、瓶 や 缶類を 出せない 曜日が あるし、ある 場所では、毎月 第1・第3火曜日に、瓶や 缶類 を 出せるのに、第2火曜日は 古紙類しか 出せません。

瓶は、ラベルを はがして、蓋も 取って、瓶だけ 捨てますが、ラベルも 蓋も 資源ゴミ に なります。また、紙と プラスチックは 混ぜて 出せません。

だから、家庭ゴミの 収集カレンダーを 見ながら、うまく 分別して 出します。みな さんは 間違わずにちゃんと ゴミが 出せますか。

たくさん 買いものをして、部屋に ゴミが いっぱいになる人が います。瓶や ペット ボトルを コンビニのゴミ箱に 捨てに 行く 人が いますが、それは よくないですね。

Gomi no bunbetsu

Nihon de gomi o umaku suteraremasu ka. Mazu, moeru gomi to moenai gomi o wakeru koto wa chotto muzukashī desu ga, tatoeba, koshirui shika dasenai yōbi ga aru shi, bin ya kanrui o dasenai yōbi ga aru shi, aru basho de wa, maitsuki dai ichi dai san kayōbi ni, bin ya kanrui o daseru no ni, dai ni kayōbi wa koshirui shika dasemasen.

Bin wa raberu o hagashite, futa mo totte, bin dake sutemasu ga, raberu mo futa mo shigen gomi ni narimasu. Mata, kami to purasuchikku wa mazete dasemasen.

Dakara, katei gomi no shūshū karendā o minagara, umaku bunbetsu shite dashimasu. Minasan wa machigawazuni chanto gomi ga dasemasu ka.

Takusan kaimono o shite, heya ni gomi ga ippai ni naru hito ga imasu. Bin ya pettobotoru o konbini no gomibako ni suteni iku hito ga imasu ga, sore wa yoku nai desu ne.

Separating the Garbage

Can you dispose of garbage properly in Japan? First, it is slightly difficult to separate burnable from non-burnable garbage; for example, there are days of the week when you can only put out used paper, or when you can't put out bottles or cans. In some places you can put out bottles and cans on the first and third Tuesdays of every month, but on the second Tuesday you can only put out used paper.

Though we remove the labels and also take off the lids and only throw away the bottles, the labels and the lids can be recycled. Also, you can't put out garbage with paper and plastic mixed.

So, looking at the collection calendar of household garbage, you separate it properly and put it out. Can everyone put out the garbage properly without making a mistake?

There are some people who buy a lot of things and their living space gets filled with trash. Some people throw away their glass or plastic bottles in the convenience store trash can, but that's bad.

QUESTIONS
Answers with their suggested sentence structure can be found on page 203.

1. どのように ゴミを 分けますか。
   Dono yō ni gomi o wakemasu ka.

2. どうやって 瓶の ラベルを 捨てますか。
   Dō yatte bin no raberu o sutemasu ka.

3. 毎日 ゴミを捨てられなくて どうなる人がいますか。
   Mainichi gomi o suterarenakute dō naru hito ga imasu ka.

CHAPTER 5

I Have a Headache Because I Couldn't Sleep Last Night

夕べ 寝られなかったから 頭が 痛いです

Cause and Effect

In this chapter you'll learn how to use constructions to express cause and effect including **KARA**, **NODE**, **TAME (NI)** and **-N/NO DESU**, as well as various forms of the suffix verb **-SUGIRU** to express consequence. We'll look at different scenarios you might encounter so that you can learn how to communicate appropriately in a variety of friendly, formal, polite or emotive situations.

🎧 KEY SENTENCE PATTERNS

1. 夕べ 寝られなかったから 頭が 痛いです。
   Yūbe nerarenakatta kara atama ga itai desu.   *Because...*
   I have a headache because I couldn't sleep last night.

2. 電車が 遅れた ので、遅刻 しました。
   Densha ga okureta node, chikoku shimashita.   *Because...*
   Because the train was delayed, I was late.

3. 事故が ありました から、遅刻 しました。
   Jiko ga arimashita kara, chikoku shimashita.   *Because...*
   Because there was an accident, I was late.

4. なぜかというと、最近 ちょっと 働きすぎた からです。
   Nazeka to iu to, saikin chotto hataraki sugita kara desu.   *It is because...*
   It is because I have recently worked a little too hard.

5. ちょっと 気分が 悪いん です。
   Chotto kibun ga warui n desu.   *Reason, cause, explanation*
   In fact, it's because I feel rather ill.

Formation of Cause and Effect Sentences

❶ Clause 1 (plain form) + **KARA**, Clause 2.
   [Because + Clause 1], Clause 2.
❷ Clause 1 + **NODE**, Clause 2.
   [Because + Clause 1], Clause 2.   **NOTE: NODE** cannot follow **DA**.
❸ Clause 1 (polite form) + **KARA**, Clause 2.
   [Because + Clause 1], Clause 2.
❹ **NAZE KA TO IU TO** + explanation.
   [It is because] + explanation (gives emphasis to the explanation).
❺ Clause (ending with the plain form) + **N DESU**.
   [Something is in a condition that means] + Clause.

GRAMMAR AND USAGE NOTES

🎧 5.1 Giving a reason using から／ので **KARA/NODE**

The conjunction **KARA** may replace **GA** in the **GA** table on page 56 and expresses the meaning "because." When **KARA** follows the plain form, the sentence can sound rude or emotional, so save this usage for very casual or informal situations:

お腹が 空いたから、 何か 食べようよ！
Onaka ga suita kara, nanika tabeyō yo!
Let's eat something, because I'm hungry!

Compare the following three sentences, which all mean *I was late because the train was delayed.*

❶ 電車が 遅れたから、 遅刻した。
   Densha ga okureta kara, chikoku shita.

❷ 電車が 遅れたから、 遅刻しました。
   Densha ga okureta kara, chikoku shimashita.

❸ 電車が 遅れたので、 遅刻しました。
   Densha ga okureta node, chikoku shimashita.

Sentence ❶ sounds as if the speaker is insisting their lateness was caused by the delayed train.

Sentence ❷ sounds odd, because the verb in the main clause is in the polite form and the verb in the subordinate clause is in the plain form. Both verbs should have the same form. As mentioned above, using the plain form before **KARA** sounds casual or emotional, so should be avoided in formal situations. If both verbs are in the plain form, it's fine for casual conversation with friends. (However, it is not unusual to hear Japanese people using the plain form before **KARA** and the polite form in the main clause in both friendly and polite situations.)

Sentence ❸ neutrally expresses an objective reason. **NODE** normally follows the plain form.

When **KARA** follows the polite form, as in the following example, the whole sentence sounds formal and polite. Note that the final verb of the sentence must also take the polite form.

電車が 来ますから、黄色の線の後ろまで下がります。
Densha ga kimasu kara, kīro no sen no ushiro made sagarimasu.
Move behind the yellow line because a train is coming.

NODE usually follows the plain form (but it cannot follow **da**. In such cases **da** becomes **na**.) The plain form + **NODE** sounds slightly less polite than the polite form + **KARA**.

危ないので ／危険なので、入らないで下さい。
Abunai node / kiken na no node, hairanaide kudasai.
Please do not enter because it is dangerous.

EXERCISE SET 1
Translate the sentences into Japanese using **KARA** or **NODE**. See suggested answers on page 203.

❶ *Mom, buy that for me because I want it!*

_____

❷ *Put on your seatbelts because it's dangerous.*

_____

❸ *I'm drawing blood, so please don't move.*

_____

❹ *I'll help you, so don't worry.*

_____

🎧 5.2 Giving a reason using ため(に) TAME (NI)

TAME (NI), more formal than **NODE**, can also express a reason. It is mostly used in written language such as reports, or in formal speeches. Because **TAME** is a noun, it follows the plain form of the verb or **-I** adjective, the adjectival noun + **NA**, or the noun + **NO**.

日本は 地震が あるために、多くの 建物を 耐震化している。
Nihon wa jishin ga aru tame ni, ōku no tatemono o taishinka shite iru.
Many buildings are quakeproofed in Japan due to frequent earthquakes.

事故が あったために、高速道路は ７キロの 渋滞です。
Jiko ga atta tame ni, kōsoku dōro wa nana kiro no jūtai desu.
Traffic is backed up for 7 kilometers along the expressway due to an accident.

海抜が 低いために、津波が 入ってきた。
Kaibatsu ga hikui tame ni, tsunami ga haitte kita.
The tsunami swept in because the altitude is low.

渋谷は 有名なために 友だちと 待ち合わせする人が いつも多いです。
Shibuya wa yūmei na tame ni tomodachi to machiawase suru hito ga itsumo ōi desu.
Since Shibuya is so famous, there are always crowds of people waiting to meet their friends.

人身事故のため、電車が 遅れている。
Jinshin jiko no tame, densha ga okurete iru.
Trains are delayed due to a fatal accident.

Note that **TAME (NI)** also expresses purpose. See section 9.3.

EXERCISE SET 2
Create sentences with **TAME (NI)**, following the prompts. See suggested answers on page 203.

❶ [USE:] 計算／ミス／仕事／休む／ことができる
       keisan / misu / shigoto / yasumu / koto ga dekiru

_____

❷ [USE:] 不況／タクシーのお客さん／減る
       fukyō / takushī no okyakusan / heru

_____

❸ [USE:] うまく／行く／ボス／悩んでいる
       umaku / iku / bosu / nayande iru

_____

❹
  [USE:] 水不足／水／もらっている
       mizubusoku / mizu / moratte iru

_____

🎧 5.3 Giving a reason using ん です N DESU

This phrase gives the reason for, explanation for, or background of a situation. **N DESU** is the short form of **NO DESU**, which is also widely used. **N/NO** follows the plain form and is a nominalizer that makes the preceding phrase into a noun phrase.

あの2人は 付き合って いる<u>ん</u>です。
Ano futari wa tsukiatte iru <u>n desu</u>.
Those two have a close relationship.

In the previous example the speaker uses **N DESU** to explain the situation that is being observed.

すみません。
地下鉄が 遅れた <u>ん です</u>。
Sumimasen.
Chikatetsu ga okureta <u>n desu</u>.
I'm sorry. The subway was delayed.

In the above situation the phrase **chikatetsu ga okureta <u>kara desu</u>** would sound as though the man is blaming his lateness on the subway. By using the neutral **N DESU** he sounds polite and unemotional.

🎧 5.4   ん です N DESU with nouns and adjectival nouns

When the final element of an explanatory sentence is a noun or adjectival noun, the present-tense ending form must be **NA N DESU** instead of **DESU**.

これは マイボトル<u>な ん です</u>。 (showing it)
Kore wa mai botoru <u>na n desu</u>.
This is a reusable bottle.

とても エコ<u>な ん です</u>。 (explaining about it)
Totemo eko <u>na n desu</u>.
It is very ecological (so I use it).

EXERCISE SET 3
Use the prompts to create explanatory sentences using **N DESU**. See suggested answers on page 203.

❶ [USE:] 迷惑メール／たくさん／来る
    meiwaku mēru / takusan / kuru

_____

❷ [USE:] 仕事／締め切り／間に合う
    shigoto / shimekiri / maniau

_____

❸ [USE:] 今日／太郎／誕生日
    kyō / tarō / tanjōbi

_____

④ [USE:] 津波／から／逃げる
tsunami / kara / nigeru

🎧 5.5 Giving a reason using から だ／から です KARA DA/KARA DESU

KARA can be put with the linking verb **DA/DESU** at the end of a sentence to state a reason. When speaking informally, **DA/DESU** can be omitted.

いつも インスタントラーメンを。
食べてるね
Itsumo insutanto rāmen o tabeteru ne.
You always eat instant ramen, don't you?

うん、今 お金が ない<u>から</u> (だよ)。
Un, ima okane ga nai <u>kara</u> (da yo).
Yes, that's because I have no money now.

Compare the following two structures:

私は 生ものが ダメだ <u>から</u>、
└ subordinate clause ┘
Watashi wa namamono ga dame da <u>kara</u>,
Because I react badly to raw food,

刺身を 食べません。
└ main clause ┘
sashimi o tabemasen.
I don't eat sashimi.

刺身を 食べないですね。
└ independent sentence ┘
Sashimi o tabenai desu ne.
You don't eat sashimi, do you?

私は 生ものが ダメだ <u>からです</u>。
└ independent sentence ┘
Watashi wa namamono ga dame da <u>kara desu</u>.
It's because I react badly to raw food.

🎧 5.6 Emphasizing a reason using なぜかというと NAZE KA TO IU TO

NAZE KA TO IU TO, or its more informal version **NANDE KA TO IU TO**, means "because" and may be put at the beginning of the sentence to emphasize a reason. Its literal meaning is "if I say why it is."

遊ばないよ。<u>なんでかというと</u> 今 お金がないから。
Asobanai yo. <u>Nande ka to iu to</u> ima okane ga nai kara.
I'm not socializing because I have no money right now.

Its formal written version is **NAZE NARA(BA)**, which sounds odd in casual conversation.

たくさんの人が 避難した。<u>なぜなら(ば)</u> 原発事故が あったからだ。
Takusan no hito ga hinan shita. <u>Naze nara(ba)</u> genpatsu jiko ga atta kara da.
Many people took refuge. That's because there was a nuclear power plant accident.

EXERCISE SET 4
Use the pictures and the prompts to create dialogues with **N DESU KA**, **NAZE KA TO IU TO** and **KARA DESU**. See suggested answers on page 203.

A: *Why is Yoko absent?*
よう子さんは どうして 休みなん ですか。
Yōko san wa dōshite yasumi na n desuka.

B: *Because she got a fever.*
なぜか というと 熱が 出た からです。
Nazeka to iu to netsu ga deta kara desu.

❶ A: [USE:] どうして／腕／赤い
　　　　 dōshite / ude / akai

_____

B: [USE:] アレルギー／ある
　　　　 arerugī / aru

_____

❷ A: [USE:] どうして／入院する
　　　　 dōshite / nyūin suru

_____

B: [USE:] 足／折る
　　　　 ashi / oru

_____

❸ A: [USE:] どうして／ドライバー／困っている
　　　　 dōshite / doraibā / komatte iru

_____

B: [USE:] ガソリン／高い
　　　　 gasorin / takai

_____

❹ A: [USE:] どうして／機械で／草／刈っている
      dōshite / kikai de / kusa / katte iru

_____

B: [USE:] 手で／刈る／難しい
      te de / karu / muzukashī

_____

🎧 **5.7   Emphasizing a reason using じつは JITSU WA**

JITSU WA means "to tell the truth," or "the fact is" and may be put at the beginning of the sentence that ends in **N DESU** to emphasise the truth of an explanation. In response, the words **TSUMARI** ("in other words") or **JĀ**, ("then") may be used to clarify and confirm the explanation.

部下：　　すみません。実は ちょっと 用事が ある ん です。
Buka:　　**Sumimasen. Jitsu wa chotto yōji ga aru n desu.**
Employee: _I'm sorry. To tell the truth, I have things to do._

上司：　　うん？じゃあ、 今日は 飲みに 行かない ん ですね。
Jōshi:　　**Un? Jā, kyō wa nomi ni ikanai n desu ne.**
Boss:　　_Huh? Then you mean you're not going drinking with us today, right?_

EXERCISE SET 5
Look at the pictures and use the prompts to create dialogues with **JITSU WA ... N DESU** and **JĀ ... N DESU NE**, following the pattern above. See suggested answers on page 203.

❶ A: [USE:] 実は／ 歯／痛い
      jitsu wa / ha / itai

_____

B: [USE:] じゃあ／いまは／食べられない
      jā / ima wa / taberarenai

_____

❷ A: [USE:] 実は／ タブレット／初めて／使う
      jitsu wa / taburetto / hajimete / tsukau

_____

B: [USE:] じゃあ／まだ／できない
      jā / mada / dekinai

_____

❸ A: [USE:] 実は／カメラ／買った
jitsu wa / kamera / katta

_____

B: [USE:] じゃあ／いい／写真／撮れる
jā / ī / shashin / toreru

_____

🎧 5.8 Giving a reason for going using verb + に きます NI IKIMASU

To express one's purpose in going somewhere, use the front part of the **-MASU** form + **NI IKIMASU**. The front part of the **-MASU** form becomes like a destination/goal/target, and so this kind of structure can only be used with verbs of coming and going, such as **ikimasu**, **kimasu**, and **dekakemasu** (to go out).

回転寿司を	食べ	に	行きます
kaiten zushi o	**tabe**	**ni**	**ikimasu**
conveyor-belt sushi	eat	(target marker)	go

[I'm] go[ing] to eat conveyor-belt sushi.

EXERCISE SET 6
Read the questions and use the prompts in brackets to create a reply with the front part of the **-MASU** form + **NI** + verb. See suggested answers on page 203.

❶ 何を 食べに 行きましょうか。（牛丼）
Nani o tabe ni ikimashō ka. (gyūdon)

_____

❷ どこへ 何を しに 行きますか。（公園／バーベキューをする）
Doko e nani o shi ni ikimasu ka. (kōen / bābekyū o suru)

_____

❸ お父さんは どこへ 何を しに 行きますか。（ダンスホール／踊る）
Otōsan wa doko e nani o shini ikimasu ka. (dansu hōru / odoru)

_____

🎧 5.9 Expressing doing something to excess using 〜すぎる（過ぎる） -SUGIRU

To expresses doing something to excess we use the following structure:

verb/**-I** adjective/adjectival noun + **-SUGIRU**.

飲みすぎる	**nomisugiru**	to drink too much
切りすぎる	**kirisugiru**	to cut too short
言いすぎる	**īsugiru**	to speak too strongly/be way out of line
やりすぎる	**yarisugiru**	to overdo
汚すぎる	**kitanasugiru**	to be too dirty
簡単すぎる	**kantan sugiru**	to be too easy

SUGIRU means something passes a certain point. The point passed is marked with the particle **O**.

うとうと していたら、降りる駅<u>を</u> 電車が すぎました。
Utō-uto shite itara, oriru eki <u>o</u> densha ga sugimashita.
While I was dozing, my train passed the station where I had to get off.

The adjective **ī** (good) becomes **yo** before **-SUGIRU**:

これは 僕には ちょっと <u>よ</u>すぎます。贅沢は いけないです。
Kore wa boku ni wa chotto <u>yo</u>sugimasu. Zeitaku wa ikenai desu.
This is a little too good as far as I'm concerned. We shouldn't be extravagant.

The negative adjective **-nai** is changed into **-nasa** before **-SUGIRU**.

USJ に 行きたい けど、暇が <u>なさ</u>すぎます。
Yūesujei ni ikitai kedo, hima ga <u>nasa</u>sugimasu.
I want to go to USJ [Universal Studios Japan] but I have too little spare time.

EXERCISE SET 7
Fill in the blanks with the **-SUGIMASU** form of each verb or adjective phrase. Answers on page 203.

-MASU form/-DESU form	-SUGIMASU form
1. 働きます **hatarakimasu** (to work)	
2. 買います **kaimasu** (to buy)	
3. 休みます **yasumimasu** (to rest)	
4. 寝ます **nemasu** (to sleep)	
5. 見ます **mimasu** (to see)	
6. 練習します **renshū shimasu** (to practice)	
7. 安いです **yasui desu** (cheap)	
8. 遅いです **osoi desu** (slow/late)	
9. 退屈です **taikutsu desu** (dull/boring/bored)	

To express the consequence of doing something to excess we use the following structure:

verb/-**I** adjective/adjectival noun + -**SUGITE** + the main sentence

❶ The front part of the -**MASU** form of verb + -**SUGITE**

食べすぎて 食べたものを 吐きます。
Tabesugite tabeta mono o hakimasu.
I ate so much that I may throw up what I have eaten.

頑張りすぎて とても 疲れました。
Ganbarisugite totemo tsukaremashita.
I tried so hard that now I'm very tired.

愛しすぎて もう 別れられません。
Aishisugite mō wakareraremasen.
I love her so much that I can't be apart from her now.

❷ -**I** adjective/adjectival noun + **SUGITE**

美しすぎて 君が 怖い。
Utsukushisugite kimi ga kowai.
You are so beautiful that I'm afraid of you.

AKB 48 は有名すぎて 先生でも 知っていますよ。
Ēkēibī fōtī eito wa yūmei sugite sensei demo shitte imasu yo.
(The J-Pop group) AKB 48 are so famous that even the teacher knows them.

EXERCISE SET 8
Use the prompts to create sentences with -**SUGITE**. See suggested answers on page 203.

❶ [USE:] ソフト／むずかしい／うまく／使える
    sofuto / muzukashī / umaku / tsukaeru

_____

❷ [USE:] 太郎／ゲーム／おもしろい／やめる
    tarō /gēmu / omoshiroi / yameru

_____

❸ [USE:] 疲れる／朝まで／ぐっすり／寝られる
    tsukareru / asa made / gussuri / nerareru

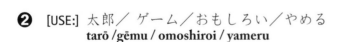

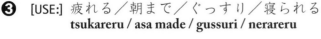

_____

🎧 5.11 Expressing "too (difficult) to (do)" using には …すぎます NI WA … -SUGIMASU

To express that something is too (adjective) to (verb), use the following structure:

Subject **WA** + plain form of verb + **NI WA** + **-I** adjective/adjectival noun + **-SUGIMASU**.

漢字は 書くには むずかしすぎます。
Kanji wa kaku ni wa muzukashisugimasu.
Kanji are too difficult to write.

ユニバーサルスタジオジャパンは 1 日で 見るには アトラクションが 多すぎます。
Yunibāsaru sutajio japan wa ichi nichi de miru ni wa atorakushon ga ōsugimasu.
Universal Studios Japan has too many attractions to see in one day.

EXERCISE SET 9
Use the prompts to create sentences with **-NI WA … -SUGIMASU**. See suggested answers on page 204.

❶ [USE:] 海岸／ゴミ／全部／拾う／広い
　　　　 kaigan / gomi / zenbu / hirou / hiroi

_____

❷ [USE:] 先生／説明／理解する／難しい
　　　　 sensei / setsumei / rikai suru / muzukashī

_____

🎧 5.12 Using ～すぎ -SUGI to express doing something too much

To talk about doing something too much, the following structure can be used:

verb + **-SUGI**, used as a noun or followed by **DA/DESU** at the end of a sentence.

飲みすぎ ですよ。食べすぎも よくないですよ。
Nomisugi desu yo. Tabesugi mo yokunai desu yo.
You're drinking too much. Eating too much isn't good either.

In the following example, note the particle **no** that connects the nouns **arubaito** and **shisugi**.

アルバイトのしすぎで 眠いです。
Arubaito no shisugi de nemui desu.
I am sleepy because of working too hard at my part-time job.

EXERCISE SET 10
Use **-SUGI** (as a noun) + **DESU NE** to rephrase the sentences below. Suggested answers on page 204.

❶ お菓子を ちょっと 買いすぎて いますね。
Okashi o chotto kaisugite imasu ne.

_____

❷ ゲームを しすぎて いますね。
Gēmu o shisugite imasu ne.

_____

🎧 CONVERSATION PRACTICE

アルバイトを したい ん ですが

マイク： アルバイトを したい ん ですが、いい アルバイトは ありませんか。
けんじ： でも、勉強が 忙しいし、家も 遠いし、時間が ないでしょ？
マイク： 遊ばないで 勉強するから、大丈夫なん です。
よう子： へぇ、どうして そんなに アルバイトが したい ん ですか。
マイク： なんでかというと、いろいろと 体験を して 社会について 学びたい から です。
けんじ： たしかに。アルバイトを しながら いろいろと 体験できますね。
よう子： でも、アルバイトを しすぎないで、勉強も しっかりと して下さいね。
マイク： はい。とにかく アルバイトを 探しに 行きたい ん ですが。
けんじ： よし、分かりました。いっしょに ハローワークへ 探しに 行きましょう。

Arubaito o shitai n desu ga

Mike: **Arubaito o shitai n desu ga, ī arubaito wa arimasen ka.**
Kenji: **Demo, benkyō ga isogashī shi, ie mo tōi shi, jikan ga nai desho?**
Mike: **Asobanai de benkyō suru kara, daijōbu na n desu.**
Yoko: **Hē, dōshite sonnani arubaito ga shitai n desu ka.**
Mike: **Nandeka to iu to, iroiro to taiken o shite shakai ni tsuite manabitai kara desu.**
Kenji: **Tashikani. Arubaito o shinagara iroiro to taiken dekimasu ne.**
Yoko: **Demo, arubaito o shisuginai de, benkyō mo shikkari to shite kudasai ne.**
Mike: **Hai. Tonikaku, arubaito o sagashini ikitai n desu ga.**
Kenji: **Yoshi, wakarimashita. Isshoni harōwāku e sagashini ikimashō.**

I'd Like to Work Part-Time

Mike: I'd like to work part-time. Aren't there any good part-time jobs?

Kenji: But you are busy with your studies, your house is far away, and you don't have time, do you?

Mike: Since I study and don't go out with friends, it's no problem.

Yoko: Hmmm, why do you want to work part-time so much?

Mike: Because I want to have different experiences and learn about society.

Kenji: You can certainly experience many things working part-time, can't you?

Yoko: But don't do too much part-time work, and please study hard.

Mike: Yes. Anyhow, I would like to go and look for a part-time job.

Kenji: OK. I see. Let's go together to Hello Work [*a job-placement office*] and have a look.

TASK

Create a dialogue with **N DESU GA** and **KARA DESU** and practice it.

_____ : _____

_____ : _____

🎧 READING PRACTICE

日本の祭り

日本では あちこちに たくさん 祭りがあるので、どこでも いろいろな 祭りを 見て 楽しめます。京都の祇園祭、大阪の天神祭、東京の神田祭を 日本三大祭と言います。ほかにも 日本中に 祭りが たくさん ありすぎて 数えられません。

祭りの時は、子供から お年寄りまで、祭りを 見に来る人が 多すぎて、どこも 座る場所 が ありません。祭りでは、参加する人が 山車を 引いたり、御輿を 担いだりします。

夏には、多くの花火大会が あります。数十万発の花火が、港や川から 上がりますが、人が 多すぎて ときどき 見る場所が 取れません。

東京ディズニーランドの ミッキーたちの キャラクター行進は 現代的な祭りと 言えます。山車である電飾パレードが 行進し、花火も 上がり、大勢の人が それを見ます。今 も 昔も たくさんの人が 一緒に 楽しむ様子は 同じです。

Nihon no matsuri

Nihon de wa achikochi ni takusan matsuri ga aru node, doko demo iroirona matsuri o mite tanoshimemasu. Kyōto no gion matsuri, ōsaka no tenjin matsuri, tōkyō no kanda matsuri o nihon sandai matsuri to īmasu. Hoka ni mo nihonjū ni wa matsuri ga takusan arisugite kazoeraremasen.

Matsuri no toki wa, kodomo kara otoshiyori made, matsuri o mini kuru hito ga ōsugite, doko mo suwaru basho ga arimasen. Matsuri de wa, sanka suru hito ga dashi o hītari, mikoshi o katsuidari shimasu.

Natsu ni wa, ōkuno hanabi taikai ga arimasu. Sūjū manpatsu no hanabi ga, minato ya kawa kara agarimasu ga, hito ga ōsugite tokidoki miru basho ga toremasen.

Tōkyō dizunīrando no mikkī tachi no kyarakutā kōshin wa gendaitekina matsuri to iemasu. Dashi de aru denshoku parēdo ga kōshin shi, hanabi mo agari, ōzei no hito ga sore o mimasu. Ima mo mukashi mo takusan no hito ga isshoni tanoshimu yōsu wa onaji desu.

Japanese Festivals

Since there are many festivals throughout Japan, you can enjoy watching them wherever you are. Kyoto's Gion Festival, Osaka's Tenjin Festival and Tokyo's Kanda Festival are said to be the three main festivals of Japan. There are too many festivals all over Japan to count.

At the time of a festival many people, from children to old people, come to watch so there is no place to sit down. At a festival, participants pull a festival float or shoulder a mikoshi.

There are many firework displays in summer. Hundreds of thousands of fireworks are set off from a harbor or a river, and there are lots of people, so sometimes you can't find a viewing place.

The parade with Mickey Mouse and other characters at Tokyo Disneyland can be said to be a modern festival. There is an electrical parade, which is like a festival float parade, fireworks are also set off, and many people watch. Many people enjoy themselves together as they did a long time ago.

QUESTIONS
Answers with their suggested sentence structure can be found on page 204.

1. 日本には 祭りが どれぐらい ありますか。
   Nihon ni wa matsuri ga dore gurai arimasu ka.

2. 祭りの時は どんな人が 見に 来ますか。
   Matsuri no toki wa donna hito ga mini kimasu ka.

3. 花火は どこから 上がりますか。
   Hanabi wa doko kara agarimasu ka.

CHAPTER 6

I Think I'll Go to Itsukushima Shrine Next Time

今度 宮島の 厳島神社に 行こうと 思います

Expressing Intentions and Plans and Giving Advice

In this chapter you'll learn how to use the structures **TO OMOIMASU, TO OMOTTE IMASU, TSUMORI DESU**, and **YOTEI DESU** to express intentions and plans. You'll learn to give advice using the construction **-TA HŌ GA Ī DESU,** and to express how to do something using the suffix **-KATA.**

In Japanese grammar, the verb form used for expressing intentions and plans and giving advice is called the volitional form. When a verb is described as "volitional," it means the action is intended. In a non-volitional verb, such as "understand," "(can) see," or "(can) hear," for example, the action is beyond the control of the speaker. Keep this in mind as you study the grammar of this chapter.

🎧 KEY SENTENCE PATTERNS

1. 今度 宮島の 厳島神社に 行こうと 思います。
   Kondo miyajima no itsukushima jinja ni ikō to omoimasu.   *I think I will...*
   I think I'll go to Itsukushima Shrine next.

2. でも、友だちは 高野山に 行こうと 思っています。
   Demo, tomodachi wa kōyasan ni ikō to omotte imasu.   *the third person thinks he/she will...*
   But my friend thinks he will go to Mount Koya.

3. もう 健康に 悪い タバコは やめる つもりです。
   Mō kenkō ni warui tabako wa yameru tsumori desu.   *I intend to...*
   I intend to give up smoking because it is bad for my health.

4. 帰国して また 来年 来日する 予定です。
   Kikoku shite mata rainen rainichi suru yotei desu.   *I am scheduled to...*
   I'm scheduled to go home to my country and return to Japan next year.

5. 京都だけ でなく 奈良(に)も 行った方が いいですよ。
   Kyōto dake de naku nara (ni) mo itta hō ga ī desu yo.   *it might be better to...*
   It might be better to visit not only Kyoto but also Nara.

6. 将棋の 次は 囲碁の やり方を 覚える つもりです。
   Shōgi no tsugi wa igo no yarikata o oboeru tsumori desu.   *how to...*
   I'm going to learn how to play go after shogi.

Formation of the Volitional Form

	Dictionary Form	→	Plain Volitional Form			
-U Verbs	行く **iku**	→	行こう **iko-**	+ **o**	**ikō**	
-RU Verbs	見る **miru**	→	見よう **mi-**	+ **yō**	**miyō**	
Irregular Verbs	する **suru**	→	しよう **shi-**	+ **yō**	**shiyō**	
	来る **kuru**	→	来よう **ko-**	+ **yō**	**koyō**	

GRAMMAR AND USAGE NOTES

🎧 6.1 Expressing "let's ..." using 〜う／よう -O/YŌ

-ō and **-YŌ** are the plain-form verb endings used to express "let's." Their polite equivalent is **-MASHŌ**.

ゲームを やろう。
Gēmu o yarō.   *Let's play the game.* (casual)

ゲームを やりましょう。
Gēmu o yarimashō.   *Let's play the game.* (polite)

じゃ、僕が やろう。
Ja, boku ga yarō.   *Then I will do it.* (casual)

では、私が やりましょう。
Dewa, watashi ga yarimashō.   *Then I will do it.* (polite)

The sentence-ending particle **YO** may often be added to express asking for agreement.

ゲームを やろうよ。
Gēmu o yarō yo.   *Let's play the game, OK?* (casual)

EXERCISE SET 1
Fill in the blanks with the **-O/YŌ** form of each verb. Check your answers on page 204.

Dictionary form	Plain volitional form -O/YŌ
1. 走る **hashiru** (to run)	
2. 食べる **taberu** (to eat)	
3. 買う **kau** (to buy)	
4. 起きる **okiru** (get up)	
5. 確認する **kakunin suru** (to confirm)	

6.2 Expressing one's thoughts using と思います／と思っています TO OMOIMASU/ TO OMOTTE IMASU

TO + **OMOIMASU/OMOTTE IMASU** comes at the end of a clause to express "one thinks that + sentence." Note that the form **TO OMOIMASU** only expresses the speaker's thinking. To express the thinking of a third person the form **TO OMOTTE IMASU** is used (and this form may also sometimes be used to express the speaker's thinking, as in the third example below).

［太郎さんは 私が 好きだ］と 思います。
[Tarō san wa watashi ga suki da] to omoimasu.   *I think Taro likes me.*
太郎さんは ［私が 好きだ］と 思っています。
Tarō san wa [watashi ga suki da] to omotte imasu.   *Taro thinks I like him./Taro thinks he likes me.*

［太郎さんは 私が 好きだ］と 思っています。
[Tarō san wa watashi ga suki da] to omotte imasu.   *I'm thinking Taro likes me.*

6.3 Expressing one's will using 〜う／よう と思います／と思っています -O/YŌ TO OMOIMASU/TO OMOTTE IMASU

The plain volitional form (as shown in the chart at the top of the facing page) + **TO OMOIMASU/ TO OMOTTE IMASU** expresses one's will, desire, or plan. This form conveys a less fixed intention than **TSUMORI DESU**.

富士山に 登ろうと 思います。
Fuji san ni noborō to omoimasu.

I think I'll climb Mount Fuji./ I'm planning to climb Mount Fuji.

富士山に 登る つもりです。
Fuji san ni noboru tsumori desu.

I intend to climb Mount Fuji.

太郎さんも 富士山に 登ろうと 思っています。
Tarō san mo fuji san ni noborō to omotte imasu.

Taro also thinks he'll climb Mount Fuji./ Taro also plans to climb Mount Fuji.

太郎さんも 富士山に 登る つもりです。
Tarō san mo fuji san ni noboru tsumori desu.

Taro also intends to climb Mount Fuji.

やっぱり ガラケーに しようと 思います。友だちはスマホにしようと 思っています。
Yappari garakē ni shiyō to omoimasu. Tomodachi wa sumaho ni shiyō to omotte imasu.
I think I will buy a feature phone after all. My friend is going to buy a smartphone.

JLPT の N3 に 合格しようと 思います。
JLPT no N san ni gōkaku shiyō to omoimasu.   *I'll try to pass the N3 level of the JLPT.*

JLPT の N3 に 合格したいと 思います。
JLPT no N san ni gōkaku shitai to omoimasu.   *I want to pass the N3 level of the JLPT.*

In questions addressed to the second person, you should use **OMOIMASU KA**.

どの携帯電話に しようと 思いますか。
Dono keitai denwa ni shiyō to <u>omoimasu ka</u>.
Which cell phone do you think you will choose?

EXERCISE SET 2

Use the prompts to create sentences with **TO OMOIMASU** or **TO OMOTTE IMASU**. See suggested answers on page 204.

❶ [USE:] 私／彼女／ダンス／練習する
watashi / kanojo / dansu / renshū suru

_____

❷ [USE:] ピアノ／練習／やめる
piano / renshū / yameru

_____

❸ [USE:] 花子／神様に／お願いする
hanako / kamisama ni / onegai suru

_____

❹ [USE:] バレンタインデー／彼氏／チョコレート／あげる
barentain dē / kareshi / chokorēto / ageru

_____

🎧 6.4 Expressing one's firm intention using つもり TSUMORI and よてい YOTEI

TSUMORI (intention) and **YOTEI** (arrangement) are nouns that can be modified by the dictionary form or the negative **-NAI** form of the verb.

行く + つもり　　　　　　行かない + つもり
iku + tsumori　　　　　**ikanai + tsumori**
intention to go　　　　　intention not to go

行く + 予定　　　　　　　行かない + 予定
iku + yotei　　　　　　**ikanai + yotei**
arrangement to go　　　arrangement not to go

The subject can be connected to the nouns, **TSUMORI** and **YOTEI** by the linking verb **DA/DESU**.

私は 今度 世界文化遺産の 姫路城に 上る つもりです。
<u>Watashi wa</u> kondo sekai bunka isan no himejijō ni noboru tsumori <u>desu</u>.
I intend to go to the top of Himeji Castle, a World Cultural Heritage Site, next time.
[*lit.* I <u>am</u> the intention of going to the top of Himeji Castle.]

However, whereas the negative of **DESU** is usually **DEWA ARIMASEN**, when used with **TSUMORI** the negative is **WA/GA ARIMASEN**.

私は 行くつもりです。
Watashi wa iku tsumori <u>desu</u>.
I intend to go.

私は 行くつもりは／が ありません。
Watashi wa iku tsumori <u>wa/ga arimasen</u>.
I am not intending to go.

INCORRECT:
私は 行くつもりでは ありません。
Watashi wa iku tsumori <u>dewa arimasen</u>.

Therefore, the following two sentences have the same meaning.

今週末は 遊びに 行かない つもりです。
Konshūmatsu wa asobi ni ikanai tsumori desu.

今週末は 遊びに 行く つもりは ありません。
Konshūmatsu wa asobi ni iku tsumori wa arimasen.
I have no intention of going out to have fun this weekend.

EXERCISE SET 3

Use the prompts to create sentences with **TSUMORI/YOTEI + DESU** or **TSUMORI/YOTEI WA ARIMASEN**. See suggested answers on page 204.

❶ [USE:] 今日も／仕事／頑張る
kyō mo / shigoto / ganbaru

_____

❷ [USE:] これから／両社／協力する
kore kara / ryōsha / kyōryoku suru

_____

❸ [USE:] 銀行／百万円／貯金する
ginkō / hyaku-man en / chokin suru

_____

❹ [USE:] 車／乗る
kuruma / noru

_____

⑤ [USE:] 人間ドック／検査する
ningen dokku / kensa suru

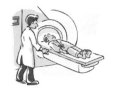

🎧 6.5 Giving friendly advice using ～た方が いいです -TA HŌ GA Ī DESU

The word **hō** means "option," thus the above phrase literally means that the option mentioned is better. The dictionary form of the verb may also precede **HŌ** + **GA Ī DESU**, but this sounds more forceful and frank than the **-TA** form. To soften the tone, the sentence-ending particle **YO** may be added.

特急で 行った方が いいですよ。
Tokkyū de itta hō ga ī desu yo.
It would be better to go by limited express train.

パチンコを やめる方が いいですよ。
Pachinko o yameru hō ga ī desu yo.
You had better (or *should*) *stop playing pachinko.*

Giving advice not to do something is expressed by the **-NAI** form of the verb + **HŌ GA Ī DESU**.

電車の中で 大きな声で 電話を し<u>ない</u>方がいいですよ。
Densha no naka de ōkina koe de denwa o shi<u>nai</u> hō ga ī desu yo.
You shouldn't speak loudly on your phone in the train.

To give friendly advice more indirectly, add **TO OMOIMASU (YO)**.

あんまり 飲まない方が いい<u>と 思いますよ</u>。
Anmari nomanai hō ga ī <u>to omoimasu yo</u>.
I think it would be better not to drink too much (alcohol).

EXERCISE SET 4
Use the prompts to create sentences with **-TA/-NAI HŌ GA Ī DESU YO**. Suggested answers on page 204.

❶ [USE:] 休む／よ
yasumu /yo

❷ [USE:] 無理に／食べる／よ
muri ni / taberu / yo

❸ [USE:] お父さん！／もっと／お母さん／話す／よ
Otōsan! / motto / okāsan / hanasu / yo

___

🎧 6.6 Expressing how to do something using ～方 -KATA

The front part of the **-MASU** form + **KATA** means "how to do something."

EXERCISE SET 5

Fill in the blanks with the **-KATA** form of each verb. Check your answers on page 204.

Dictionary form	-KATA form
1. 書く **kaku** (to write)	
2. 読む **yomu** (to read)	
3. 見る **miru** (to view)	
4. する **suru** (to do)	

When the verb before **-KATA** takes an element marked by a particle, **NO** must be inserted to connect the preceding element and the noun phrase **-KATA**.

［東京駅の 八重洲南口へ］の 行き方が 分かりません。
[Tōkyō eki no yaesu minamiguchi e] no ikikata ga wakarimasen.
I don't know how to get to the Yaesu south exit of Tokyo Station.

Note that the particle **NO** is placed after whichever particle marks the element:

八重洲南口へ 行く
yaesu minamiguchi e iku   *to go to the Yaesu south exit*

八重洲南口への 行き方
yaesu minamiguchi e no ikikata   *how to go to the Yaesu south exit*

日本人 と 付き合う
nihonjin to tsukiau   *to keep company with Japanese people*

日本人との 付き合い方
nihonjin to no tsukiaikata   *how to keep company with Japanese people*

However, the particle **E** can often be omitted before **NO,** and **NI** cannot precede **NO**:

CORRECT: 八重洲南口(へ)の 行き方   INCORRECT: 八重洲南口にの 行き方
    yaesu minamiguchi (e) no ikikata   **yaesu minamiguchi ni no ikikata**

The object marker **O** must be deleted before **NO**:

箸<u>を</u> 使う
hashi <u>o</u> tsukau   *to use chopsticks*

箸<u>の</u> 使い方 (INCORRECT: 箸<u>をの</u> 使い方)
hashi <u>no</u> tsukaikata   *how to use chopsticks*

When the verb is a action noun + **suru,** the particle **NO** must be inserted between the noun and the word **shikata,** meaning *way of doing.* Thus, a double or triple **NO** occurs in this type of phrase. (Note that the word **shikata** has its own kanji, 仕方.)

日本語を 勉強する   →   日本語<u>の</u> 勉強<u>の</u> し方(= 仕方)
nihongo o benkyō suru   **nihongo <u>no</u> benkyō <u>no</u> shikata**
to study Japanese   *how to study Japanese*

写真を 添付する   →   写真<u>の</u> 添付<u>の</u> 仕方
shashin o tenpu suru   **shashin <u>no</u> tenpu <u>no</u> shikata**
to attach a photo (to an e-mail)   *how to attach a photo*

ファイルを メールに 添付する → ファイル<u>の</u> メール<u>への</u> 添付<u>の</u>仕方
fairu o mēru ni* tenpu suru   **fairu <u>no</u> mēru <u>e no</u>* tenpu <u>no</u> shikata**
to attach a file to an e-mail   *how to attach a file to an e-mail*

*Note that **NI** must be changed to **E** because **NI** + **NO** is ungrammatical.

EXERCISE SET 6
Use **-KATA** to rephrase or translate the sentences, as in the examples. Answers on page 204.

Example
1) 成田空港へ 行きます。   **Narita kūkō e ikimasu.**   <u>成田空港への行き方</u>
2) *how to eat sushi*   <u>寿司の食べ方</u>

❶ 日本語で 手紙を 書きます。
   Nihongo de tegami o kakimasu.   _____

❷ ホテルを 予約します。
   Hoteru o yoyaku shimasu.   _____

❸ ソフトを インストールします。
   Sofuto o insutōru shimasu.   _____

❹ 新幹線に 乗ります。
   Shinkansen ni norimasu.   _____

❺ how to learn kanji   _____

❻ how to get in a Japanese bath   _____

❼ how to live in Tokyo _____

❽ how to send a parcel abroad _____

🎧 6.7 Expressing the method for doing something using 方法 HŌHŌ

HŌHŌ (方法) is a noun meaning "method." To express the method for doing something, we can use the following structure:

dictionary form of the verb + HŌHŌ

This structure has the same function as -KATA in 6.6. Note the difference in the particle that marks "the photocopier" in each of the following sentences:

［コピー機を 使う］方法が 分かりません。
[Kopīki o tsukau] hōhō ga wakarimasen.
I don't know the method for using the photocopier.

コピー機の 使い方が 分かりません。
Kopīki no tsukaikata ga wakarimasen.
I don't know how to use the photocopier.

EXERCISE SET 7
Rephrase the sentences using HŌHŌ. See suggested answers on page 204.

❶ 私は 泳ぎ方を 知りません。
Watashi wa oyogikata o shirimasen.

_____

❷ 東京駅の 八重洲南口への 行き方が 分かりません。
Tōkyō eki no yaesu minamiguchi e no ikikata ga wakarimasen.

_____

❸ 日本人との 付き合い方は ちょっと むずかしいです。
Nihonjin to no tsukiaikata wa chotto muzukashī desu.

_____

❹ 箸の 使い方を いつ 覚えましたか。
Hashi no tsukaikata o itsu oboemashita ka.

_____

EXERCISE SET 8
Look at the pictures and create sentences with **NO SHIKATA**. See suggested answers on page 204.

❶ [USE:] タブレット／操作／分かる
taburetto / sōsa / wakaru

_____

❷ [USE:] 花／デザイン／覚える
hana / dezain / oboeru

_____

❸ [USE:] 花子／ 田植え／よく／知っている
Hanako / taue / yoku / shitte iru

_____

🎧 **CONVERSATION PRACTICE**

割り勘
けんじ： 来日して 2週間 経ちましたが、日本での 生活の仕方は どうですか。
マイク： 大丈夫ですよ。けっこう 面白い ことが ありますね。
よう子： 面白い ことって、どんな ことですか。
マイク： お金の 払い方です。先日、友だち3人と 一緒に 居酒屋で 飲んだり 食べたり
しましたが、レジの前で みんな 自分の料理のお金だけ 払っていました。
けんじ： 割り勘のことですね。みんなは 自分の お金だけ 払おうと 思っていますね。
マイク： そうです。それに、計算が とても 正確で 驚きました。私は、自分が 食べた
料理を 計算したら、2,982円 だったので、3,000円 出す つもりでした。
よう子： 18円の お釣りですね。
マイク： ええ。確かに 18円の お釣りを もらいました。レジの前で 小さな 計算を して、
時間が かかりました。
けんじ： 店に 迷惑ですね。もっと お金の 出し方を 考えた方が いいと 思いますね。

Warikan

Kenji: **Rainichi shite ni shūkan tachimashita ga, nihon de no seikatsu no shikata wa dō desu ka.**

Mike: **Daijōbu desu yo. Kekkō omoshiroi koto ga arimasu ne.**

Yoko: **Omoshiroi koto tte, donna koto desu ka.**

Mike: **Okane no haraikata desu. Senjitsu, tomodachi san nin to isshoni izakaya de nondari tabetari shimashita ga, reji no mae de minna jibun no ryōri no okane dake haratte imashita.**

Kenji: **Warikan no koto desu ne. Minna wa jibun no okane dake haraō to omotte imasu ne.**

Mike: **Sō desu. Soreni, keisan ga totemo seikaku de odorokimashita. Watashi wa jibun ga tabeta ryōri o keisan shitara, ni sen kyūhyaku hachi jū ni en datta node, san zen en dasu tsumori deshita.**

Yoko: **Jūhachi en no otsuri desu ne.**

Mike: **Ē. Tashikani jū hachi en no otsuri o moraimashita. Reji no mae de chīsana keisan o shite, jikan ga kakarimashita.**

Kenji: **Mise ni meiwaku desu ne. Motto okane no dashikata o kangaeta hō ga ī to omoimasu ne.**

Splitting the Bill

Kenji: It's been two weeks since you came to Japan. What do you think about living here?

Mike: It's ok. There are some interesting things, aren't there?

Yoko: And what are the things that you find interesting?

Mike: The way you pay for things. When I went eating and drinking with my three friends at an izakaya the other day, everyone paid only for their own dish at the cash register.

Kenji: It's a Dutch treat, isn't it? Everyone thinks they will pay only for what they had.

Mike: Right. The calculation was so exact that I was surprised. Since it was 2,982 yen when I calculated how much my food cost, I was going to put in 3,000 yen.

Yoko: And you got 18 yen change, didn't you?

Mike: Yes, that's right, 18 yen change. We spent a long time standing at the cash register while they made these small calculations.

Kenji: It is a nuisance for the shop, isn't it? I think they should find a better way of paying.

TASK

Create a dialogue with **-O/YŌ TO OMOIMASU** or **TSUMORI/YOTEI DESU** and practice it.

_____ : _____

_____ : _____

日本の食事のマナー

日本での 食事の 仕方を 説明しようと 思います。まず、食事の 始めに 「いただきます」と 言います。これは 仏教の 教えで、「いただく」は 「もらう」という意味の 謙譲語です。米や 野菜や 肉、魚などの 命を もらうので、「いただきます」と 言いながら、手を 合わせます。

私も これから もっと 食べ物に 感謝しながら 食べる つもりです。日本では 「いただきます」と 言わずに 食べない方が いいでしょう。食事が 終わったら、今度は 「ごちそうさま」と 言った方が いいと思います。

和食では、箸の 使い方も 大切だと 思います。食事の 時には 箸使いの タブーに 気を 付けた方が いいでしょう。例えば、「刺し箸」と 言う言葉が ありますが、食べ物を 箸で 刺しながら 食べない方が いいです。もう一つ 意味も漢字も 違う 「指し箸」があって、箸で 人や 物を 指したりするのも しない方が いいです。箸から 箸へ 食べ物を 渡す 「拾い箸」（箸渡し）も タブーです。

それから、ずるずると 音を 立てながら 汁物を 飲まない方が いいでしょう。それは 下品ですね。でも、実は、ラーメンや うどんや そばを 食べながら 音を 立てる 日本人は 多いのです。

Nihon no shokuji no manā

Nihon de no shokuji no shikata o setsumei shiyō to omoimasu. Mazu, shokuji no hajime ni "itadakimasu" to īmasu. Kore wa bukkyō no oshie de, "itadaku" wa "morau" to iu imi no kenjōgo desu. Kome ya yasai ya niku, sakana nado no inochi o morau node, "itadakimasu" to īnagara, te o awasemasu.

Watashi mo korekara motto tabemono ni kansha shinagara taberu tsumori desu. Nihon de wa "itadakimasu" to iwazuni tabenai hō ga ī deshō. Shokuji ga owattara, kondo wa "gochisōsama" to itta hō ga ī to omoimasu.

Washoku de wa, hashi no tsukaikata mo taisetsu da to omoimasu. Shokuji no toki ni wa hashizukai no tabū ni ki o tsuketa hō ga ī deshō. Tatoeba, "sashibashi" to iu kotoba ga arimasu ga, tabemono o hashi de sashinagara tabenai hō ga ī desu. Mo hitotsu imi mo kanji mo chigau "sashibashi" ga atte, hashi de hito ya mono o sashitari suru mono shinai hō ga ī desu. Hashi kara hashi e tabemono o watasu "hiroibashi" (hashiwatashi) mo tabū desu.

Sorekara, zuruzuru to oto o tatenagara shirumono o nomanai hō ga ī deshō. Sore wa gehin desu ne. Demo, jitsu wa, rāmen ya udon ya soba o tabenagara oto o tateru nihonjin wa ōi no desu.

Japanese Table Manners

I'd like to explain how to have a meal in Japan. First, we say **itadakimasu** at the beginning of a meal. This is Buddhist teaching, and **itadaku** is the humble word for "to receive." We pray with hands together, saying, "I will receive," because we are taking the life of rice, vegetables, meat, fish, etc.

I intend to appreciate food more from now on. In Japan you shouldn't eat without saying **itadakimasu**. When you have finished eating, you should say **gochisōsama**.

I think the way you use chopsticks is also important for Japanese-style food. You should be careful about taboos when using chopsticks at mealtimes. For example, there is a word **sashibashi** (stabbing with chopsticks), and you shouldn't eat while stabbing your food with chopsticks. There is another word **sashibashi**, with a different meaning and different kanji, which means pointing at people or food with chopsticks. This is also something you shouldn't do. **Hiroibashi** (or **hashiwatashi**), meaning to pass food from chopsticks to chopsticks, is also taboo.

Also, you probably shouldn't make a slurping noise when you drink soup from the bowl. It's vulgar. But in fact, there are many Japanese people who make a noise when eating ramen, udon and soba.

QUESTIONS

Answers with their suggested sentence structure can be found on page 205.

1. 日本では なぜ 食事の前に 「いただきます」 と 言いますか。
   Nihon dewa naze shokuji no mae ni "itadakimasu" to īmasu ka.

2. 箸の使い方で、例えば、どう しない方が いいですか。
   Hashi no tsukaikata de, tatoeba, dō shinai hō ga ī desu ka.

3. 何を 食べながら 音を 立てる 日本人が 多いですか。
   Nani o tabenagara oto o tateru nihonjin ga ōi desu ka.

CHAPTER 7

I'll Keep the Air Conditioner Set at 28°C
エアコンの設定を 28 度 にして おきます

Keeping Things in the Same State

In this chapter you'll learn how to talk about keeping things in the same state, or creating a state, using the constructions **-TE OKIMASU**, **-TE IMASU**, **-TE ARIMASU**, **-PPANASHI** and **MAMA**. These sentences can be tricky, as the subject is often understood rather than stated explicitly, but this chapter will help you grasp the nuance and appropriate usage of each construction.

🎧 KEY SENTENCE PATTERNS

1. エアコンの設定を 28度 にして おきます。
   Eakon no settei o ni jū hachi do ni shite okimasu. *Keeping a thing in a certain condition*
   I'll keep the air conditioner set at 28°C.

2. コーヒーを 入れて おきます。
   Kōhī o irete okimasu. *The speaker doing something beforehand*
   I'll make some coffee and keep it (for you).

3. コーヒーが 入って います。
   Kōhī ga haitte imasu. *Something being in a certain state*
   (Coffee was made and) the coffee is there (for you).

4. コーヒーが 入れて あります。
   Kōhī ga irete arimasu. *Somebody having done something*
   (Somebody made coffee and) the coffee is there (for you).

5. コーヒーを 入れて あります。
   Kōhī o irete arimasu. *The speaker having done something*
   I made coffee (and have been keeping it for you).

6. ファンヒーターを つけっ放しに しないで下さい。
   Fan hītā o tsukeppanashi ni shinaide kudasai. *Leaving something in a specified state*
   Please don't leave the fan heater turned on.

7. 屋台で 立ったまま ラーメンを 食べました。
   Yatai de tatta mama rāmen o tabemashita. *Doing two things at the same time*
   I ate ramen noodles standing up at a food stall.

Formation of Sentences Expressing a State

❶ Keeping something or something being kept in the same state

Agent	Object Marker	Verb		
The speaker	+ **O/WA**	+ transitive verb* (**-TE**)		+ **OKIMASU**
Someone/the speaker	+ **GA**	+ intransitive verb (**-TE**)		+ **IMASU**
Someone	+ **GA**	+ transitive verb (**-TE**)		+ **ARIMASU**
The speaker	+ **O**	+ transitive verb (**-TE**)		+ **ARIMASU**

*a transitive verb takes an object; an intransitive verb does not take an object

❷ Leaving something in a particular state

Agent	Object Marker	Verb	
Someone/the speaker	+ **O**	+ front of **-MASU** form	+ **-PPANASHI NI SHIMASU**

GRAMMAR AND USAGE NOTES

🎧 7.1 Expressing a state using ～て おきます -TE OKIMASU

The verb **OKU** means to put (something in a certain state). The implication is as follows:

O/WA + **-TE** form of transitive verb   + **OKU**
The speaker does something and...   keeps/puts it in a state for a specified purpose.

Sentence 1 on page 97 implies that the purpose of setting the air conditioner at 28°C is to save energy. Sentence 2 implies that the purpose of making the coffee is to serve it to the other person. Consider also the following sentences and their implied meanings.

燃える ゴミと 燃えない ゴミを 分けて おきます。
Moeru gomi to moenai gomi o wakete okimasu.
I'll separate the combustible from the non-combustible trash (so that we can dump it later).

食べた お皿は 返却口に 戻して おいて下さい。
Tabeta osara wa henkyakuguchi ni modoshite oite kudasai.
Please return the plates to the drop-off point after eating (and keep the table clean).

いすは そのままに して おいて下さい。
Isu wa sonomama ni shite oite kudasai.
Please leave the chairs (you used) as they are (so that I can place them as I like).

The subject in a question may be ambiguous, but the verb ending **-MASHŌ KA** clearly implies the subject is the speaker.

エアコンはつけておきますか。
Eakon wa tsukete okimasu ka.
Shall I leave the air conditioner turned on?/Do you leave the air conditioner turned on?

エアコンはつけておきましょうか。
Eakon wa tsukete okimashō ka.
Shall I leave the air conditioner turned on?

EXERCISE SET 1

Translate the sentences using **-TE OKIMASU**. Check your answers on page 205.

❶ *I have kept the oil fan heater on for you.*
[USE:] 石油ファンヒーター／つける
sekiyu fan hītā / tsukeru

_____

❷ *I'll do the shopping beforehand at the 100 yen shop.*
[USE:] 100 円ショップ／買い物／する
hyaku en shoppu / kaimono / suru

_____

❸ *I'll sleep tight (ready for tomorrow).*
[USE:] ぐっすり／寝る
gussuri / neru

_____

❹ *I'll shovel snow off the roof (for safety's sake).*
[USE:] シャベル／雪／屋根／から／下ろす
shaberu / yuki / yane / kara / orosu

_____

🎧 7.2 Expressing a temporary state using (が) ～て います (GA) -TE IMASU

The verb **IRU** means to temporarily be in a certain state. The implication is as follows:

GA + **-TE** form of intransitive verb   **+ IRU**
Something attains a certain state and...   it remains in that state for a specified purpose.

The literal translation of the sentence below shows the underlying meaning of this structure:

コーヒーが 入って   います。
Kōhi ga haitte   **imasu.**
Coffee comes (into the cup) and...   *it remains (in the cup so as to be drunk by you).*

Note that who made the coffee is not mentioned. In many cases somebody else may have made the coffee, though the speaker could use this structure as a humble way of saying they made the coffee.

抹茶が できています。　　　　　　　*できる **dekiru** (to be made)
Matcha ga dekite imasu.
Matcha tea has been made.

彼女に 告白する 覚悟が できていますか。
Kanojo ni kokuhaku suru kakugo ga dekite imasu ka.
Are you ready to declare your love to her?

私たちが 乗る 新幹線が もう ホームに 来ています。
Watashitachi ga noru shinkansen ga mō hōmu ni kite imasu.
The bullet train we are going to take has already arrived at the platform (and it is there).

EXERCISE SET 2

Use the prompts to create sentences with **(... GA) ... -TE IMASU** following the examples above. See suggested answers on page 205.

❶ [USE:] パソコン／壊れる
　　　　pasokon / kowareru

_____

❷ [USE:] 店／閉まる
　　　　mise / shimaru

_____

❸ [USE:] パン／焼ける
　　　　pan / yakeru

_____

❹ [USE:] あそこ／防犯カメラ／付く
　　　　asoko / bōhan kamera / tsuku

_____

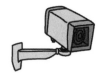

🎧 7.3 Expressing an ongoing state using （が）〜て あります (GA) -TE ARIMASU

The verb **ARU** means to be standing still (in a certain state). The implication is as follows:

GA + **-TE** form of transitive verb　　+ **ARU** (**GA ARU** = there is)
Somebody does something and...　　it remains in the resulting state for a specified purpose.

The literal translation of the sentence below shows the underlying meaning of this structure:

コーヒーが 入れて　　　　あります。
Kōhi ga irete　　　　arimasu.
Somebody made coffee and...　　it remains (in the cup so as to be drunk by you).

Who made the coffee is not mentioned. Thus, in many cases somebody else has made the coffee.

掲示に 「禁煙」 と 書いて あります。
Keiji ni "kin'en" to kaite arimasu.
The notice says "No Smoking."
(Somebody wrote "No Smoking," and it is on the notice.)

車両に 「女性専用車両」 と 書いて あります。
Sharyō ni "josei sen'yō sharyō" to kaite arimasu.
The car says that it is for women only.
(Somebody wrote, "women-only train car.")

EXERCISE SET 3

Translate the sentences using **(... GA) ... -TE ARIMASU**. See suggested answers on page 205.

❶ *The documents have been printed.*
　[USE:] 資料／印刷する
　　　shiryō / insatsu suru

_____

❷ *Lots of apps are installed on my phone.*
　[USE:] スマホ／たくさん／アプリ／インストールする
　　　sumaho / takusan /apuri / instōru suru

_____

❸ *My locker's (been) locked!*
　[USE:] ロッカー／鍵／かける
　　　rokkā / kagi / kakeru

_____

❹ *The dollars have been changed into yen.*
　[USE:] ドル／円／替える
　　　doru / en / kaeru

_____

🎧 7.4 Expressing creating a state with （を）〜て あります (O) -TE ARIMASU

The implication is as follows:

O + **-TE** form of transitive verb   + **ARU**
I did something and...   it remains in the resulting state for a specified purpose.

The literal translation of the sentence below shows the underlying meaning of this structure:

コーヒーを 入れて　　　　　　　　あります。
Kōhi o irete　　　　　　　　　　　**arimasu.**
Somebody made coffee and...　　*it remains (in the cup so as to be drunk by you).*

Note that the use of the object particle **O** usually implies that the speaker has made the coffee.

🎧 7.5 Describing an ongoing state using 〜っ放し です -PPANASHI DESU

This structure comes from the verb **hanasu** 放す, which means to turn loose or set free. It is used to describe something that has been left in an ongoing state. The structure is as follows:

front part of the **-MASU** form of the verb with the suffix **-PPANASHI** + **DESU**

私は いつも ゲームで 負けっぱなし です。
Watashi wa itsumo gēmu de makeppanashi desu.
I have been having a losing streak in the game.

ラッシュアワーの 電車の 中で ずっと 立ちっぱなしでした。
Rasshu awā no densha no naka de zutto tachippanashi deshita.
I was standing up the whole way on the rush-hour train.

夫は いつも お皿を 出しっぱなし です。
Otto wa itsumo osara o dashippanashi desu.
My husband always leaves the dishes lying around.

🎧 7.6 Carelessly leaving something in a certain state using （を）〜っ放し にします (O) -PPANASHI NI SHIMASU

The phrase **-PPANASHI NI SHIMASU** must follow a transitive verb with an object marked by **O**. The phrase **NI SHIMASU** means to leave something as it is. The structure is as follows:

object + **O** + front part of the **-MASU** form of the verb with the suffix **-PPANASHI** + **NI SHIMASU**

The implication is as follows:

O + **-PPANASHI**　　　　　　　　　　**NI SHIMASU**
One does something and...　　　　　　carelessly leaves something in the resulting state.

The literal translation of the sentence below shows the underlying meaning of this structure:

ファンヒーターを つけっ放し　　　　に します。
Fan hītā o tsukeppanashi　　　　　　**ni shimasu.**
One turns on the fan heater and...　　*leaves it on / forgets to turn it off.*

Who turns on the fan heater is not mentioned. The subject may be the first, second or third person.

スマホを 机の上に 置きっぱなし にしていますよ。
Sumaho o tsukue no ue ni okippanashi ni shite imasu yo.
You've left your smartphone on the desk.

疲れて よく テレビを つけっぱなし にして 寝てしまいます。
Tsukarete yoku terebi o tsukeppanashi ni shite nete shimaimasu.
I often fall asleep with the TV on when I'm tired.

NOTE: The adverbial phrase **-PPANASHI DE** is used to modify a following verb.

テレビを つけっぱなし<u>で</u>寝ていました。
Terebi o tsukeppanashi <u>de</u> nete imashita.
I was sleeping with the TV on.

EXERCISE SET 4

Use the prompts to create sentences with **... O ... -PPANASHI NI SURU**. Suggested answers on page 205.

❶ [USE:] 資料／コピー機／置く
       shiryō / kopīki / oku

_____

❷ [USE:] 本／開く／寝る／てしまう
       hon / hiraku / neru / te shimau

_____

❸ [USE:] テレビ／つける／ください
       terebi / tsukeru / kudasai

_____

EXERCISE SET 5

Use the pictures to create sentences with **-PPANASHI DE** + verb. See suggested answers on page 205.

❶ [USE:] 携帯電話／充電する／忘れている
       keitai denwa / jūden suru / wasurete iru

_____

❷ [USE:] 本／開く／寝る／てしまう
hon / hiraku / neru / te shimau

🎧 7.7 Describing a resulting state that stays the same using まま MAMA

MAMA resembles **-PPANASHI**. It indicates a resulting state that remains as it is. The structure is as follows: **-TA** form of the verb + **MAMA** + **NI SURU**.

ファンヒーターを つけっ放し に する
fan hītā o tsukeppanashi ni suru
leave the fan heater turned on (possibly as a result of carelessness)

ファンヒーターを 付けたまま に する
fan hītā o tsuketa mama ni suru
leave the fan heater turned on (and definitely intending to keep it on)

The implication is as follows:

〜た まま -TA MAMA	に する NI SURU
the state of something that occurred	keep/leave it as it is in the resulting state

The phrase **MAMA (DE)** can be used to modify the verb that follows:

屋台で 立ったまま(で) ラーメンを 食べました。
Yatai de tatta mama (de) rāmen o tabemashita.
I ate ramen standing up at a food stall.

活作りは、魚を 生きたまま 食べます。
Ikezukuri wa, sakana o ikita mama tabemasu.
Ikezukuri is when they eat fish that are still alive.

ニートは 社会から 引きこもったまま 生活しています。
Nīto wa shakai kara hikikomotta mama seikatsu shite imasu.
NEETs [young people Not in Education, Employment, or Training] live their lives withdrawn from society.

Unlike **-PPANASHI**, **MAMA** can also follow an **-I** adjective, an adjectival noun + **NA**, or a noun + **NO**.

多くの 日本人は 牛乳を 冷たいまま 飲みます。
Ōku no nihonjin wa gyūnyū o tsumetai mama nomimasu.
Many Japanese drink milk cold.

仕事を 中途半端なまま にして おかないで下さい。
Shigoto o chūtohanpa na mama ni shite okanaide kudasai.
Please don't leave your work half finished.

日本の家には 靴のままで 上がれません。
Nihon no ie ni wa kutsu no mama de agaremasen.
You can't go into a Japanese house with your shoes on.

MAMA also means "as," as in the following sentence. In this structure **MAMA** is followed by **NI**.

社長の 言うままに した方が いいですよ。

Shachō no iu mama ni shita hō ga ī desu yo.

It would be better to (obediently) do as the company president tells you.

The above **MAMA** may replace **YŌ NI** or **TŌRI (NI)** meaning "in the same way." The **-TA** form may also precede this phrase. Unlike the two sentences below that use these constructions, **IU MAMA NI** in the above sentence implies that the person being addressed should stop being disobedient.

社長の 言う通りに／言うように した方が いいですよ。

Shachō no iu tōri ni / iu yō ni shita hō ga ī desu yo.

社長の 言った通りに／言ったように した方が いいですよ。

Shachō no itta tōri ni / itta yō ni shita hō ga ī desu yo.

EXERCISE SET 6

Use the prompts to translate the sentences using **MAMA**. See suggested answers on page 205.

❶ *The windmills stand still and do not spin around.*
[USE:] 風車／止まる／回る
    fūsha / tomaru / mawaru

_____

❷ *The driver just put down the delivery parcel and left it.*
[USE:] 運転手／配達の荷物／置く
    untenshu / haitatsu no nimotsu / oku

_____

❸ *Please do not leave the light on.*
[USE:] 電気／つける／ないで／ください
    denki / tsukeru / nai de / kudasai

_____

❹ *Please don't leave the washed dishes [in the dishwasher].*
[USE:] 食器／洗う／ないで／ください
    shokki / arau / nai de / kudasai

_____

梅雨が 来た

マイク： テレビで、梅雨入りしたって 言ってましたが、あまり 雨が 降らないですね。
これでも 梅雨なん ですか。

よう子： 梅雨でも 毎日 降らないん です。台風の 時には 時々 洪水に なりますが。

マイク： そうなん ですか。毎日 大雨が 降ると 思ってました。

けんじ： でも、傘は 持って おいた方が いいですよ。雨が しとしと 降ったり、急に
大雨に なったりするから。

よう子： 私も 今日は かばんに 傘を 入れて あります。

けんじ： あ、ほんと ですね。きれいな 折りたたみ傘が 入って いますね。

よう子： 梅雨の 時は 傘を 入れたままに しています。

マイク： 梅雨は だいたい 5月から 7月に かけての 40、50日ぐらい ですね。

けんじ： そう。梅雨に 入ったら 初夏だけど、梅雨明けに なったら 本当の 夏に なるん
ですよ。

よう子： この時期は 湿気が 高くなるから、食べ物に カビが 生えます。ちゃんと 冷蔵庫
に 入れておきましょう。

けんじ： 食べ物を 出しっ放しに しない方が いいです。カビが 生えなくても、O157とか
も あるし。いつも 手を よく 洗おうと 思います。

マイク： あ、今朝 洗濯物を 出しっ放し にして 来ました。（笑）

Tsuyu ga kita

Mike: **Terebi de, tsuyuiri shita tte ittemashita ga, amari ame ga furanai desu ne. Kore demo tsuyu na n desuka.**

Yoko: **Tsuyu demo mainichi furanai n desu. Taifū no toki ni wa tokidoki kōzui ni narimasu ga.**

Mike: **Sō na n desu ka. Mainichi ōame ga furu to omottemashita.**

Kenji: **Demo, kasa wa motte oita hō ga ī desu yo. Ame ga shitoshito futtari, kyūni ōame ni nattari suru kara.**

Yoko: **Watashi mo kyō wa kaban ni kasa o irete arimasu.**

Kenji: **A, honto desu ne. Kirei na oritatamigasa ga haitte imasu ne.**

Yoko: **Tsuyu no toki wa kasa o ireta mama ni shite imasu.**

Mike: **Tsuyu wa daitai go gatsu kara shichi gatsu ni kakete no shi, go jū nichi gurai desu ne.**

Kenji: **Sō. Tsuyu ni haittara shoka da kedo, tsuyuake ni nattara hontō no natsu ni naru n desu yo.**

Yoko: **Kono jiki wa shikke ga takaku naru kara, tabemono ni kabi ga haemasu. Chanto reizōko ni irete okimashō.**

Kenji: **Tabemono o dashippanashi ni shinai hō ga ī desu. Kabi ga haenakutemo, ō ichi gō nana* toka mo aru shi. Itsumo te o yoku araō to omoimasu.**

Mike: **A, kesa sentakumono o dashippanashi ni shite kimashita. (wara)**

The Rainy Season Has Come

Mike: Although it said on television that the rainy season has begun, it doesn't rain much, does it? Is this really the rainy season?

Yoko: Even in the rainy season it doesn't rain every day. But when there's a typhoon, we sometimes have floods.

Mike: Is that right? I thought it rained heavily every day.

Kenji: But it is better to have an umbrella with you. That's because light rain can suddenly turn into a storm.

Yoko: I've also put my umbrella in my bag today.

Kenji: Oh, so you have. That's a beautiful folding umbrella you've got in there, isn't it?

Yoko: I keep my umbrella in my bag during the rainy season.

Mike: The rainy season lasts for about 40 to 50 days from May to July, doesn't it?

Kenji: Yes. It's early summer when the rainy season begins, and when the rainy season ends, the real summer will come.

Yoko: Food gets moldy during this season because of the high humidity. Make sure you put your food in the fridge.

Kenji: It is better not to leave food out. Even if it doesn't get moldy, it can develop E. coli.* I make sure I always wash my hands well.

Mike: Oh, I left the washing out this morning. (LOL)

* The Japanese term for E. coli is O157, referring to the particular strain that causes sickness.

TASK

Create a dialogue with **... O ... -TE OKIMASU / ... O ... -TE ARIMASU** and practice it.

_____ : _____

_____ : _____

いろいろな　エコ活動

日本は　エコ意識が　高いと　思いますが、買い物の　時の　包装や　袋は　無駄が　多いと　思います。品物が　新しい　包み紙で　二重に　包んで　あったり、新しい袋に　入れて　あったりします。

しかし、スーパーでは　エコバッグを　持ってきたり、コンビニでは　レジ袋は　要らないと　言ったりする　人も　増えました。マイバッグを　用意して　おく　人が　増えているからです。

エネルギーの　節約も　しますね。東北大震災の　後、原発事故の　問題が　あって、いろいろと　節電して　いました。駅の　照明を　全部　つけっ放しに　しないで、電気を　少し　暗くして　あったり、エスカレータも　一部　止めた　ままに　していたり　しました。

昔から　「もったいない」という　意識が　あるからです。だから、店で　包み紙は　要らないと　言ったら、店員が　「ありがとう　ございます」と　丁寧に　言います。

ペットボトルや　空き缶は、リサイクルできますが、最近は　マイボトルを　買っておいて、それに　飲み物を入れておく人も　います。実は、弁当文化も　エコと　言えます。容器を　リユースできるからです。最近の弁当は　使い捨ての　容器が　多くて、ゴミに　なりますから、昔の　方が　エコでした。使い捨ての　容器は、食べっ放しに　しないで、ゴミ箱まで　持って　行きましょう。

Iroirona eko katsudō

Nihon wa eko ishiki ga takai to omoimasu ga, kaimono no toki no hōsō ya fukuro wa muda ga ōi to omoimasu. Shinamono ga atarashī tsutsumigami de nijū ni tsutsunde attari, atarashī fukuro ni irete attari shimasu.

Shikashi, sūpā de wa ekobaggu o motte kitari, konbini de wa rejibukuro wa iranai to ittari suru hito mo fuemashita. Maibaggu o yōi shite oku hito ga fuete iru kara desu.

Enerugī no setsuyaku mo shimasu ne. Tōhoku daishinsai no ato, genpatsu jiko no mondai ga atte, iroiro to setsuden shite imashita. Eki no shōmei o zenbu tsukeppanashi ni shinaide, denki o sukoshi kuraku shite attari, esukarētā mo ichibu tometa mama ni shite itari shimashita.

Mukashi kara "mottainai" to iu ishiki ga aru kara desu. Dakara, mise de tsutsumigami wa iranai to ittara, ten'in ga "arigatō gozaimasu" to teinei ni īmasu.

Petto botoru ya akikan wa, risaikuru dekimasu ga, saikin wa maibotoru o katte oite, soreni nomimono o irete oku hito mo imasu. Jitsu wa, bentō bunka mo eko to iemasu. Yōki o riyūsu dekiru kara desu. Saikin no bentō wa tsukaisute no yōki ga ōkute, gomi ni narimasu kara, mukashi no hō ga eko deshita. Tsukaisute no yōki wa, tabeppanashi ni shinaide, gomibako made motte ikimashō.

Various Eco-Activities

Although I think that Japan's eco-consciousness is high, there is a lot of waste of packaging and bags when shopping. Articles are double-wrapped in new wrapping paper, or are put into a new bag.

However, more people are bringing a reusable bag to the supermarket, or refuse a plastic bag at the convenience store. It is because those who have their own reusable bags, called **maibaggu**, are increasing in number.

We are saving energy too. After the Tohoku earthquake and the problem of the accident at the nuclear power plant, electricity is being saved in various ways. All the electric lights are no longer kept on at train stations, the lighting has been made a little dimmer, and some escalators have been stopped.

This is because there has been an awareness of **mottainai** [wastefulness] since ancient times. So, if you tell a shop assistant in a store that your wrapping paper is not necessary, they will say "thank you" politely.

Although plastic bottles and empty cans are recyclable, these days there are some people who buy a reusable **maibotoru** and put their drink into it. In fact, a bento lunch box culture can also be said to be eco-friendly. This is because the container can be reused. These days, lunch boxes are often disposable containers, which become garbage, so it was more ecological in the old days. After eating, we should take disposable containers to the trash can rather than just leaving them.

QUESTIONS
Answers with their suggested sentence structure can be found on page 205.

1. 日本で 買い物を すると、どんな 無駄が ありますか。
   Nihon de kaimono o suru to, donna muda ga arimasu ka.

2. 駅の 照明を 少し 暗くしたのは どうしてですか。
   Eki no shōmei o sukoshi kuraku shita no wa dōshite desu ka.

3. 昔の 弁当と 今の弁当では 何が 違いますか。
   Mukashi no bentō to ima no bentō de wa nani ga chigaimasu ka.

CHAPTER 8

Looking at Traditional Japanese Things
Is Something I Like
日本の 伝統的なものを 見るのが 好きです

Making Verbs into Noun Phrases

In this chapter you'll learn how to make verbs into noun phrases using constructions with
NO, NO O, KOTO and **MONO**, exploring the differences in expressing physical actions, perception
and concepts. Mastering these grammatical constructions will allow you to express opinions,
observations and statements of fact with improved fluency.

🎧 KEY SENTENCE PATTERNS

1. 日本の 伝統的なものを 見るのが 好きです。
   Nihon no dentōteki na mono o miru no ga suki desu. *Like doing something*
   Looking at traditional Japanese things is something I like.

2. タバコを 吸うのも お酒を 飲むのも やめました。
   Tabako o sū no mo osake o nomu no mo yamemashita. *Give up doing something*
   I gave up smoking as well as drinking sake.

3. データを 自分で 確認することが 大切です。
   Dēta o jibun de kakunin suru koto ga taisetsu desu. *Doing something is ...*
   Confirming the data yourself is important.

4. 趣味は あちこちの 温泉を 巡ることです。
   Shumi wa achikochi no onsen o meguru koto desu. *Is doing something*
   My hobby is traveling to hot springs all over the place.

5. ノミニケーションは 飲みながら 交流することです。
   Nominikēshon wa nominagara kōryū suru koto desu. *... means ...*
   Nomication* means communicating over drinks.
   *a Japanese-coined word created by connecting **nomi** (drinking) and communication.

111

Formation of Noun Phrases Using Verbs and Adjectives

	Example Noun Phrase		Meaning
Dictionary Form of the Verb	見るの／見ること	**miru no/miru koto**	seeing
-TA Form of the Verb	見たの／見たこと	**mita no/mita koto**	having seen
-I Adjective	面白いの／ 面白いこと	**omoshiroi no/ omoshiroi koto**	being interesting
Adjectival Noun + **NA**	便利なの／ 便利なこと	**benri na no/ benri na koto**	being convenient

GRAMMAR AND USAGE NOTES

8.1 Making noun phrases using の NO and こと KOTO

The nominalizers **NO** and **KOTO** change the preceding verb, **-I** adjective, or adjectival noun into a noun phrase. The most commonly used pattern is:

dictionary form or **-TA** form of the verb + **NO/KOTO**.

The phrase nominalized by **NO** or **KOTO** functions as the noun element of a sentence. **NO** is better than **KOTO** to talk about factual events. **KOTO** tends to be used for concepts or imaginary events.

Used as the subject:

[相撲を 見るの]は けっこう 面白いです。
[Sumō o miru no] wa kekkō omoshiroi desu.
Watching sumo is really interesting.

[日本文化を 知ること]は 大切です。
[Nihon bunka o shiru koto] wa taisetsu desu.
It is important to know Japanese culture.

[ここで 雪が 降ったの]は めずらしい。
[Koko de yuki ga futta no] wa mezurashī.
It's unusual that it snowed here.

Used as the object:

[世界が 平和に なること]を 希望します。
[Sekai ga heiwa ni naru koto] o kibō shimasu.
We hope that the world will be at peace.

日本人は [花見を するの]が 好きです。
Nihonjin wa [hanami o suru no] ga suki desu.
Japanese people like cherry-blossom viewing.

二郎は [娘が うまく やったの]を 喜んでいた。
Jirō wa [musume ga umaku yatta no] o yorokonde ita.
Jiro was pleased that his daughter had made a success of herself.

Used as the complement (note that **NO/N** cannot be used with **DESU** here, because **NO/N** + **DESU** has a different function, see section 5.3), or adverbial element:

趣味は［アニメの キャラクターを 描くこと］です。(INCORRECT: 描くのです)
Shumi wa [anime no kyarakutā o kaku koto] <u>desu</u>.
My hobby is drawing anime characters.

私の 目標は［日本語能力試験 N2 を 取ること］です。(INCORRECT: 取るのです)
Watashi no mokuhyō wa [nihongo nōryoku shiken enu tsū o toru koto] <u>desu</u>.
My goal is to pass the N2 level of the Japanese Language Proficiency Test.

夜中は コンビニが［食べ物を 買うの］に 便利です。
Yonaka wa konbini ga [tabemono o kau no] <u>ni</u> benri desu.
Convenience stores are handy for buying food in the middle of the night.

EXERCISE SET 1

Create one sentence with **NO** and one sentence with **KOTO**, as illustrated in the examples. See suggested answers on page 205.

> **Examples**
>
> 1. *Making tea is easy.*
>   お茶を 点てるのは 簡単ですよ。
>   **Ocha o tateru no wa kantan desu yo.**
>
> 2. *Her job is to teach tea ceremony.*
>   彼女の仕事は 茶道を 教える こと です。
>   **Kanojo no shigoto wa sadō o oshieru koto desu.**

❶ 1. [USE:] 花／生ける／芸術 **hana / ikeru / geijutsu**

_____

_____

2. [USE:] 趣味 **shumi**

_____

_____

❷ 1. [USE:] ダンスをする **dansu o suru**

_____

_____

2. [USE:] 男の子たち／部活 **otoko no kotachi / bukatsu**

_____

_____

🎧 8.2 Modified noun phrases using の NO and もの MONO

The pronoun **NO** and noun **MONO** can be used with a verb, an **-I** adjective, or an adjectival noun.

	NO or **MONO**	meaning
dictionary form of verb	見るの／見るもの **miru no / miru mono**	*what one sees*
-TA form of verb	見たの／見たもの **mita no / mita mono**	*what one saw*
dictionary form of **-I** adjective	面白いの／面白いもの **omoshiroi no / omoshiroi mono**	*what is interesting*
the adjectival noun + **NA**	便利なの／便利なもの **benri na no / benri na mono**	*what is convenient*

As seen above, **NO** is used as a pronoun. The pronoun **NO** can indicate not only a thing but also a person, a place, time, etc.

今日 紹介する<u>の</u>は 私の 友人の けんじです。 (the person)
Kyō shōkai suru <u>no</u> wa watashi no yūjin no kenji desu.
The person I will introduce today is my friend, Kenji.

私が 生まれた<u>の</u>は 神戸です。 (the place)
Watashi ga umareta <u>no</u> wa kōbe desu.
The place where I was born is Kobe.

都合が いい<u>の</u>は いつですか。 (the time)
Tsugō ga ī <u>no</u> wa itsu desu ka.
When is (the time that is) convenient for you?

NO often refers to the same kind of thing as previously mentioned, whereas **MONO** is used to indicate anything in general and things that have not already been specified. In the sentence below, **NO** clearly refers to **sumaho** as a specific (not general) thing, so **MONO** is not suitable.

君が 買った スマホはiOS ですが、 私が 買った<u>の</u>は アンドロイド です。
Kimi ga katta sumaho wa aioesu desu ga, watashi ga katta <u>no</u> wa andoroido desu.
The smartphone you bought runs on iOS, but the one I bought is an Android.

In the sentence below, the word **MONO** refers to a general thing not already specified:

私が 買ったものは 靴です。
Watashi ga katta mono wa kutsu desu.
What I bought was shoes.

However, **NO** may replace **MONO** when the kind of thing the speaker is talking about is clear from the general context, even if it hasn't been discussed previously. In the following example, the general context (things that can be bought in a shop) is clear, so either word may be used:

いつも コンビニで 買う<u>の</u>は おにぎりです。 [**NO** used as a pronoun]
いつも コンビニで 買う<u>もの</u>は おにぎりです。 [**MONO** used as a pronoun]
Itsumo konbini de kau <u>no</u> (<u>mono</u>) wa onigiri desu.
What I usually buy at a convenience store is onigiri rice balls.

EXERCISE SET 2

Complete the sentences using **NO**, as illustrated in the example. Suggested answers on page 205.

> **Example**
>
> *The piece of furniture Mike wants to buy is a sofa, but what I want to buy is a massage chair.*
> マイクさんが 買いたい 家具は ソファーですが、私が
> 買いたい のはマッサージチェア です。
> **Maiku san ga kaitai kagu wa sofā desu ga, watashi ga kaitai no wa massāji chea desu.**
>
>

❶ *The animals Yoko likes are dogs, but (Kenji / cats)*
[USE:] よう子さんが 好きな 動物は 犬ですが、
Yoko san ga sukina dōbutsu wa inu desu ga,

_____

❷ *What my friend often drinks is draft beer, but (I / sake)*
[USE:] 友だちが よく 飲むものは 生ビールですが、
Tomodachi ga yoku nomu mono wa nama bīru desu ga,

_____

🎧 8.3 Using の を NO o to express a physical action

NO, unlike **KOTO**, can express a physical action, as in the following sentences.

❶ When the noun phrase is followed by a perception verb. **KOTO** is not correct here.

> ［マイク<u>が</u> コンビニで アルバイトを している の ］を 見ました。
> **[Maiku <u>ga</u> konbini de arubaito o shite iru <u>no</u>] o mimashita.**
> *I saw Mike working at his part-time job in a convenience store.* (something seen)

Note that the agent must be marked by **GA** in the noun phrase.

> ［けんじさん<u>が</u> カラオケで 上手に 歌う の］を 聞きました。
> **[Kenji san <u>ga</u> karaoke de jōzu ni utau <u>no</u>] o kikimashita.**
> *I heard Kenji sing well in the karaoke box.* (something heard)

❷ **KOTO** is not used if the noun phrase is followed by verbs such as **tomeru** (to stop), **yameru** (to stop/give up), **fusegu** (to prevent), **tasukeru** (to help/rescue), **tetsudau** (to assist), etc.

> 今は ［彼女を 作る の］を やめて 勉強だけします。
> **Ima wa [kanojo o tsukuru <u>no</u>] o yamete benkyō dake shimasu.**
> *Now I will give up getting a girlfriend and only study.*

> ［スマホを 買う の］を 手伝って下さい。
> **[Sumaho o kau <u>no</u>] o tetsudatte kudasai.**
> *Please help me to buy a smartphone.*

NOTE: Akirameru (to give up) can follow **NO + O** and **KOTO + O** as it is a verb of mental action:

［漢字を　覚える　の／こと］を　あきらめないで　がんばりましょう。
[Kanji o oboeru no / koto] o akiramenaide ganbarimashō.
Do not give up on memorizing kanji and do your best.

EXERCISE SET 3

Use the prompts to create sentences with **NO O**, as illustrated in the example. See suggested answers on page 205.

> **Example**
>
> *I heard Yoko play Chopin on the piano.*
> よう子さんが　ピアノで　ショパンを　弾くのを　聞きました。
> **Yoko san ga piano de shopan o hiku no o kikimashita.**

❶ [USE:] けんじ／タブレット／音楽／聞く／見る
    Kenji / taburetto / ongaku / kiku /miru

_____

❷ [USE:] 花子／発表する／聞く
    Hanako / happyō suru / kiku

_____

❸ [USE:] けんじ／迷惑メール／困る／見る
    Kenji / meiwaku mēru / komaru / miru

_____

❹ [USE:] 娘／お母さん／お皿／洗う／手伝う
    musume / okāsan / osara / arau / tetsudau

_____

🎧 **8.4 "Looking forward to ..." using** の／こと を 楽しみにしています **NO/KOTO O TANOSHIMI NI SHITE IMASU**

The idiom **O TANOSHIMI NI SURU** (to look forward to) expresses a mental action, so it may take a noun phrase marked by either **NO** or **KOTO**.

また 会える　の／ことを 楽しみにしています。
Mata aeru no/koto o tanoshimi ni shite imasu.
I'm looking forward to seeing [*lit.* being able to meet] *you again.*

EXERCISE SET 4

Use the prompts to create sentences with **NO/KOTO O TANOSHIMI NI SHITE IRU**. See suggested answers on page 205.

❶ [USE:] 来週／バーベキューをしに行く
raishū / bābekyū o shi ni iku

---

❷ [USE:] お寺／写真／撮る
otera / shashin / toru

---

❸ [USE:] 赤ちゃん／出かける
akachan / dekakeru

EXERCISE SET 5

Create sentences with **... WA ... KOTO DESU**, as in the example. Suggested answers on page 206.

> **Example**
>
> *Taro's job is assembling cars.*
> 太郎さんの　仕事は　車を　組み立てることです。
> **Tarō san no shigoto wa kuruma o kumitateru koto desu.**

❶ [USE:] お父さん／日課／毎朝／ジョギングする
otōsan / nikka / maiasa / jogingu suru

---

❷ [USE:] お母さん／日課／激安／商品／探す
okāsan / nikka / gekiyasu / shōhin / sagasu

---

❸ [USE:] 私たち／担当／ゴミ／分別する
watashitachi / tantō / gomi / bunbetsu suru

---

❹ [USE:] クラウドサービス／ネットで／データ／利用する
kuraudo sābisu / netto de / dēta / riyō suru

🎧 CONVERSATION PRACTICE

コンパ

けんじ： 今度 居酒屋で コンパを します。みんなにも 参加して ほしいんだ。
マイク： コンパ？何ですか。
よう子： あ、コンパは 日本語じゃないですね。コンパは、元々 ドイツ語の **kompanie** です。日本語では いっしょに お酒を 飲んで 交流することですよ。
けんじ： 新入生を 歓迎するのは、新入生 歓迎 コンパ、つまり、新歓 コンパと言って 新入生といっしょに 食べたり 飲んだりすることだよ。
マイク： 楽しい でしょうね。僕も 参加しようと思います。飲みながら 食べるのが 好きですから。
よう子： 二次会って いうのも ありますよ。
けんじ： そう。場所を 変えて また 飲み会を することだよ。二次会で もっと コミュニケーションをすることが 大切だね。
マイク： 楽しみです。僕には 日本語で コミュニケーションすることが 大事ですね。
けんじ： 「話し上手は 聞き上手」と 言うよ。自分が 3割 話して、相手が 7割 しゃべるの がいいね。

Kompa

Kenji: **Kondo izakaya de kompa o shimasu. Minna ni mo sanka shite hoshī n da.**
Mike: **Kompa? Nan desu ka.**
Yoko: **A, kompa wa nihongo ja nai desu ne. Kompa wa motomoto doitsugo no "kompanie" desu. Nihongo de wa isshoni osake o nonde kōryū suru koto desu yo.**
Kenji: **Shinnyūsei o kangei suru no wa, shinnyūsei kangei kompa, tsumari, shinkan kompa to itte shinnyūsei to isshoni tabetari nondari suru koto da yo.**
Mike: **Tanoshī deshō ne. Boku mo sanka shiyō to omoimasu. Nominagara taberu no ga suki desu kara.**
Yoko: **Nijikai tte iu no mo arimasu yo.**
Kenji: **Sō. Basho o kaete mata nomikai o suru koto da yo. Nijikai de motto komyunikēshon o suru koto ga taisetsu da ne.**
Mike: **Tanoshimi desu. Boku ni wa nihongo de komyunikēshon suru koto ga daiji desu ne.**
Kenji: **"Hanashijōzu wa kikijōzu" to iu yo. Jibun de san wari hanashite, aite ga nana wari shaberu no ga ī ne.**

A **Kompa** Party

Kenji: I'm going to have a **kompa** party next time in an izakaya. And I want everybody to come.

Mike: A **kompa**? What's that?

Yoko: Ah, **kompa** isn't a Japanese word, right. **Kompa** is from the German word "kompanie." In Japanese it means drinking alcohol and getting to know each other.

Kenji: When we welcome new students we have a **shinnyusei kangei kompa**, or **shinkan kompa** for short, where we eat and drink together.

Mike: That sounds fun! I think I'll come because I love eating and drinking.

Yoko: There's also an afterparty.

Kenji: Right. That's when we change the venue and hold another drinking session. Communicating more deeply at the second party is important.

Mike: I'm looking forward to it. Communicating in Japanese is important to me.

Kenji: We say, "A good talker is a good listener." It is good for you to talk for 30 percent of the time and for your partner to talk for 70 percent.

TASK

Create a dialogue with **NO/KOTO** and practice it.

_____ : _____

_____ : _____

🎧 READING PRACTICE

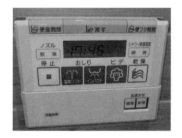

日本の家

日本の 住宅には、マンション、アパート、一戸建て等が あります。マンションや アパートの場合、間取りを 「2LDK」 等と 表しています。LDK は、リビング・ダイニング・キッチンのことで、例えば、2DK は、部屋が 2 つと ダイニング・キッチンです。

しかし、多くの日本人は 木造の 一戸建てに 住むのが 好きです。理由は 木の家の中で 落ち着けることです。多くの人の 夢は 庭付きの 一戸建てを 建てることでしょう。

さて、便器は、最近では 和式の 人気が なくなって、洋式が 一般的に なりました。今は 多くの人は 和式便器を 使うのは 嫌でしょう。進化した便器は、便座が 温熱式なので、冬でも 暖かく 用を足せます。そのあとに、温水で お尻を 洗うことができます。便利なのは ふたが自動で 開いたり 水が自動で 流れたり するものも あることです。便器が これほど 良くなったのは 驚くことでしょう。

Nihon no ie

Nihon no jūtaku ni wa, manshon, apāto, ikkodate nado ga arimasu. Manshon ya apāto no bāi, madori o "nī eru dī kē" nado to arawashite imasu. Eru dī kei wa, ribingu, dainingu, kitchin no koto de, tatoeba, nī dī kē wa, heya ga futatsu to dainingu kitchin desu.

Shikashi, ōku no nihonjin wa mokuzō no ikkodate ni sumu no ga suki desu. Riyū wa ki no ie no naka de ochitsukeru koto desu. Ōku no hito no yume wa niwa tsuki no ikkodate o tateru koto deshō.

Sate, benki wa, saikin de wa washiki no ninki ga nakunatte, yōshiki ga ippanteki ni narimashita. Ima wa ōku no hito wa washiki benki o tsukau no wa iya deshō. Shinka shita benki wa, benza ga onnetsushiki na node, fuyu demo atatakaku yō o tasemasu. Sono ato ni, onsui de oshiri o arau koto ga dekimasu. Benri na no wa futa ga jidō de hiraitari mizu ga jidō de nagaretari suru mono mo aru koto desu. Benki ga korehodo yoku natta no wa odoroku koto deshō.

A Japanese House

There are various kinds of housing in Japan, such as condominiums, apartments and single-family houses. In the case of condominiums or apartments, the room arrangement is called 2LDK, etc. LDK means living-dining-kitchen area. For example, 2DK means two rooms and a dining-kitchen area.

However, many Japanese people like living in a wooden detached house. This is because it is quiet and peaceful in a wooden house. Many people dream of building a detached house with a garden.

Moving on to bathrooms – these days, Japanese-style [squat] toilets are no longer popular, and the Western style has gained popularity. Now, it seems that many people don't like using a Japanese-style toilet. Since the modern toilet has a heated seat, you can stay warm even when using the toilet in winter. After, you can wash yourself with warm water. Other convenient functions include automatic lids and automatic flushing. It's surprising how much the toilet has improved!

QUESTIONS

Answers with their suggested sentence structure can be found on page 206.

1. 2LDK は どのような 住宅ですか。
   Nī eru dī kē wa dono yō na jūtaku desu ka.

2. 多くの日本人は どのような家に 住むのが 好きですか。
   Ōku no nihonjin wa dono yō na ie ni sumu no ga suki desu ka.

3. どのような 便器が 人気が ありますか。
   Dono yō na benki ga ninki ga arimasu ka.

CHAPTER 9

Now I Can Understand "Manga" Japanese!
マンガの 日本語が 分かるように なりました

Resulting States

In this chapter you'll learn how to talk about resulting states using the constructions **YŌ NI NARU**, **YŌ NI NARIMASHITA**, **NO TAME NI**, **NO NI**, **YŌ NI SHITE IMASU** and **KOTO NI NARIMASHITA**.

When studying the constructions in this chapter, you'll come across the terms "volitional" and "non-volitional," which also cropped up in chapter 6. When a verb is described as "volitional," it means that the action is intended. In a non-volitional verb (such as "understand," "see" or "hear," for example), the action is beyond the control of the speaker.

Another grammatical term that is key to this chapter is the "potential form" that you studied in chapter 2. This refers to verb forms that describe one's ability (or inability) to do something.

🎧 KEY SENTENCE PATTERNS

1. マンガの 日本語が 分かるように なりました。
   Manga no nihongo ga wakaru yō ni narimashita.
   Now I can understand "manga" Japanese.

   Become able to do

2. コレステロールを 減らすために 魚を 食べるように しています。
   Koresuterōru o herasu tame ni sakana o taberu yō ni shite imasu.
   I'm trying to eat fish to lower my cholesterol.

   So as to; be trying to do

3. もっと 話せるように 単語を 覚えることに しています。
   Motto hanaseru yō ni tango o oboeru koto ni shite imasu.
   I make a rule of memorizing words so that I can speak more.

   So that ... can; make a rule of doing

4. 日本の 会社で 仕事を することになりました。
   Nihon no kaisha de shigoto o suru koto ni narimashita.
   It has been arranged that I will work at a Japanese firm.

   It has been arranged that

5. ポイントを ためるのに ポイントカードが 必要です。
   Pointo o tameru no ni pointo kādo ga hitsuyō desu.
   To accumulate points you need a rewards card.

   Something is necessary in order to do something

Formation of Verb Phrases Expressing Resulting States

	...YŌ NI NARIMASU	...YŌ NI SHITE IMASU	...TAME NI	...NO NI
書きます kakimasu	書けるようになります kakeru yō ni narimasu	書くようにしています kaku yō ni shite imasu	書くために kaku tame ni	書くのに kaku no ni
食べます tabemasu	食べられるように なります taberareru yō ni narimasu	食べるようにして います taberu yō ni shite imasu	食べるために taberu tame ni	食べるのに taberu no ni
見ます mimasu	見られるようになります mirareru yō ni narimasu	見るようにしています miru yō ni shite imasu	見るために miru tame ni	見るのに miru no ni
します shimasu	できるようになります dekiru yō ni narimasu	するようにしています suru yō ni shite imasu	するために suru tame ni	するのに suru no ni
来ます kimasu	来られるようになります korareru yō ni narimasu	来るようにしています kuru yō ni shite imasu	来るために kuru tame ni	来るのに kuru no ni

GRAMMAR AND USAGE NOTES

🎧 9.1 Expressing a resulting state using ように なります YŌ NI NARIMASU

The noun **YŌ** preceded by the plain form of the non-volitional verb (usually a potential verb) expresses a resulting state, and is followed by **NI NARU** (to become able to).

> ステージ 3 で ターゲットを 全部 打ち落とせる ように なりました。
> **Sutēji san de tāgetto o zenbu uchiotoseru yō ni narimashita.**
> *I can now* [*lit.* I became able to] *shoot down all the targets at stage 3.*

Non-volitional verbs like **WAKARU** (to [be able to] understand), **MIERU** (can be seen), **KIKOERU** (can be heard), etc., also precede **YŌ NI NARU**.

> めがねをかけたら、よく見えるようになります。
> **Megane o kaketara, yoku mieru yō ni narimasu.**
> *If I put on my glasses, I'll be able to see well* [*lit.* I'll come to be able to see well].

> 日本語のコメディーが 分かるように なりました。
> **Nihongo no komedī ga wakaru yō ni narimashita.**
> *Now I can* [*lit.* have come to be able to] *understand Japanese comedy.*

However, in the negative expression, **NAKU** (the **-KU** form of the negative auxiliary **-NAI**) replaces **YŌ NI**.

> いつも タイプを していて、あまり 漢字が 書け<u>なく</u> なりました。
> **Itsumo taipu o shite ite, amari kanji ga kake<u>naku</u> narimashita.**
> *I always type, so I can't write kanji well any more* [*lit.* I became unable to write kanji well].

EXERCISE SET 1

Use the prompts to create sentences with verb + **YŌ NI NARIMASHITA** (or **NAKU NARIMASHITA**).
Suggested answers on page 206.

❶ [USE:] けんじ／ギター／弾く
Kenji / gitā / hiku

_____

❷ [USE:] 私／陶器／作る
watashi / tōki / tsukuru

_____

❸ [USE:] 補聴器／よく／聞こえる
hochōki / yoku / kikoeru

_____

❹ [USE:] スマホ／起動しない
sumaho / kidō shinai

_____

❺ [USE:] ガソリン／高すぎる／買えない
gasorin / takasugiru / kaenai

_____

🎧 9.2 Expressing purpose using ように YŌ NI

YŌ preceded by the dictionary form or **-NAI** form of the non-volitional verb (usually a potential verb) expresses a purpose. It is followed by the target marker **NI** and a clause that explains the action that relates to the purpose. A non-volitional verb indicates the subject is not in control of the action.

Dictionary form or **-NAI** form of the non-volitional verb   + **YŌ NI**
one may/can do something   so that

箸が うまく 使えるように 中指の 筋肉を 鍛えました。
Hashi ga umaku tsukaeru <u>yō ni</u> nakayubi no kin'niku o kitaemashita.
I trained the muscles of my middle finger so that I can use chopsticks well.

花火が もっと 見えるように 前に 行きましょう。
Hanabi ga motto mieru <u>yō ni</u> mae ni ikimashō.
Let's move forward so that we can see the fireworks better.

聞いたことを 忘れないように、携帯に メモして おきます。
Kīta koto o wasurenai <u>yō ni</u>, keitai ni memo shite okimasu.
I put memos into my mobile phone so that I don't forget what I've heard.

アニメのことばが 分かるように、何度も ビデオを 見ます。
Anime no kotoba ga wakaru <u>yō ni</u>, nando mo bideo o mimasu.
I watch anime videos as often as I can so that I understand the language.

EXERCISE SET 2

Use the prompts to create sentences with verb + **YŌ NI**. See suggested answers on page 206.

❶ [USE:] みなさん／分かる／よく／説明する
minasan / wakaru / yoku / setsumei suru

_____

❷ [USE:] 自分で／立てる／サポートする
jibun de / tateru / sapōto suru

_____

❸ [USE:] 本／きちんと／並ぶ／置く
hon / kichinto / narabu / oku

_____

❹ [USE:] 風邪／ひかない／マスクをする
kaze / hikanai / masuku o suru

_____

🎧 9.3 Expressing purpose using ために TAME NI

TAME is a noun meaning "advantage, benefit, profit." The noun **TAME** preceded by the dictionary form or **-NAI** form of a volitional verb expresses a purpose. It is followed by the target marker **NI** and a clause that explains the action that relates to the purpose.

Dictionary form or **-NAI** form of the volitional verb   + **TAME NI**
one may/can do something   so that

世界文化遺産 の 写真 を 撮る ために ここ を 訪れました。
Sekai bunka isan no shashin o toru tame ni koko o otozuremashita.
I came on a visit here to take photos of the World Heritage Site.

もっと 運動する ために フィットネス・クラブ に 行っています。
Motto undo suru tame ni fittonesu kurabu ni itte imasu.
I've been going to the fitness club so that I can exercise more.

TAME NI should not be used when the outcome is not easily or intentionally controlled by the speaker. In the following example (which relates to one's natural ability), **YŌ NI** is more suitable.

日本語 が 上手 に ［なる ように／なれる ように］ 毎日 練習 しています。
Nihongo ga jōzu ni [naru yō ni/nareru yō ni] mainichi renshū shite imasu.
I'm practicing Japanese every day so that I'll be good at it.

However, when one can intentionally pursue an outcome (such as studying for a qualification) **TAME NI** is good, as in the following example:

通訳者 に なる ために 毎日 日本語 を 練習 しています。
Tsūyakusha ni naru tame ni mainichi nihongo o renshū shite imasu.
I'm practicing Japanese every day so that I can become a translator.

Volitional and non-volitional verbs cannot always be easily told apart, thus, **YŌ NI** and **TAME NI** are occasionally interchangeable. The **-NAI** form tends to be followed by **YŌ NI** rather than **TAME NI**.

日本語能力試験 N2 に 合格する <u>ように</u>／<u>ために</u> 勉強 しています。
Nihongo nōryoku shiken enu tsū ni gōkaku suru <u>yō ni</u>/<u>tame ni</u> benkyō shite imasu.
I'm studying so that I can pass the JLPT N2.

交通事故 に あわない <u>ように</u> 気 を つけてください。
Kōtsū jiko ni awa<u>nai yō ni</u> ki o tsukete kudasai.
Pay careful attention so that you don't have a traffic accident.

EXERCISE SET 3

Use the prompts to create sentences with verb + **TAME NI**. See suggested answers on page 206.

❶ [USE:] 家を建て替える／荷物／移す
     ie o tatekaeru / nimotsu / utsusu

_____

❷ [USE:] 鬼／追い払う／豆／まく
     oni / oiharau / mame / maku

_____

🎧 9.4. "For the sake of / for the benefit of / because of" using のために
NO TAME NI

Noun + **NO TAME NI** means "for the sake of," "for the benefit of," or "because of."

高度経済成長期には 会社のために 働く人が 多かったです。
Kōdo keizai seichōki ni wa kaisha <u>no tame ni</u> hataraku hito ga ōkatta desu.
There were a lot of people who worked for the good of their company during the period of high economic growth.

便宜のために この用語を 使います。
Bengi <u>no tame ni</u> kono yōgo o tsukaimasu.
I'll use this phrase for convenience's sake.

体調不良のために しばらく 休みます。
Taichō furyō <u>no tame ni</u> shibaraku yasumimasu.
I'll take a rest from my job for a while owing to bad health.

EXERCISE SET 4
Look at the pictures and create sentences with noun + **NO** + **TAME NI**. See suggested answers on page 206.

❶ [USE:] 父／ネクタイ／買う
chichi / nekutai / kau

_____

❷ [USE:] 熱／寝込む
netsu / nekomu

_____

❸ [USE:] 明日／発表／レポート／準備
ashita / happyō / repōto / junbi

_____

🎧 9.5 Expressing a purpose using のに NO NI

The dictionary form of the verb + **NO NI** expresses a purpose when followed by adjectives that express a value judgment like **hitsuyō desu** (it is necessary) and **jūyō desu / taisetsu desu / daiji desu** (it is important).

ネット・ショッピングで 注文するのに クレジット・カードが 必要です。
Netto shoppingu de chūmon suru <u>no ni</u> kurejitto kādo ga hitsuyō desu.
A credit card is necessary for ordering online.

セキュリティーを 万全にする<u>のに</u> ウイルス対策ソフトが 重要です。

Sekyuritī o banzen ni suru <u>no ni</u> uirusu taisaku sofuto ga jūyō desu.

Antivirus software is important to be fully secure.

EXERCISE SET 5

Use the prompts to create sentences with **NO NI + HITSUYŌ DESU/JŪYŌ DESU**. Suggested answers on page 206.

❶ [USE:] 発表する／プロジェクター／必要
   happyō suru / purojekutā / hitsuyō

_____

❷ [USE:] それ／ 決める／会議／重要
   sore / kimeru / kaigi / jūyō

_____

🎧 9.6 Expressing the acquisition of a habit using ようになります YŌ NI NARIMASU

When a volitional verb expressing a controllable action precedes **YŌ NI NARIMASU**, this phrase indicates that the subject of the sentence is acquiring the habit of doing something.

最近は 早寝早起きを するように なりました。

Saikin wa hayane hayaoki o suru yō ni narimashita.

Recently I have gotten into the habit of keeping early hours.

Its negative expression takes **NAKU** (the **-KU** form of the negative auxiliary **-NAI**) instead of **YŌ NI**.

インターネットを するから、テレビを 見<u>なく</u> なりました。

Intānetto o suru kara, terebi o mi<u>naku</u> narimashita.

I use the Internet, so I've stopped watching TV.

EXERCISE SET 6

Use the prompts to create sentences with verb + **YŌ NI NARIMASU** (or **NAKU NARIMASU**). See suggested answers on page 206.

❶ [USE:] けんじ／よく ／学校／遅刻する
   Kenji / yoku / gakkō / chikoku suru

_____

❷ [USE:] おばあさん／カートを押す／歩く
obāsan / kāto o osu / aruku

_____

❸ [USE:] 最近／マイボトル／使う
saikin / maibotoru / tsukau

_____

🎧 9.7 Expressing trying to acquire a habit using ようにしています YŌ NI SHITE IMASU

When a volitional verb precedes **YŌ NI SHITE IMASU**, this phrase indicates that the subject is trying to acquire the habit of doing something.

毎日 1 万歩 歩くように しています。
Mainichi ichiman po aruku yō ni shite imasu.
I'm trying to walk ten thousand steps every day.

日本人と 日本語で たくさん 話すようにしています。
Nihonjin to nihongo de takusan hanasu yō ni shite imasu.
I'm trying to speak with Japanese people in Japanese.

The **-NAI** form may also precede **YŌ NI SHITE IMASU**.

肥えないように あまり 肉を 食べない ように しています。
Koenai yō ni amari niku o tabe<u>nai</u> yō ni shite imasu.
I'm trying not to eat much meat so I don't get fat.

集合時間に 遅れない ように して下さい。
Shūgō jikan ni okure<u>nai</u> yō ni shite kudasai.
Please try not to be late for the appointed time.

EXERCISE SET 7
Use the prompts to create sentences with verb + **YŌ NI SHITE IMASU**. Suggested answers on page 206.

❶ [USE:] 先生に／挨拶する
sensei ni / aisatsu suru

_____

❷ [USE:] 先生の質問に／すぐに／答える
sensei no shitsumon ni / sugu ni / kotaeru

_____

❸ [USE:] お風呂の水／洗濯に／使う
ofuro no mizu / sentaku ni / tsukau

_____

🎧 9.8 Expressing habit or determination using ことに しています KOTO NI SHITE IMASU

When a volitional verb precedes **KOTO NI SHITE IMASU**, the phrase indicates that the subject has a habit of doing something or is determined to do something. Thus, **KOTO NI SHITE IMASU** may sometimes replace **YŌ NI SHITE IMASU** (see section 9.7) as shown in the first example below. However, **YŌ NI SHITE IMASU** cannot be used in the second sentence, which expresses a settled habit, or determination.

毎年 元旦には 神社に 初詣に 行くことに しています／ようにしています。
Maitoshi gantan ni wa jinja ni hatsumōde ni iku koto ni shite imasu / yō ni shite imasu.
I make a habit of paying the first visit to a shrine of the New Year's on New Year's Day.

卒業したら 大学院に 進学することに しています。
Sotsugyō shitara daigakuin ni shingaku suru koto ni shite imasu.
I am determined to enter graduate school after I graduate.

Note that **koto ni shita** means to have just determined to do something.

大学院に 進学することに しました。
Daigakuin ni shingaku suru koto ni shimashita.
I have just decided to enter graduate school.

EXERCISE SET 8
Translate the sentences using verb + **KOTO NI SHITE IMASU**. See suggested answers on page 206.

❶ _I'm getting into the habit of using an electric fan instead of the air conditioner._
[USE:] エアコン／つける／扇風機／使う
eakon / tsukeru / senpūki / tsukau

_____

❷ _I made it a rule to study, even on the train._
[USE:] 電車／中／でも／勉強
densha / naka / demo / benkyō

_____

9.9 Expressing something that has been decided using ことに なりました KOTO NI NARIMASHITA

The dictionary form of the verb + **KOTO NI NARIMASHITA** indicates that it has been decided that some event will occur or that a person is due/scheduled to do something.

今度 インターンで 日系企業で 働くことに なりました。
Kondo intān de nikkei kigyō de hataraku koto ni narimashita.
I am due to work at a Japanese-affiliated company shortly.

🎧 CONVERSATION PRACTICE

[1画]
一 乙
[2画]
二 七 八 九 人 入 了 丁 刀 力 十 又
[3画]
下 三

川 山 工 己 巾 弓 才
[4画]
不 中 丹 乏 予 五 互 井 介 今

双 反 友 太 天 夫 孔 少 尺 屯 幻 引 弔 心 戸 手 支 文 斗

[5画]
巨 世 丙 丘 主 丼 以 仕 仙 他 代 付 令 兄 冊 写 処 凹 出

圧 冬 甘 央 失 奴 尻 巧 左 市 布 平 幼 広 庁 弁 込 辺

外 生 用 田 甲 申 由 白 皮 血 目 矛 矢 石 示 礼 穴 立
[6画]

常用漢字

けんじ： マイク、漢字は どのぐらい 書けるようになった？
マイク： そうね。だいたい 百字ぐらい 読んだり 書いたり できるようになったかな。
よう子： へえ、まだ もっと 覚えなきゃね。
マイク： うん、どれぐらい 覚えたらいいかな？
けんじ： 日本語で 新聞を 読むためには、常用漢字の 二千字ぐらいは 要るよ。
マイク： え〜っ、新聞を読むのに 二千も 必要なの？大変だなぁ。
よう子： 毎日 漢字を いくつか 覚えることにしたら どう？
マイク： 実は、僕は マンガを 読みながら 覚えることにしているんだよ。
けんじ： へぇ、マンガで どんな漢字を 覚えた？
マイク： 「俺」とか 「最悪」とか。マンガは、ちょっと 乱暴な 言葉が 多いよね。
よう子： じゃ、マンガが だいたい 読めるようになった？
マイク： まだまだです。マンガに 出てくる 漢字の方が むずかしいね。
けんじ： なるほど。たしかに マニアックな 言葉が 多いからだね。

Jōyō kanji

Kenji: **Maiku, kanji wa dono gurai kakeru yō ni natta?**

Mike: **Sōne. Daitai hyaku ji gurai yondari kaitari dekiru yō ni natta kana.**

Yoko: **Hē, mada motto oboenakya ne.**

Mike: **Un, dore gurai oboetara ī kana?**

Kenji: **Nihongo de shinbun o yomu tame ni wa, jōyō kanji no ni sen ji gurai wa iru yo.**

Mike: **Ē! Shinbun o yomu no ni ni sen mo hitsuyō nano? Taihen da nā.**

Yoko: **Mainichi kanji o ikutsuka oboeru koto ni shitara dō?**

Mike: **Jitsuwa, boku wa manga o yominagara oboeru koto ni shite iru n da yo.**

Kenji: **Hē, manga de donna kanji o oboeta?**

Mike: **"Ore" toka "saiaku" toka. Manga wa, chotto ranbō na kotoba ga ōi yo ne.**

Yoko: **Ja, manga ga daitai yomeru yō ni natta?**

Mike: **Madamada desu. Manga ni dete kuru kanji no hō ga muzukashī ne.**

Kenji: **Naruhodo. Tashikani, maniakku na kotoba ga ōi kara da ne.**

Commonly Used Kanji Characters

Kenji: Mike, how many kanji characters are you able to write now?

Mike: Well. I'm now able to read and write about 100 characters.

Yoko: Oh, you have to memorize more, don't you?

Mike: Yes, I wonder how many I should memorize.

Kenji: To read a newspaper in Japanese, you need about 2,000 commonly used kanji.

Mike: Wow, you need as many as 2,000 to read a newspaper? That's hard.

Yoko: How about memorizing several kanji every day?

Mike: Actually, I make it a rule to memorize them while reading comics.

Kenji: Oh, what kind of kanji have you memorized through comics?

Mike: **Ore** and **saiaku**, and so on. Comics have lots of quite violent words, don't they?

Yoko: So, are you able to read comics fairly well now?

Mike: Not yet. The kanji that appear in comics are more difficult.

Kenji: That's right. That's because they include many geeky words.

TASK

Create a dialogue with one of the phrases **YŌ NI NARIMASU**, **YŌ NI SHITE IMASU** or **KOTO NI SHITE IMASU** and practice it.

_____ : _____

_____ : _____

オノマトペの音

日本語で 音を 表すのに、オノマトペという 言葉を たくさん 使う。例えば、「どんどん」とか「パリパリ」のような 語は、漢字で 書こうと 思っても 書けない。

日本語の オノマトペが うまく 使えるように なるのに、千語 程度 覚えることが 必要だ。日本人は、昔から とても たくさん 自然の 音を 真似する ようになり、様子を 言葉で 表すように なった。

多くの マンガ家は、様子が うまく 表せるように、オノマトペを 使うように している。例えば、「ギョエー」と 言えば、気持ちが 悪いことを 表し、「ギンギン」と 言えば、やる気が 強いことを 表す。これらは 新しく 作った オノマトペだ。

日本語の オノマトペには 少しだけ ルールがある。[a] や [o] には、大きいとか 遅いという 意味がある。大きな 音を 表すのに「がんがん」と 言うし、「のろのろ」は ゆっくりしていることを 表す。

「かんかん」や「とんとん」のように、[k] や [t] を 使ったら、かたい音を 表すことになる。「めろめろ」のように、柔らかい 様子を 表すのに [m] の 音が 必要だ。「さっと」や「どっと」のように、急な 動きや変化を 表すのに、促音が 必要だ。

「ころころ」と「ごろごろ」、「すたすた」と「ずたずた」、「とろとろ」と「どろどろ」、「とんとん」と「どんどん」のように、清音は 明るくて リズミカルな イメージを 表し、濁音は 粗くて 重いものを 表す ようになっている。

Onomatope no oto

Nihongo de oto o arawasu no ni, onomatope to iu kotoba o takusan tsukau. Tatoeba, "dondon" toka "paripari" no yō na go wa, kanji de kakō to omottemo kakenai.

Nihongo no onomatope ga umaku tsukaeru yō ni naru no ni, sen go teido oboeru koto ga hitsuyō da. Nihonjin wa, mukashi kara totemo takusan shizen no oto o mane suru yō ni nari, yōsu o kotoba de arawasu yō ni natta.

Ōku no mangaka wa, yōsu ga umaku arawaseru yō ni, onomatope o tsukau yō ni shite iru. Tatoeba, "gyoē" to ieba, kimochi ga warui koto o arawashi, "gingin" to ieba, yaruki ga tsuyoi koto o arawasu. Korera wa atarashiku tsukutta onomatope da.

Nihongo no onomatope ni wa sukoshi dake rūru ga aru. [A] ya [o] ni wa, ōkī toka osoi to iu imi ga aru. Ōkina oto o arawasu no ni "gangan" to iu shi, "noronoro" wa yukkuri shite iru koto o arawasu.

"Kankan" ya "tonton" no yō ni, [k] ya [t] o tsukattara, katai oto o arawasu koto ni naru. "Meromero" no yō ni, yawarakai yōsu o arawasu no ni [m] no oto ga hitsuyō da. "Satto" ya "dotto" no yō ni, kyū na ugoki ya henka o arawasu no ni, sokuon ga hitsuyō da.

"Korokoro" to "gorogoro," "sutasuta" to "zutazuta," "torotoro" to "dorodoro," "tonton" to "dondon" no yō ni, seion wa akarukute rizumikaru na imēji o arawashi, dakuon wa arakute omoi mono o arawasu yō ni natte iru.

The Sounds of Onomatopoeia

In order to express sounds in Japanese, we use a lot of onomatopoeia. These kinds of words, like **dondon** or **paripari**, for example, cannot be written in kanji.

In order to become able to use Japanese onomatopoeia well, you have to memorize about 1,000 words. Japanese people have been able to imitate a vast number of natural sounds since ancient times, and have become able to express situations using these words.

Many cartoonists try to use onomatopoeia to convey a situation well. For example, if they say **gyoē**, this expresses an unpleasant feeling. **Gingin** expresses strong motivation. These are newly made onomatopoeia.

There are only a few rules for Japanese onomatopoeia. Words with *a* and *o* sounds mean that something is big or late respectively. **Gangan** expresses a loud sound, and **noronoro** expresses doing something slowly.

If you use *k* and *t* as in **kankan** and **tonton**, you can convey a hard sound. The *m* sound expresses a softness, as in **meromero**. In **satto** and **dotto**, the doubled consonant is used to express a sudden motion and change.

A voiceless sound conveys a bright and rhythmical image and a voiced consonant expresses something coarse and heavy as in **korokoro** and **gorogoro**, **sutasuta** and **zutazuta**, **torotoro** and **dorodoro**, **tonton** and **dondon**.

QUESTIONS

Answers with their suggested sentence structure can be found on page 206.

1. 日本語の オノマトペが うまく 使えるように なるには どうしたらいいですか。
   Nihongo no onomatope ga umaku tsukaeru yō ni naru ni wa dō shitara ī desu ka.

2. どうしたら かたい 音を 表すことができますか。
   Dō shitara katai oto o arawasu koto ga dekimasu ka.

3. 「ころころ」と 「ごろごろ」の イメージの 違いは 何ですか。
   "Korokoro" to "gorogoro" no imēji no chigai wa nan desu ka.

CHAPTER 10

I Was Praised by the Neighbors for Helping with the Cleaning

掃除を手伝って 近所の人に ほめられました

The Giving and Receiving of Actions

In this chapter you'll learn how to express the giving and receiving of actions using the passive voice and using the verbs of giving and receiving: **ageru**, **kureru**, **morau**, **sashiageru** and **itadaku**. The ability to use the correct form of the correct verb in the correct situation is key to maintaining harmonious social relationships in your daily interactions with Japanese people.

🎧 KEY SENTENCE PATTERNS

1. 掃除を手伝って 近所の人に ほめられました。
   Sōji o tetsudatte, kinjo no hito ni homeraremashita.   *The direct passive*
   I was praised by the neighbors for helping with the cleaning.

2. 茶道の 師匠に ほめられたり 叱られたりします。
   Sadō no shishō ni homeraretari shikararetari shimasu.   *The direct passive*
   I am praised and scolded by my tea ceremony teacher.

3. 店先の 傘立てで 傘を 取られました。
   Misesaki no kasatate de kasa o toraremashita.   *The owner's passive*
   I had my umbrella taken from the umbrella stand in front of the store.

4. 大雨に 降られて 今日は どうしようもないです。
   Ōame ni furarete kyō wa dōshiyō mo nai desu.   *The indirect passive*
   Because of the heavy rain I don't feel like doing anything today.
   [*lit.* I suffer from the heavy rain and cannot do anything today.]

5. まとめて 買って 値段を まけて もらいました。
   Matomete katte nedan o makete moraimashita.   *The receiving of an action*
   I bought them all and got the price reduced.

6. 弟の 誕生日に 新しいゲーム機を 買ってあげました。
   Otōto no tanjōbi ni atarashī gēmu ki o katte agemashita.   *The giving of an action*
   I bought a new game console for my younger brother's birthday.

Formation of the Passive Form

Dictionary Form (examples)	-NAI Form	Passive Form
-U Verbs	置く (to put)	置かない	置かれる (to be put)
	oku	**okanai**	**okareru**
-U Verbs	揉む (to massage)	揉まない	揉まれる (to have a massage)
	momu	**momanai**	**momareru**
-RU Verbs	ほめる (to praise)	ほめない	ほめられる (to be praised)
	homeru	**homenai**	**homerareru**
-RU Verbs	見る (to see)	見ない	見られる (to be seen *or* have sth. seen)
	miru	**minai**	**mirareru**
Irregular Verbs	する (to do)	しない	される (to be done)
	suru	**shinai**	**sareru**
	来る (to come)	来ない	来られる (to suffer from one's coming)
	kuru	**konai**	**korareru**

GRAMMAR AND USAGE NOTES

10.1 Creating the passive form of the verb

The passive form of the verb is created by adding **-RERU** to the front part of the **-NAI** form of a **-U** verb, or by adding **-RARERU** to the front part of the **-NAI** form of an **-RU** verb and the irregular verb **kuru**. The irregular verb **suru** has its own passive form, **sareru**. The passive form looks the same as the **-ARERU** potential form, but the variations below should be noted:

Verb Type	Example	Potential Form				Passive Form
-U Verbs	取る	取られる	>	取れる		取られる
	toru	**torareru**	>	**toreru** (commonly used)		**torareru**
-RU Verbs	見る	見られる	>	見れる		見られる
	miru	**mirareru**	>	**mireru** (slang)		**mirareru**
Irregular Verbs	来る	来られる	>	来れる		来られる
	kuru	**korareru**	>	**koreru** (widely used slang)		**korareru**
	する	できる				される
	suru	**dekiru**				**sareru**

EXERCISE SET 1

Fill in the blanks with the passive form of each verb. Check your answers on page 206.

-MASU form	-MASU form of the passive
1. 読みます **yomimasu** (to read)	
2. 壊します **kowashimasu** (to break)	
3. 売ります **urimasu** (to sell)	
4. 食べます **tabemasu** (to eat)	
5. 作ります **tsukurimasu** (to make)	

-MASU form	-MASU form of the passive
6. 聞きます **kikimasu** (to hear)	
7. 飲みます **nomimasu** (to drink)	
8. 知っています **shitte imasu** (to know)	
9. 攻撃します **kōgeki shimasu** (to attack)	
10. 批判します **hihan shimasu** (to criticize)	

🎧 10.2 Sentence structures using the passive form of the verb

In each example the first sentence is in the active form; the second sentence is in the passive form.

❶ The Direct Passive

師匠は 私を ほめます。
Shishō wa <u>watashi o</u> homemasu.　　　　　*The instructor praises me.*

私は 師匠に ほめられます。
<u>Watashi wa</u> shishō <u>ni</u> homeraremasu.　　　*I am praised by the instructor.*

NOTE: The particle **NI** is the agent marker that is equivalent to the English "by."

❷ The Owner's Passive

誰かが 私の 傘を 取りました。
Dareka ga <u>watashi no</u>　kasa o torimashita.　　*Someone took my umbrella.*

私は （誰かに） 傘を 取られました。
<u>Watashi wa</u> (dareka ni) <u>kasa o</u> toraremashita.　*I had my umbrella taken (by someone).*

先生は 私のレポートを ほめました。
Sensei wa <u>watashi no</u> repōto o homemashita.　*The teacher praised my report.*

私は 先生にレポートをほめられました。
<u>Watashi wa</u> sensei <u>ni</u> <u>repōto o</u> homeraremashita.　*I had my report praised by the teacher.*

NOTE: The subject "I" is the owner of the object (the umbrella, the report). This extends to body parts, as in the following example:

誰かが （私の）足を 踏みました。
Dareka ga (<u>watashi no</u>) <u>ashi o</u> fumimashita.　*Someone stepped on my foot.*

私は （誰かに） 足を 踏まれました。
<u>Watashi wa</u> (dareka ni) <u>ashi o</u> fumaremashita.　*I had my foot stepped on (by someone).*

❸ The Indirect Passive

大雨が 降りました。
Ōame ga furimashita.

It rained heavily. (A heavy rain fell on me.)

（私は）大雨に 降られました。
(Watashi wa) ōame ni furaremashita.

It rained heavily (so I got soaked.)
(I suffered <u>from</u> the heavy rain.)

母が 死にました。
Haha ga shinimashita.

My mother died.

私は 母に 死なれました。
Watashi wa <u>haha ni</u> shinaremashita.

My mother died. (I suffered <u>from my mother's</u> death.)

隣の人が 大声で 話して…。
Tonari no hito ga ōgoe de hanashite...

<u>*A man next to me*</u> *was talking loudly, so...*

隣の人に 大声で 話されて…。
Tonari no hito ni ōgoe de hanasarete...

(I suffered from) <u>*a man next to me*</u> *talking loudly, so...*

In the last example, the indirect passive implies that the subject person suffers from the agent's doing something. Therefore it is called **meiwaku no ukemi** (the nuisance passive).

EXERCISE SET 2

Use the prompts to translate the sentences using the passive voice, using the structure of the example sentence as a model. Suggested answers on page 207.

Example

Our team had the ball taken by the opposing team.
うちのチームが 相手の チームに ボールを 取られました。
Uchi no chīmu ga aite no chīmu ni bōru o toraremashita.

---

❶ *The younger brother was punched in the face by the older brother.*
[USE:] 弟／兄／顔／殴る
    otōto / ani / kao / naguru

_____

❷ *We had our ball received by the opposing team.*
[USE:] 相手チーム／ボール／レシーブする
    aite / chīmu / bōru / reshību suru

_____

③ *The boy was grabbed by the arm by a stranger.*
[USE:] 男の子／知らない人／腕／つかむ
otoko no ko / shiranai hito / ude / tsukamu

_____

④ *I was distracted by her sleeping beside me while I was studying.*
[USE:] 勉強中／隣で／寝る
benkyō chū / tonari de / neru

_____

10.3 Using verbs of giving and receiving

The verbs of giving and receiving (**ageru, kureru, morau**) follow the **-TE** form of the verb and express giving and receiving of profit, advantage, kindness, etc., between the subject person [S] and the agent [A] as follows:

❶ [S] **wa/ga**   [A] **ni**   **-te ageru.**
S kindly does something for A. S brings a profit, etc. to A by doing something.
NOTE: A cannot be the first person or someone close to the first person.

❷ [S] **wa/ga**   [A] **ni**   **-te kureru.**
S kindly does something for A. S brings a profit, etc. to A by doing something.
NOTE: S cannot be the first person or someone close to the first person.

❸ [S] **wa/ga**   [A] **ni**   **-te morau**
A kindly does something for S. S receives a profit, etc. from A by A's doing something.
NOTE: A cannot be the first person or close to the first person.

EXERCISE SET 3
Correct the underlined verbs of giving or receiving in the following sentences. Answers on page 207.

❶ 太郎さんは 私に プレゼントを 買って あげました。
Tarō san wa watashi ni purezento o katte <u>agemashita</u>. _____

❷ 太郎さんは 私の 妹に プレゼントを 買って あげました。
Tarō san wa watashi no imōto ni purezento o katte <u>agemashita</u>. _____

❸ 太郎さんは 自分の妹に プレゼントを 買って くれました。
Tarō san wa jibun no imōto ni purezento o katte <u>kuremashita</u>. _____

❹ 私は 友だちを 町に 案内して くれました。
Watashi wa tomodachi o machi ni an'nai shite <u>kuremashita</u>. _____

❺ 私は 友だちに 町を 案内して くれました。
Watashi wa tomodachi ni machi o an'nai shite <u>kuremashita</u>. _____

🎧 10.4 Expressing giving and receiving help

Beware of using the verb **tetsudau** to express the giving or receiving of help. The first sentence below is objectively correct but sounds unnatural. To express that someone profits or is benefited by doing something, the verbs of giving and receiving are used.

INCORRECT: 同僚は 私を 手伝いました。
Dōryō wa watashi o <u>tetsudaimashita</u>. (unnatural or odd)
My coworker helped me.

CORRECT: 同僚は 私を 手伝って くれました。
Dōryō wa watashi o tetsudatte <u>kuremashita</u>.
My coworker [kindly] helped me.

CORRECT: 私は 同僚に 手伝って もらいました。
Watashi wa dōryō ni tetsudatte <u>moraimashita</u>.
I had my coworker [kindly] help me.

EXERCISE SET 4

Use a verb of giving or receiving to rephrase the underlined part of each sentence. See suggested answers on page 207.

❶ （私に）駅まで 行く道を <u>教えますか</u>。
(Watashi ni) eki made iku michi o <u>oshiemasu ka</u>. _____

❷ 私は 妹 に 絵本を <u>買いました</u>。
Watashi wa imōto ni ehon o <u>kaimashita</u>. _____

❸ 私は 師匠に 柔道を <u>教えられました</u>。
Watashi wa shishō ni judo o <u>oshieraremashita</u>. _____

EXERCISE SET 5

Use the prompts to translate both sentences with the **-TE** form of the verb + a verb of giving or receiving, as illustrated in the examples. See suggested answers on page 207.

Examples

Taro (kindly) cleaned the floor for us.
太郎が 床を きれいにして くれました。
Tarō ga yuka o kirei ni shite kuremashita.

We had the floor cleaned by Taro.
太郎に 床を きれいにして もらいました。
Tarō ni yuka o kirei ni shite moraimashita.

---

❶ *The students cleaned the classroom for us.*
We had the classroom cleaned by the students.
[USE:] 学生／教室／掃除する **gakusei / kyōshitsu / sōji suru**

_____

_____

❷ *The tutor taught me math.*
I was taught math by the tutor.
[USE:] 家庭教師／数学／教える
  katei kyōshi / sūgaku / oshieru

_____

_____

❸ *The caregiver (kindly) pushed my wheelchair.*
I was (kindly) pushed in my wheelchair by the caregiver.
[USE:] 介護士／車椅子／押す
  kaigoshi / kuruma isu / osu

_____

_____

❹ *The doctor [kindly] saw my child off the clock.*
I had my child kindly seen by the doctor off the clock.
[USE:] 医者／見る／時間外に
  isha / miru / jikangai ni

_____

_____

🎧 10.5 Polite forms of giving and receiving

The verbs of giving and receiving have their more polite forms as below:

Verb of Giving/Receiving	Respectful Form	Humble
あげます (to give) **agemasu**	あげられます［あげられる］ **agerareru (ageraremasu)**	さしあげます［さしあげる］ **sashiagemasu (sashiageru)**
くれます (to give) **kuremasu**	くださいます［くださる］ **kudasaimasu (kudasaru)**	—
もらいます (to receive) **moraimasu**	もらわれます（もらわれる） **morawaremasu (morawareru)**	いただきます［いただく］ **itadakimasu (itadaku)**

Replace the normal form of giving-receiving verbs with the verbs on the previous page to express respect or a humble attitude toward the agent or the other person.

❶ When the agent kindly does something for you or helps you, you can express the agent's act and your respect for or gratitude to the agent as below:

太郎さんが 手伝って くださいました。
Tarō san ga tetsudatte kudasaimashita.
Taro (kindly) helped me.

❷ When the agent kindly does something for you or helps you, you can state the agent's act and your humble attitude toward the agent as below:

(私は) 太郎さんに 手伝って いただきました。
(Watashi wa) Tarō san ni tetsudatte itadakimashita.
I was helped by Taro.
[*lit.* I humbly received Taro's kind help.]

❸ When you sincerely do something for someone or help someone whom you respect, you can express your act and your humble attitude toward him or her as below:

(私は) 先生を 手伝って さしあげました。
(Watashi wa) sensei o tetsudatte sashiagemashita.
I helped my teacher.

❹ When you request someone to do something (e.g., tell you the way to the bank), the verb of receiving takes the potential form as below:

銀行へ 行く道を 教えて いただけませんか。　　(dictionary form = いただける)
Ginkō e iku michi o oshiete itadakemasen ka.
Could you kindly tell me the way to the bank?
[*lit.* Couldn't I receive your kindly telling me the way to the bank?]

Yarimasu/yaru is the casual form of **agemasu/ageru**. It can also sound arrogant, so take care when using.

このマンガ 見たかったら、貸して やるよ。
Kono manga mitakattara, kashite yaru yo.
If you want to read this comic book, I'll lend it to you.

EXERCISE SET 6

Use the polite verbs of giving or receiving and rephrase the underlined part of the sentence. See suggested answers on page 207.

❶ (私は) 駅まで 行く道を <u>教えてもらえませんか</u>。
(Watashi wa) eki made iku michi o <u>oshiete moraemasen ka</u>. _____

❷ (私は) 師匠に 華道を <u>教えてもらいました</u>。
(Watashi wa) shishō ni kadō o <u>oshiete moraimashita</u>. _____

❸ 店長は 給料を <u>上げてくれました</u>。
Tenchō wa kyūryō o <u>agete kuremashita</u>. _____

ジェスチャー

よう子：日本では 当たり前の ことでも、外国人には そうではない ことが
　　　　ありますね。
けんじ：それを 知ることが、異文化を 理解する ことにも なりますね。
マイク：そうですね、日本人は 話しながら 意味もなく よく 手を 動かしますね。
けんじ：手の 動かし方の 意味を 分かって もらうのは むずかしいですね。
よう子：じゃ、ジェスチャーの 使い方 によって、相手に 誤解される ことも
　　　　ありますか。
マイク：日本人は 手の平を 下にして 手招き しますが、アメリカでは 「向こうへ
　　　　行け」 という 意味に なります。
よう子：へぇ。外国人と 話す 友だちに 教えて あげた方が いいですね。
けんじ：ほかにも 教えて くれませんか。
マイク：親指と人指し指で 丸い 輪を 作るサインは、日本では OK やお金の 意味
　　　　です。
けんじ：あ、知ってます。それは 外国では 悪い意味に とられますね。
よう子：小指を 立てるのは、日本では、恋人や愛人を 指しますよ。
マイク：それは 外国では バカにされたと 思いますよ。
よう子：へえ、じゃ、間違われないように 手を 止めて 話そうと 思います。（笑）

Jesuchā

Yoko: **Nihon de wa atarimae no koto demo, gaikokujin ni wa sō de wa nai koto ga arimasu ne.**

Kenji: **Sore o shiru koto ga, ibunka o rikai suru koto ni mo narimasu ne.**

Mike: **Sō desu ne, nihonjin wa hanashinagara imi mo naku yoku te o ugokashimasu ne.**

Kenji: **Te no ugokashikata no imi o wakatte morau no wa muzukashī desu ne.**

Yoko: **Ja, jesuchā no tsukaikata ni yotte, aite ni gokai sareru koto mo arimasu ka.**

Mike: **Nihonjin wa te no hira o shita ni shite temaneki shimasu ga, amerika de wa "mukō e ike" to iu imi ni narimasu.**

Yoko: **Hē. Gaikokujin to hanasu tomodachi ni oshiete ageta hō ga ī desu ne.**

Kenji: **Hoka ni mo oshiete kuremasen ka.**

Mike: **Oyayubi to hitosashiyubi de marui wa o tsukuru sain wa, nihon de wa ōkē ya okane no imi desu.**

Kenji: **A, shittemasu. Sore wa gaikoku de wa warui imi ni toraremasu ne.**

Yoko: **Koyubi o tateru no wa, nihon de wa, koibito ya aijin o sashimasu yo.**

Mike: **Sore wa gaikoku de wa baka ni sareta to omoimasu yo.**

Yoko: **Hē, ja, machigawarenai yō ni te o tomete hanasō to omoimasu. (wara)**

Gestures

Yoko: There are things that seem obvious to Japanese people but not always to foreigners, aren't there?

Kenji: Knowing about these things helps you understand foreign culture, doesn't it?

Mike: Yes. Like when Japanese people often meaninglessly move their hands while talking.

Kenji: It's difficult for me to let you know how I move my hands and what it means.

Yoko: Can we be misunderstood by the other person depending on how we use gestures?

Mike: Japanese people turn their palm down to beckon, but that could mean "go away" in the United States.

Yoko: Aha. You should tell that to your friends who talk with foreigners.

Kenji: Would you teach me other examples?

Mike: Making a circle with your thumb and forefinger means "OK" or "money" in Japan.

Kenji: Yes, I know. But in some countries it is interpreted as having a bad meaning.

Yoko: Raising your little finger refers to a sweetheart or a lover in Japan.

Mike: In other countries I think it means the other person is a fool.

Yoko: Oh, right then, I think I'll stop moving my hands when I talk so I'm not misunderstood. (LOL)

TASK

Create a dialogue with the passive form or **-TE** + verb of giving or receiving, and practice it.

_____ : _____

_____ : _____

🎧 READING PRACTICE

異文化間理解

それぞれの 国には いろいろな 文化が あります。相手の 習慣に 反しないように、文化の 違いを 理解することが 大事です。予想外の トラブルを 起こしたり、いやな 気持ちを 与えたりしないように、正しく 理解して もらうことが 大切です。

異文化間コミュニケーションには ユーモアも 大事です。ユーモアを 言わずに 話すのは、人と 親しくなれず、コミュニケーションが スムーズに できません。言いたいことを 間違われないように、気を 遣いながら、冗談を 少し 言うことで、楽しくなり、異文化間でも コミュニケーションが うまく できるように なります。

文化の 違いを 分かってもらうためには、自分の 文化を うまく 説明できることも 必要
でしょう。手や顔でも コミュニケーションが できますが、きちんと 分かってもらうた
めには、やはり、言語の 勉強は 手が抜けません。

Ibunka kan rikai

Sorezore no kuni ni wa iroiro na bunka ga arimasu. Aite no shūkan ni hanshinai yō ni, bunka no chigai o rikai suru koto ga daiji desu. Yosōgai no toraburu o okoshitari, iya na kimochi o ataetari shinai yō ni, tadashiku rikai shite morau koto ga taisetsu desu.

Ibunkakan komyunikēshon ni wa yūmoa mo daiji desu. Yūmoa o iwazuni hanasu no wa, hito to shitashiku narezu, komyunikēshon ga sumūzu ni dekimasen. Ītai koto o machigawarenai yō ni, ki o tsukainagara, jōdan o sukoshi iu koto de, tanoshiku nari, ibunkakan demo komyunikēshon ga umaku dekiru yō ni narimasu.

Bunka no chigai o wakatte morau tame ni wa, jibun no bunka o umaku setsumei dekiru koto mo hitsuyō deshō. Te ya kao demo komyunikēshon ga dekimasu ga, kichinto wakatte morau tame ni wa, yahari gengo no benkyō wa te ga nukemasen.

Intercultural Understanding

There are various cultures in each country. It is important to understand cultural differences so that we do not violate the customs of others. It is important that we make ourselves understood correctly so as not to cause unexpected trouble or arouse disagreeable feelings.

Humor is also important for intercultural communication. If we talk without humor, we can't become close to each other and we can't achieve smooth communication. We will achieve pleasant and better communication between cultures by joking a little and taking care not to be misunderstood.

In order to gain understanding of cultural differences it's a good idea to properly explain one's own culture. Although communication is possible with your hands or face, in order to be understood precisely, we cannot cut corners in our language studies.

QUESTIONS
Answers with their suggested sentence structure can be found on page 207.

1. 正しく 理解してもらわなかったら どうなりますか。
   Tadashiku rikai shite morawanakattara dō narimasu ka.

2. ユーモアを 言うことで、何が できるように なりますか。
   Yūmoa o iu koto de, nani ga dekiru yō ni narimasu ka.

3. 文化の違いを分かってもらうために どうすることが 必要ですか。
   Bunka no chigai o wakatte morau tame ni dō suru koto ga hitsuyō desu ka.

CHAPTER 11

The E-mail Address Must Be Wrong
メアドが 間違っている に違いないです

Degrees of Difficulty and Expressions of Probability

In this chapter you'll learn how to talk about degrees of difficulty using the constructions **-YASUI/-NIKUI**. You'll learn to express possibility using **KAMO SHIREMASEN, HAZU DESU, NI CHIGAI NAI DESU** and **JA NAI**. When you've mastered the use of these phrases, you'll find yourself able to express complex physical or mental difficulties with greater fluency.

🎧 KEY SENTENCE PATTERNS

1. ガラケーの方が キーボードが あって 使いやすいです。
   Garakē no hō ga kībōdo ga atte tsukaiyasui desu. *To be easy to do*
   A cell phone with a keyboard is easier to use.

2. スマホは 画面タッチが しにくくて 私には 使いにくいです。
   Sumaho wa gamen tatchi ga shinikukute watashi ni wa tsukainikui desu. *To be difficult to do*
   A smartphone is difficult for me to use, as it is hard to touch the screen.

3. 人身事故で 電車が 遅れるかもしれません。
   Jinshin jiko de densha ga okureru kamo shiremasen. *May/might*
   The train might be delayed due to the fatal accident.

4. 夜行バスに 間に合わない かもしれません。
   Yakō basu ni maniawanai kamo shiremasen. *I'm afraid that...*
   I'm afraid we'll miss the night bus./We might miss the night bus.

5. こうやったら うまくいく はずです。
   Kō yattara umaku iku hazu desu. *I'm sure that...*
   I'm sure it'll go well if you do this.

6. メアドが 間違っている に違いないです。
   Meado ga machigatte iru ni chigai nai desu. *This must be..*
   The e-mail address must be wrong.

7. 携帯電話の 値段が 100円て、それ、変じゃない？
   Keitai denwa no nedan ga hyaku en te, sore, hen ja nai? *Don't you think so?*
   They say the mobile phone is ¥100, but I think it's suspicious, don't you?

Formation of Expressions of Probability

	Examples of Combinations
Front part of the -MASU form	使いやすいです (easy to use) **tsukaiyasui desu**
Front part of the -MASU form	しにくいです (difficult to do) **shinikui desu**
Plain form of verb/-I adjective	遅れる かもしれません (might be delayed) **okureru kamo shiremasen**
-NAI form of verb/-I adjective	間に合わない かもしません (I'm afraid we'll be late) **maniawanai kamo shiremasen**
(Adjectival) noun	だめ かもしれません (I'm afraid it's hopeless) **dame kamo shiremasen**
Plain form of verb/-I adjective	うまくいく はずです (I'm sure it's going well) **umaku iku hazu desu**
Adjectival noun + NA	元気な はずです (I'm sure he is well) **genki na hazu desu**
Noun + NO	休みの はずです (I'm sure today is a holiday) **yasumi no hazu desu**
Plain form of verb/-I adjective	高い に違いないです (It must be expensive) **takai ni chigai nai desu**
(Adjectival) noun	学生 に違いないです (He must be a student) **gakusei ni chigai nai desu**
Plain form of verb/-I adjective + N	落としたん じゃない？ (I guess you dropped it, right?) **otoshita n ja nai?**
Adjectival noun (+ NA N)	勘違い (なん) じゃない？ (Isn't that wrong?) **kanchigai (nan) ja nai?**

GRAMMAR AND USAGE NOTES

🎧 11.1 Indicating something is easy using 〜やすいです -YASUI DESU

The front part of the -MASU form is followed by -YASUI (easy) to indicate that something is easy to do. Bear in mind that the vocabulary word **yasui**, meaning "easy" can seldom be used separately from the verb. **Yasashī** or **kantan da** are used separately instead to mean "easy." When **yasui** is used separately from the verb, it usually means "cheap."

このゲームは やすいなあ。
Kono gēmu wa yasui nā.
This game is cheap, isn't it?

このゲームは 簡単だなあ。
Kono gēmu wa kantan da nā.
This game is easy, isn't it?

The agent of the action is marked by **NI WA** or, more formally, **NI TOTTE**.

この漢字は 私には 書きやすいです。
Kono kanji wa watashi <u>ni wa</u> kakiyasui desu.
This kanji is easy for me to write.

羽田空港は 駅に近くて 飛行機に すぐに 乗りやすいです。
Haneda kūkō wa eki ni chikakute hikōk ni sugu ni noriyasui desu.
Haneda Airport is close to the station so it is easy to immediately board a plane there.

IC 乗車券は 電車に 乗りやすいです。
Ai shī jōshaken wa densha ni noriyasui desu.
An IC ticket is convenient when taking the train. (It is easy to take the train with an IC ticket.)

日本人にとって ナイフとフォークより 箸の方が 食べやすいです。
Nihonjin <u>ni totte</u> naifu to fōku yori hashi no hō ga tabeyasui desu.
Chopsticks are easier for Japanese people to eat with than a knife and fork.

🎧 11.2 Indicating something is difficult using 〜にくいです -NIKUI DESU

The front part of the **-MASU** form is followed by **-NIKUI** (hateful, difficult) to indicate that something is difficult to do (and the speaker might hate doing it). The agent of the action is marked by **NI WA** or, more formally, **NI TOTTE**.

私には スマホは 使いにくいです。
Watashi <u>ni wa</u> sumaho wa tsukainikui desu.
A smartphone is difficult for me to use.

日本語のサイトは 漢字が 多くて 外国人にとって 分かりにくいです。
Nihongo no saito wa kanji ga ōkute gaikokujin <u>ni totte</u> wakarinikui desu.
Japanese websites have lots of kanji which make them difficult for foreigners to understand.

東京の 地下鉄は 複雑で 乗り換えにくいです。
Tōkyō no chikatetsu wa fukuzatsu de norikaenikui desu.
The Tokyo subway system is complex, and changing trains is difficult.

The endings **-GATAI** (psychologically hard) and **-TSURAI** (painful, difficult) can replace **-NIKUI**.

彼女は 忘れがたい人です。
Kanojo wa wasure<u>gatai</u> hito desu.
She is an unforgettable person.

思い出の 品は 捨てがたい です。
Omoide no shina wa sute<u>gatai</u> desu.
The things associated with memories are difficult to throw away.

筆は 書きづらいです。
Fude wa kaki<u>zurai</u> desu.
A calligraphy brush is difficult to write with.

ちょっと それは 言いづらいです。
Chotto sore wa ī<u>zurai</u> desu.
I can't tell you that [because it's emotionally difficult for me].

EXERCISE SET 1

Translate the sentences using **-YASUI DESU** and **-NIKUI DESU**, following the example. See suggested answers on page 207.

See suggested answers on page 207.

> **Example**
>
> *A USB is easy to copy files to, but a CD is difficult.*
> USB はファイルをコピーしやすいですが，CD は
> しにくいです。
> **Yūesubī wa fairu o kopī shiyasui desu ga, sīdī wa shinikui desu.**

① *Cigarettes are easy to quit, but it's difficult to refrain from alcohol.*
[USE:] タバコ／やめる／アルコール／控える
tabako / yameru / arukōru / hikaeru

_____

② *A cat is easy to keep, but a snake is difficult.*
[USE:] 猫／飼う／蛇
neko / kau / hebi

_____

③ *A calligraphy brush is difficult to write with, but a tablet is easy to type into.*
[USE:] 筆／書く／タブレット／タイプする
fude / kaku / taburetto / taipu suru

_____

④ *Pills are easy to take but powder is difficult.*
[USE:] カプセル／飲む／粉
kapuseru / nomu / kona

_____

🎧 11.3 Indicating possibility using かもしれません KAMO SHIREMASEN

When the speaker judges that some event may or might occur within a range of possibilities, the auxiliary **KAMO SHIRENAI** or its polite form **KAMO SHIREMASEN/KAMOSHIRENAI DESU** is used. If the speaker thinks the possibility is getting a little higher, **DESHŌ**, the conjecture form of **DESU**, may occasionally replace this **KAMO SHIREMASEN**.

> 行くかもしれませんが、行かないかもしれません。
> **Iku kamo shiremasen ga, ikanai kamo shiremasen.**
> *I may or may not go.*

そうかもしれませんが、そうでないかもしれません。
Sō kamo shiremasen ga, sō de nai kamo shiremasen.
It may or may not be so.

今度の 日本語能力試験に 合格できない かもしれません。
Kondo no nihongo nōryoku shiken ni gōkaku dekinai kamo shiremasen.
I'm afraid I may not be able to pass the next JLPT test.

When the speaker guesses that some past event may have occurred, the **-TA** form normally precedes **KAMO SHIRENAI**.

彼女と 恋に 落ちたかもしれません。
Kanojo to koi ni ochita kamo shiremasen.
I might have fallen in love with her.

そう 言った かもしれない けど、今は そう 思わないです。
Sō itta kamo shirenai kedo, ima wa sō omowanai desu.
I may have said so, but now I don't think so.

言って くれなかったら、損を した かもしれない。
Itte kurenakattara, son o shita kamo shirenai.
If you had not told me that, (I'm afraid) I might possibly have lost money.

EXERCISE SET 2

Use the prompts to create sentences with **KAMO SHIREMASEN**. Suggested answers on page 207.

Suggested answers on page 207.

Example
If I get that, I may be able to cook tasty takoyaki.   あれがあったら おいしい たこ焼きを 作れる かもしれません。   **Are ga attara oishī takoyaki o tsukureru kamo shiremasen.**

❶ [USE:] 花粉症／になる
     kafunshō / ni naru

_____

❷ [USE:] バーガー／大きすぎる／口／入らない
     bāgā / ōkisugiru / kuchi / hairanai

_____

❸ [USE:] 地震／岩／家／ぶつかる
     jishin / iwa / ie / butsukaru

_____

🎧 11.4 Expressing probability using はずです HAZU DESU

When the speaker judges that some event ought to, or is expected/supposed to occur, the auxiliary **HAZU DA** or its polite form **HAZU DESU** is used. If the speaker thinks the possibility is higher, **NI CHIGAI NAI** or its polite form **NI CHIGAI NAI DESU/ NI CHIGAI ARIMASEN** may replace **HAZU DA/DESU** (see 11.5). However, if the speaker judges that some past event ought to have occurred, the **-TA** form normally precedes **HAZU DA/DESU**. Note that the negative form is not **HAZU DE WA NAI/ARIMASEN**, but **HAZU GA/WA NAI/ARIMASEN**.

台風 18 号は あさって 来る はずです。
Taifū jū hachi gō wa asatte kuru hazu desu.
Typhoon No.18 is supposed to come the day after tomorrow.

うそ！本当のことは 分かっている はずだ。
Uso! Hontō no koto wa wakatte iru hazu da.
Don't lie! You ought to know the truth.

もう 搭乗できる はずです。チェックイン しましょう。
Mō tōjō dekiru hazu desu. Chekku in shimashō.
Now they should have started boarding. Let's check in.

太郎さんは アルバイトを 辞めた はずです。
Tarō san wa arubaito o yameta hazu desu.
I'm sure Taro has given up his part-time job.

分からない はずは ないでしょう。
Wakaranai hazu wa nai deshō.
You can't not understand it! [You must understand it.]

こんな **konna** and そんな **sonna** (such ... as this/that) can directly precede **HAZU**.

まさか！そんな はずは ないよ。
Masaka! Sonna hazu wa nai yo.
You're kidding! It can't be.

こんな はずでは なかった。
Konna hazu de wa nakatta.
*It couldn't have been so./I didn't expect this.**

*はずではない **hazu dewa nai** is a set phrase of regret.

EXERCISE SET 3
Use the prompts to create sentences with **HAZU DESU**, as illustrated in the example. See suggested answers on page 207.

Example
I'm sure Kenji and Yoko will get married. けんじと よう子は 結婚する はすです。 **Kenji to Yōko wa kekkon suru hazu desu.**

❶ [USE:] きっと／よくなる
kitto / yoku naru

_____

❷ [USE:] 新聞／トイレットペーパー／リサイクル
shinbun / toiretto pēpā / risaikuru

_____

❸ [USE:] おいしい／餅／できる
oishī / mochi / dekiru

_____

❹ [USE:] レールパス／どの電車／乗れる
rēru pasu / dono densha / noreru

_____

🎧 11.5 Expressing "must" or "must have" using にちがいないです NI CHIGAI NAI DESU

When the speaker judges that some event is sure to happen, the auxiliary **NI CHIGAI NAI** or its polite form **NI CHIGAI NAI DESU** or **NI CHIGAI ARIMASEN** is used. When stating that some event must have happened, the **-TA** form precedes **NI CHIGAI NAI**.

いい考え です が、実行するのは むずかしい にちがいないです。
Ī kangae desu ga, jikkō suru no wa muzukashī ni chigai nai desu.
It's a good idea, but it must be difficult to put into practice.

あれ？ない。どっかで 落とした にちがいない。
Are? Nai. Dokka de otoshita ni chigai nai.
Oh dear. It's gone. I must have dropped it somewhere.

EXERCISE SET 4

Use the prompts to create sentences with **NI CHIGAI NAI DESU /ARIMASEN**, as illustrated in the example. See suggested answers on page 207.

> **Example**
>
> _The caterpillar must be turning into a chrysalis soon._
> 青虫は もうすぐ さなぎに なる にちがい ありません。
> **Aomushi wa mōsugu sanagi ni naru ni chigai arimasen.**

❶ [USE:] ここから／入れない
koko kara / hairenai

_____

❷ [USE:] ここで／タクシー／乗れる
koko de / takushī / noreru

_____

❸ [USE:] 今日／天気／晴れる
kyō / tenki / hareru

_____

❹ [USE:] 父／怒っている
chichi / okotte iru

_____

🎧 11.6 Asking for agreement or opinion using ん じゃない? N JA NAI?

When the speaker is not sure and is asking for the other person's agreement or opinion, **JA NAI** with a rising intonation is very casually used as follows:

❶ the plain form of the verb or the **-I** adjective + **N** + **JA NAI**

間に合わない ん じゃない?
Maniawanai n ja nai?
I'm afraid we'll be late, don't you think so?

ちょっと 高い ん じゃない?
Chotto takai n ja nai?
I feel it's expensive, don't you think so?

忘れた ん じゃない?
Wasureta n ja nai?
I guess you forgot it, right?

今日は 雨が 降る ん じゃない?
Kyō wa ame ga furu n ja nai?
I guess today will be rainy, don't you think so?

❷ a noun (+ **NA N**) + **JA NAI** (see also section 5.4)

> バカ じゃ ない？
> **Baka ja nai?**
> *You're kidding, right?*

> 閉店 なん じゃ ない？
> **Heiten na n ja nai?**
> *The shop is closed, isn't it?*

❸ an adjectival noun + (**NA N**) + **JA NAI**

> 無理（なん）じゃ ない？
> **Muri (na n) ja nai?**
> *It's impossible, don't you think so?*

❹ a noun/adjectival noun + **JA NAI/DATTA/JA NAKATTA** + **N** + **JA NAI**

> これ、山手線 じゃ ない ん じゃ ない？
> **Kore, yamanotesen ja nai n ja nai?**
> *This is not the Yamanote line, right?*

> 事故 だった ん じゃ ない？
> **Jiko datta n ja nai?**
> *There was an accident, right?*

> 間違い じゃ なかった ん じゃ ない？
> **Machigai ja nakatta n ja nai?**
> *It wasn't a mistake, right?*

The following adverbs may collocate with the auxiliaries that express judgment of possibility.

Adverbs that collocate	Meaning	Auxiliary verb
もしかしたら／もしかすると **moshikashitara/moshikasuruto**	perhaps/maybe/possibly	かもしれない／じゃない？ **kamo shirenai/ja nai?**
たぶん／おそらく **tabun/osoraku**	perhaps/maybe	だろう／じゃない？ **darō/ja nai**
きっと／必ず **kitto/kanarazu**	surely/certainly/ undoubtedly	はずだ／にちがいない／ だろう／じゃない？ **hazu da/ni chigai nai/ darō/ja nai?**

The confidence rating is as follows:

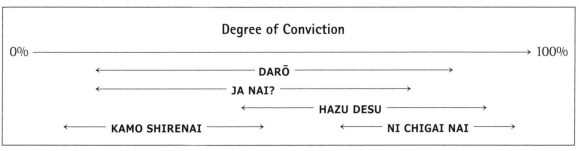

EXERCISE SET 5

Look at the pictures and create dialogues with **N JA NAI** as illustrated in the example. Check your ideas with the sample dialogues in the answer key on page 207.

Example

A: *What shall we do?*
どうしようか。
Dō shiyō ka?

B: *There isn't any other good way, is there?*
ほかに いい方法が ない んじゃない？
Hoka ni ī hōhō ga nai n ja nai?

---

❶ [USE:] A: どんな／味／かしら   B: すごく／おいしい
     A: **donna / aji / kashira**   B: **sugoku / oishī**

A: _____

B: _____

❷ [USE:] A: どうした／のかな   B: 駐車違反
     A: **dōshita / no kana**   B: **chūsha ihan**

A: _____

B: _____

❸ [USE:] A: 久しぶり   B: 人ちがい
     A: **hisashiburi**   B: **hito chigai**

A: _____

B: _____

❹ [USE:] A: よく／寝ている   B: 気持ちいい
     A: **yoku / nete iru**   B: **kimochi ī**

A: _____

B: _____

いいですね

よう子： コーヒーに お砂糖と ミルクは いいですか。

マイク： いいです。

よう子： 私は お砂糖も ミルクも 入れますね。甘い コーヒーが 飲みやすいです。

マイク： あれ？僕も 砂糖と ミルクも 入れたいんですが。

よう子： ああ、「いいです」って 言ったから、「要らない」かと 思いました。「いいです」は、「なくていいです」って 意味かもしれません。

マイク： 「僕は 砂糖も ミルクも あったらいいです」と 思いました。

よう子： でも、「砂糖が いいです」と 言ったら、砂糖が ほしいという意味に 違いありませんね。「いいですね」と 言ったら、気に入ったという 意味のはずですよ。

マイク： 「いいです」は 分かりにくいですね。

Ī desu ne

Yoko: **Kōhī ni osatō to miruku wa ī desu ka.**

Mike: **Ī desu.**

Yoko: **Watashi wa osatō mo miruku mo iremasu ne. Amai kōhī ga nomiyasui desu.**

Mike: **Are? Boku mo satō to miruku mo iretai n desu ga.**

Yoko: **Ā, "ī desu" tte itta kara, "iranai" ka to omoimashita. "Ī desu" wa, "nakute ī desu" tte imi kamo shiremasen.**

Mike: **Boku wa "satō mo miruku mo attara ī desu" to omoimashita.**

Yoko: **Demo, "satō ga ī desu" to ittara, satō ga hoshī to iu imi ni chigai arimasen ne. "Ī desu ne" to ittara, kini itta to iu imi no hazu desu yo.**

Mike: **"Ī desu" wa wakarinikui desu ne.**

It's Nice, Isn't It?

Yoko: Would you like sugar and milk in your coffee? [*lit.* Are sugar and milk okay for your coffee?]

Mike: Okay.

Yoko: I take sugar and milk. I like to drink sweet coffee.

Mike: What? But I want sugar and milk too.

Yoko: Ah, you said **ī desu**, so I thought you didn't want any. **Ī desu** can mean that it's okay without it.

Mike: I thought it meant "It's okay with sugar and milk."

Yoko: But if you say, **sato ga ī desu**, it means that you want sugar. And if you say "**ī desu ne**" it undoubtedly means you like something.

Mike: **Ī desu** is hard to understand!

TASK

Create a dialogue with the phrases **-NIKUI DESU** and **HAZU DESU** and practice it.

_____ : _____

_____ : _____

🎧 READING PRACTICE

曖昧な言葉

日本人は あまり はっきりと 言わないことが 多い。だから、外国人にとっては 日本語 が 曖昧な 言葉で、理解しにくい かもしれない。

日本人の 多くは、言いにくいことは、言わずに 理解してもらうことを 美徳としている かもしれない。「以心伝心」という 有名な言葉が ある。これは、言わなくても 自分の 考えや 気持ちが 理解されるという 意味である。だから、外国人は、日本語で どれぐ らい はっきりと 言ったらいいか 分かりにくい。

例えば、どのように 誘ったら いいか、どのように 断ったらいいかが むずかしいに違 いない。日本語の 曖昧な 返事は、外国人には 分かりにくい に違いない。だから、日 本人と コミュニケーションを とる時は、少し はっきりと 話してくれるように 頼んだ ら、ちょうどよい かもしれない。

Aimai na kotoba

Nihonjin wa amari hakkiri to iwanai koto ga ōi. Dakara, gaikokujin ni totte wa nihongo ga aimai na kotoba de, rikai shinikui kamo shirenai.

Nihonjin no ōku wa, īnikui koto wa, iwazuni rikai shite morau koto o bitoku to shite iru kamo shirenai. "Ishin denshin" to iu yūmei na kotoba ga aru. Kore wa, iwanakutemo jibun no kangae ya kimochi ga rikai sareru to iu imi de aru. Dakara, gaikokujin wa, nihongo de dore gurai hakkiri to ittara ī ka wakarinikui.

Tatoeba, dono yō ni sasottara ī ka, dono yō ni kotowattara ī ka ga muzukashī ni chigai nai. Nihongo no amai na henji wa, gaikokujin ni wa wakarinikui ni chigainai. Dakara, nihonjin to komyunikēshon o toru toki wa, sukoshi hakkiri to hanashite kureru yō ni tanondara, chōdo yoi kamo shirenai.

Ambiguous Language

There are many cases when Japanese people do not speak clearly. Therefore, Japanese can be ambiguous and hard to understand for foreigners.

Many Japanese people may make it a virtue to let you understand what is hard to say without saying it directly. There is the famous phrase **ishin denshin,** "tacit understanding." It means that your ideas and feelings are understood even if you don't express them. Therefore, foreigners may find it difficult to know how directly they should speak in Japanese.

For example, it must be difficult for foreigners to know how to invite or refuse. An ambiguous reply in Japanese must be hard to understand for a foreigner. Therefore, when communicating with Japanese people, it might be better to ask them to talk a little more directly.

QUESTIONS
Answers with their suggested sentence structure can be found on page 208.

1. どうして 日本人は あまり はっきりと 言わないことが 多いですか。
   Dōshite nihonjin wa amari hakkiri to iwanai koto ga ōi desu ka.

2. 外国人は 日本語を 使うとき、 何が 問題ですか。
   Gaikokujin wa nihongo o tsukau toki, nani ga mondai desu ka.

3. 日本人と コミュニケーションを とる時は、 どうしたらいいですか。
   Nihonjin to komyunikēshon o toru toki wa, dō shitara ī desu ka.

CHAPTER 12

I Hear There Was an Intensity 6 Earthquake
震度６の地震があったらしいです

Hearsay, Conjecture and Observation

In this chapter you'll learn how to express hearsay, conjecture and observation, using the auxiliary phrases and suffixes **RASHĪ**, **YŌ DESU**, **SŌ DESU**, **MITAI DESU** and **-PPOI**, and looking at appropriate sentence structures for various degrees of conviction and sureness. Mastering these structures will let you express your guesses and observations more clearly, adding credibility to what you say.

🎧 KEY SENTENCE PATTERNS

1. 震度６の地震があったらしいです。
   Shindo roku no jishin ga atta rashī desu.   *Hearsay: I hear...*
   I hear there was an intensity 6 earthquake.

2. 津波が 来るそうです。
   Tsunami ga kuru sō desu.   *Hearsay: I hear...*
   I hear that a tsunami is coming.

3. でも、人が 亡くなったみたいです。
   Demo, hito ga nakunatta mitai desu.   *Conjecture: it seems...*
   But it seems some people died.

4. 余震で 古い家が 倒れそうです。
   Yoshin de furui ie ga taore sō desu.   *Phenomenon emerging before one's eyes*
   The old houses are about to collapse due to aftershocks.

5. うわ〜、このケーキ、おいしそう！
   Uwā, kono kēki, oishisō!   *Phenomenon emerging before one's eyes*
   Wow! This cake looks delicious!

6. 連休で ホテルが 込んでそう。
   Renkyū de hoteru ga kondesō.   *Guessing about a state of affairs*
   Hotels seem to be fully booked due to the public holidays.

Formation of Expressions of Hearsay, Conjecture And Observation

Note there are two kinds of **SŌ DESU**. See usage notes for all structures in sections 12.1 to 12.8.

	Auxiliary	Example
Plain form of verb/**-I** adjective +	らしいです **RASHĪ DESU** (hearsay)	するらしいです **suru rashī desu** しないらしいです **shinai rashī desu** したらしいです **shita rashī desu** 安いらしいです **yasui rashī desu** 安かったらしいです **yasukatta rashī desu**
Adjectival noun/noun +	らしいです **RASHĪ DESU** (hearsay)	元気らしいです **genki rashī desu** 雨らしいです **ame rashī desu**
Plain form of verb/**-I** adjective +	そうです 1 **SŌ DESU 1** (reporting)	するそうです **suru sō desu** しないそうです **shinai sō desu** したそうです **shita sō desu** 安いそうです **yasui sō desu** 安かったそうです **yasukatta sō desu**
Adjectival noun/noun +	だそうです 1 **DA SŌ DESU 1** (reporting)	元気だそうです **genki da sō desu** 雨だそうです **ame da sō desu**
Plain form of verb/**-I** adjective +	ようです／ **YŌ DESU/** みたいです **MITAI DESU** (guessing)	するようです／するみたいです **suru yō desu/suru mitai desu** しないようです／しないみたいです **shinai yō desu/shinai mitai desu** したようです／したみたいです **shita yō desu/shita mitai desu** 安いようです／安いみたいです **yasui yō desu/yasui mitai desu** 安かったようです／安かったみたいです **yasukatta yō desu/yasukatta mitai desu**
Front part of **-MASU** form +	そうです 2 **SŌ DESU 2**	雨が降りそうです **ame ga furisō desu** (imminent)
Front part of **-I** adjective +	そうです 2 **SŌ DESU 2**	おいしそうです **oishisō desu** (imminent)
-TE form of the verb +	そうです 2 **SŌ DESU 2**	込んでそうです／込んでいそうです **kondesō desu / konde isō desu** (imminent)

GRAMMAR AND USAGE NOTES

12.1 Expressing hearsay using ～そうです 1/らしいです SŌ DESU 1/RASHĪ DESU

SŌ DESU 1 expresses what the speaker has heard and, without any conjecture, is simply reporting to the other person. On the other hand, **RASHĪ DESU** expresses what the speaker has heard but in this case the speaker is not sure whether it is true.

EXERCISE SET 1
Look at the pictures and create sentences with **SŌ DESU** or **RASHĪ DESU**, as illustrated in the examples. See suggested answers on page 208.

Examples

I hear a burger, fries and a drink are cheap by the set.
バーガーと フライドポテトと 飲み物が セットで
安いそうです。
Bāgā to furaido poteto to nomimono ga setto de yasui sō desu.

They say the double cheeseburger comes with a drink and fries now.
今 ダブルチーズ バーガーに ドリンクと フライドポテトが
付いている らしいです。
Ima daburu chīzu bāgā ni dorinku to furaido poteto ga tsuite iru rashī desu.

---

❶ [USE:] 雨／降る
ame / furu

_____

❷ [USE:] ペット美容／一回 ／一万円／かかる
petto biyō / ikkai / ichiman en / kakaru

_____

❸ [USE:] けんじ／自分で／弁当／作る
Kenji / jibun de / bentō / tsukuru

_____

12.2 Expressing a guess using ようです／みたいです　YŌ DESU/MITAI DESU

YŌ DESU, whose casual equivalent is **MITAI DESU**, expresses what the speaker guesses through observation, rumor, or other information like the news. Thus, the speaker is fairly sure that the situation is or will be true.

EXERCISE SET 2
Use the prompts to create sentences with **YŌ DESU** or **MITAI DESU**, as illustrated in the examples. See suggested answers on page 208.

> **Example**
>
> *It appears that years ago that husband was good-looking and his wife was beautiful.*
> あの旦那さんは 昔 イケメンで 奥さんは 美人 だった ようです。
> **Ano danna san wa mukashi ikemen de okusan wa bijin datta yō desu.**
>
> *That couple seems to be on good terms even now.*
> あの夫婦は 今でも 仲が いいみたい です。
> **Ano fūfu wa ima demo naka ga ī mitai desu.**

❶ [USE:] 外／風／強い
　　　　 soto / kaze / tsuyoi

_____

❷ [USE:] 雪／やまない
　　　　 yuki / yamanai

_____

❸ [USE:] 魚／焼けている
　　　　 sakana / yakete iru

_____

SŌ DESU 2 expresses some phenomenon that is about to emerge before one's eyes. This structure is used with a verb or an adjective.

落ちそう！
ochisō

The boxes are going to fall on me!

おいしそう！
oishisō

This is going to taste good. [*lit.* Deliciousness is going to fill my mouth!]

この自転車、壊れそうです。
Kono jitensha, kowaresō desu.
This bike may be about to break. [Because there is a crack in the frame.]

その荷物、重そうですね。
Sono nimotsu, omosō desu ne.
The bag looks heavy, doesn't it? [I will immediately know that it is heavy if I pick it up]

When **SŌ DESU 2** follows **-TE IRU**, it is often abbreviated to **-TESŌ DESU**.

あ、あの店、まだ 開いてそうです。 **A, ano mise, mada aitesō desu.**	*Oh, that shop seems to still be open.* [We will immediately know it is open if we go there.]
あの店、今日は 込んでそうです。 **Ano mise, kyō wa kondesō desu.**	*That shop seems to be crowded today.* [We will immediately know it is crowded if we go there.]

Degree of the speaker's conviction/sureness based on evidence or information	
100% ↑ Very sure	雨が降りそうです／おいしそうです **ame ga furisō desu/oishisō desu**
Quite sure	雨が降るようです／おいしいようです **ame ga furu yō desu/oishī yō desu**
I hear it and half believe it	雨が降るらしいです／おいしいらしいです **ame ga furu rashī desu/oishī rashī desu**
0 I'm just reporting what I've heard	雨が降るそうです／おいしいそうです **ame ga furu sō desu/oishī sō desu**

EXERCISE SET 3

Fill in the blanks with the **-SŌ DESU 2** form of each verb. Check your answers on page 208.

-MASU form	-SŌ DESU	-TE SŌ DESU
(E.g.) 降ります **furimasu** (to rain/snow)	降りそうです	降ってそうです
1. 空きます **sukimasu** (get less crowded)		
2. 着きます **tsukimasu** (to arrive)		
3. 勝ちます **kachimasu** (to win)		
4. 来ます **kimasu** (to come)		

EXERCISE SET 4

Use the prompts to create sentences with **-SŌ DESU 2**, as illustrated in the examples. See suggested answers on page 208.

Example

Dinner will be ready soon.
料理が もうすぐ できそうです。
Ryōri ga mōsugu dekisō desu.

That couple looks busy.
あの夫婦は 忙しそうです。
Ano fūfu wa isogashisō desu.

❶ [USE:] 宴会／楽しい
enkai / tanoshī

_____

❷ [USE:] 私たち／だいぶ／遅れる
watashitachi / daibu / okureru

_____

❸ [USE:] もうすぐ／完成する
mō sugu / kansei suru

_____

🎧 12.4 Using ～そうです 2 -SŌ DESU 2 after ～ない -NAI and いい ī

When **SŌ DESU 2** follows the **-I** adjective **-NAI**, **sa** must be added before **SŌ DESU**. When **SŌ DESU 2** follows the adjective ī, meaning "good," ī must be changed to **yo** and **sa** must be added before **SŌ DESU**.

雨が 降らない＋そうです。 → 雨が 降らな<u>さ</u>そうです。
Ame ga furanai + sō desu   **Ame ga furana<u>sa</u>sō desu.**
It doesn't look like rain.

このカバンの方がいい＋そうです。 → このカバンの方が <u>よさ</u>そうです。
Kono kaban no hō ga ī + sō desu   **Kono kaban no hō ga <u>yosa</u>sō desu.**
This bag seems better.

🎧 12.5 "So ... that ... (could ...)" using ～て ... ～そうです -TE ... -SŌ DESU 2

The phrase "so ... that ... (could) ..." can be translated by the **-TE** form of the verb + **SŌ DESU 2**.

お腹が 空い<u>て</u> 倒れそうです。
Onaka ga sui<u>te</u> taoresō desu.
I'm so hungry that I could collapse/faint.

疲れ<u>て</u> 死にそうです。
Tsukare<u>te</u> shinisō desu.
I'm so tired that I could die. (I'm tired to the extent that I may die.)

とても 安く<u>て</u> 買ってしまいそうです。
Totemo yasuku<u>te</u> katte shimaisō desu.
It is so cheap that I may buy it (in spite of myself).

EXERCISE SET 5
Use the prompts to create sentences using the **-TE** form of the verb + **SŌ DESU 2**, as illustrated in the example. See suggested answers on page 208.

Example
The flea market is so cheap that they are going to buy a lot. フリーマーケットが 安くて 二人は たくさん 買いそうです。 **Furīmāketto ga yasukute futari wa takusan kaisō desu.** 

❶ [USE:] 寒い／風邪／ひく
　　　　 samui / kaze / hiku

_____

❷ [USE:] スモッグの雨／ひどい／環境／破壊する
sumoggu no ame / hidoi / kankyō / hakai suru

🎧 12.6 Guessing something is about to change using なりそうです NARISŌ DESU

When the speaker is observing some phenomenon and guessing that something is about to change, the English phrase "(may/seem to) become" can be translated by the **-KU** form of the adjective + **NARI** + **SŌ DESU 2**, or adjectival noun/noun + **NI NARI** + **SŌ DESU 2**, as shown below.

地球が ますます 暖かく なりそうです。
Chikyū ga masumasu atataka<u>ku narisō desu</u>.
Earth seems to be getting warmer and warmer.

IC カードを 買ったら 便利になりそうです。
Ai shī kādo o kattara benri <u>ni narisō desu</u>.
If I buy an prepaid transport card it may be useful, I'm sure.

あなたのことが もっと 好きになりそうです。
Anata no koto ga motto suki <u>ni narisō desu</u>.
I feel I may come to like you more.

🎧 12.7 Other uses of らしい RASHĪ

RASHĪ DESU has another function, which is to express that the subject of the sentence has a typical distinctive feature.

けんじは ほんとに 日本人らしいです。
Kenji wa honto ni nihonjin rashī desu.
Kenji really is a typical Japanese person.

Note the following correct and incorrect sentences carefully:

CORRECT:	けんじは 男らしいです。	**Kenji wa otoko rashī desu.**	*Kenji is manly.*
INCORRECT:	けんじは 男みたいです。	**Kenji wa otoko mitai desu.**	*Kenji looks like a man.*
CORRECT:	よう子は 男みたいです。	**Yōko wa otoko mitai desu.**	*Yoko looks like a man.*
INCORRECT:	よう子は 男らしいです。	**Yōko wa otoko rashī desu.**	*Yoko is manly.*

Accordingly, the following sentence has two possible meanings:

あの人は 学生らしいです。
Ano hito wa gakusei rashī desu.
That person [a student] *is student-like.*
I hear that person is a student.

However, the negative form of this structure does not express hearsay, only the following meaning:

あの人は ぜんぜん 学生らしくないです。
Ano hito wa zenzen gakusei <u>rashiku nai</u> desu.
There is nothing of the student about him/her.

Therefore, the sentence which expresses that the speaker heard a negative sentence is as below. **RASHIKUNAI DESU** does not express hearsay.

あの人は 学生じゃ <u>ないらしい</u> です。(INCORRECT: らしくないです → see above)
Ano hito wa gakusei ja <u>nai rashī</u> desu.
I hear that person is not a student.

🎧 12.8 The casual auxiliary 〜っぽい -PPOI

The very casual auxiliary **-PPOI** may replace **YŌ DESU** or **MITAI DESU**.

子供みたいです。	→	子供っぽい [です]。
Kodomo mitai desu.		**Kodomoppoi (desu).**
He or she behaves like a child.		*He or she is childish* (immature).

Recently, many young people may add **-PPOI** not only to a noun (in standard usage) but to a verb/adjective in the plain form, making a slang word.

雨のようです。	→	雨<u>っぽい</u>。
Ame no yō desu.		**Ame<u>ppoi</u>.**
		It looks like rain.
雨が降るようです。	→	雨が降る<u>っぽい</u>。
Ame ga furu yō desu.		**Ame ga furu<u>ppoi</u>.**
		It looks like rain.
バスが来たようです。	→	バスが来た<u>っぽい</u>。
Basu ga kita yō desu.		**Basu ga kita<u>ppoi</u>.**
		Our bus seems to have come.
あの人、行かないようです。	→	あいつ、行かない<u>っぽい</u>。
Ano hito, ikanai yō desu.		**Aitsu, ikanai<u>ppoi</u>.**
		He seems not to be going.
今日は 暑いみたいです。	→	今日、暑い<u>っぽい</u>。
Kyo wa atsui mitai desu.		**Kyo, atsui<u>ppoi</u>.**
		Today seems hot.

日本の神様

マイク：この鳥居は 石で できていますが、木で 作られたのも あるみたいですね。

けんじ：赤いものも あります。

マイク：京都の 平安神宮の 鳥居は 赤くて 大きそうですね。大きくて 倒れそうです。

よう子：大丈夫。鳥居は 神社の入口で 社会と 境内を 分けるらしいです。

マイク：鳥居のない 神社も あるみたいですが？

けんじ：それは 神社じゃなくて お寺ですね。お寺は 仏教の建物で、神社は 神道 という 宗教の建物ですよ。神道は、自然や 祖先に お祈りする 宗教です。

よう子：日本人の 7割は 宗教を 信じないらしいです。でも、先祖を 思う気持ちは 9割の人が 持ってるらしいです。

けんじ：人間の力を 超えたものに対して 敬う気持ちを 持つ人も 多いです。

マイク：それで、宗教を 信じないのに、よく お参りする ん ですね。

Nihon no kamisama

Mike: **Kono torī wa ishi de dekite imasu ga, ki de tsukurareta no mo aru mitai desu ne.**

Kenji: **Akai mono mo arimasu.**

Mike: **Kyōto no heian jingū no torī wa akakute ōkīsō desu ne. Ōkikute taoresō desu.**

Yoko: **Daijōbu. Torī wa jinja no iriguchi de shakai to keidai o wakeru rashī desu.**

Mike: **Torī no nai jinja mo aru mitai desu ga?**

Kenji: **Sore wa jinja ja nakute otera desu ne. Otera wa bukkyō no tatemono de, jinja wa shintō to iu shūkyō no tatemono desu yo. Shintō wa, shizen ya sosen ni oinori suru shūkyō desu.**

Yoko: **Nihonjin no nana wari wa shūkyō o shinjinai rashī desu. Demo, senzo o omou kimochi wa kyū wari no hito ga motteru rashī desu.**

Kenji: **Ningen no chikara o koeta mono ni taishite uyamau kimochi o motsu hito mo ōi desu.**

Mike: **Sorede, shūkyō o shinjinai no ni, yoku omairi suru n desu ne.**

Japanese Gods

Mike: Although this torii gate is made of stone, it seems some are made of wood.

Kenji: There are also red ones.

Mike: The torii at Heian Jingu, which is red, looks big. It looks so big I'm afraid it might fall.

Yoko: It's safe. Apparently, a torii is the dividing line between regular society and the precincts of the shrine.

Mike: It seems that there are also shrines without torii, aren't there?

Kenji: Those aren't shrines, they're temples. A temple is a Buddhist building and a shrine is a building of the Shinto religion. Shintoism is a religion where they pray to nature and ancestors.

Yoko: I hear that 70 percent of Japanese people don't have religious beliefs. But they say that 90 percent of them have the feeling of respecting their ancestors.

Kenji: There are also many people who feel that they respect something beyond man's power.

Mike: That's why they often visit a shrine or temple, even though they don't believe in religion.

TASK
Create a dialogue with **RASHĪ DESU** and **MITAI DESU** and practice it.

_____ : _____

_____ : _____

🎧 READING PRACTICE

少子化

子供が 少なくなることを 「少子化」 という。 そして、 日本では、 これから 人口が だんだん 減りそうだと 言われている。

いろいろなニュースによると、 日本で 少子化が 進んでいく 理由は、 女性の学歴が 高くなったこと、 晩婚化、 未婚化などである ようだ。

若い男性も 最近では あまり 結婚したくない そうだ。 それは 経済的な理由で 家族を 持てないことや、 一人で 自分らしく 過ごしたい人が 増えたことのため らしい。

2030年には、 生産年齢の 人口は、 かなり 減っていそうである。 だから、 政府は、 若者や 女性の 安定した仕事だけでなく、 高齢者の仕事も 作って、 生産年齢の人口を 増やす予定のようだ。

Shōshika

Kodomo ga sukunaku naru koto o "shōshika" to iu. Soshite, nihon de wa, korekara jinkō ga dandan herisō da to iwarete iru.

Iroiro na nyūsu ni yoru to, Nihon de shōshika ga susunde iku riyū wa, josei no gakureki ga takaku natta koto, bankonka, mikonka nado de aru yōda.

Wakai dansei mo saikin de wa amari kekkon shitaku nai sō da. Sore wa, keizaiteki na riyu de kazoku o motenai koto ya, hitori de jibun rashiku sugoshitai hito ga fueta koto no tame rashī.

Nisen sanjū nen ni wa, seisan nenrei no jinkō wa, kanari hette isō de aru. Dakara, seifu wa wakamono ya josei no antei shita shigoto dake de naku, kōreisha no shigoto mo tsukutte, seisan nenrei no jinkō o fuyasu yotei no yō da.

The Declining Birth Rate

The decrease in the number of children is called **shōshika**. And in Japan, it is said that the population is likely to decrease gradually from now on.

According to various news reports, the reasons for the continuing decline in Japan's birth rate appear to be the improvement in the level of women's education, the tendency to marry later, and the tendency not to marry, etc.

It seems young men are not likely to get married these days. It is said that this is because they feel it's hard economically to support a family, or because more of them like to spend time alone, living life in their own way.

The working population may have decreased considerably by 2030. Therefore, the government seems to be planning to create not only stable work for young people and women but also work for elderly people to increase the working-age population.

QUESTIONS
Answers with their suggested sentence structure can be found on page 208.

1. どうして 日本では 少子化が 進みそうですか。
   Dōshite nihon de wa shōshika ga susumiso desu ka.

2. 社会の問題は どんなことですか。
   Shakai no mondai wa donna koto desu ka.

3. 多くの 男性は どうして 結婚をしたくないと 思っていますか。
   Ōku no dansei wa dōshite kekkon o shitaku nai to omotte imasu ka.

Japanese-English Glossary

あ

あいさつする	挨拶する	to greet
あい	愛	love
あいする	愛する	to love
あいて	相手	opponent; other person; partner
あいてチーム	相手チーム	opposing team
あいまいな	曖昧な	ambiguous
あう	遭う	to have (bad experience)
あおむし	青虫	caterpillar
あかい	赤い	red
あがる	上がる	to be set off (fireworks)
あがる	上がる	to go up; rise; enter a Japanese house
あかるい	明るい	bright
あきかん	空き缶	empty can
あきべや	空き部屋	room to let; vacancy
あきらめる	諦める	to abandon; give up
あける	開ける	to open
あげる	上げる	to give; raise; lift
あさごはん	朝ご飯	breakfast
あじ	味	taste
あそぶ	遊ぶ	to have fun; socialize
あたえる	与える	to arouse; cause
あたたかい	暖かい	warm
あたたまる	暖まる	to get warm
あたま	頭	head
あたまがいたい	頭が痛い	to have a headache
あたりまえの	当たり前の	natural; reasonable
あつさ	厚さ	thickness
あと	後	after
アトラクション		attraction
アニメ		animation
アニメぶんか	アニメ文化	anime culture
アパート		apartment
あぶない	危ない	dangerous; risky
アプリ		app
あまい	甘い	sweet
あまり/あんまり		not much; not often
あみだな	網棚	luggage rack
あらい	粗い	coarse, rough
あらう	洗う	to wash
あらわす	表す	to express; indicate
アルバイト		part-time job; part-timer
アレルギー		allergy
あんていした	安定した	stable; steady
アンドロイド		Android OS
あんないする	案内する	to guide

い

イースポーツ		e-sport
いきさき	行き先	destination
いきる	生きる	to be alive
いくつか		several; a few
イケメン		good-looking guy
いご	囲碁	go (board game)
いざかや	居酒屋	izakaya
いし	石	stone
いしき	意識	consciousness
いじょう	以上	or more than...
いそぐ	急ぐ	to dash; hurry
いたい	痛い	painful
いたずら	悪戯	mischief
いためる	痛める	to hurt
いちじ	一時	intermittent
いちにんまえ	一人前	full-fledged
いちぶ	一部	part; portion
いっしゅうする	一周する	to make a circuit
いっしょに	一緒に	together
いっぱいになる		to become full
いっぱんてき	一般的	general
いのち	命	life; life force
いびきをかく		to snore
いぶんか	異文化	different culture
いぶんかかん	異文化間	intercultural
いまでも	今でも	even now
いみ	意味	meaning
イメージ		image
いやな	嫌な	disgusting; unpleasant
いりぐち	入口	entrance
いる	要る	to need
いれる	入れる	to put in
いろいろと	色々と	variously
いろいろな	色々な	various
いわう	祝う	to celebrate
インコ		lorikeet
インスタントラーメン		instant ramen
インストールする		to install
インターン		intern
インチ		inch

う

ウィンドウズテン		Windows 10
ウィンドー・ショッピング		window-shopping
うかがう	伺う	visit; ask; hear (humble)
うける	受ける	to undergo
うごき	動き	movement; motion
うさぎ		rabbit
うそ	嘘	lie
うたう	歌う	to sing
うちおとす	打ち落とす	to knock/shoot down
うつ	撃つ	to shoot
うつ	打つ	to strike
うっかり		absent-mindedly
うつくしい	美しい	beautiful
うつす	移す	to transfer; move
うつる	写る	to appear (in a photo)
うで	腕	arm

うとうとする		to doze off
うどん		udon noodles
うまく		well; skillfully
うまくいく		to go well
うまくつかう	うまく使う	to make good use of
うまる	埋まる	to be buried
うめる	埋める	to bury; fill up
うやまう	敬う	to respect
うりあげ	売り上げ	sales
うりば	売り場	(ticket) counter
うる	売る	to sell (v.t.)
うるさい		annoying; noisy
うれる	売れる	to sell (v.i.)
うわ〜		wow!
うわさばなし	うわさ話	gossip
うんてんしゅ	運転手	driver
うんてんする	運転する	to drive
うんどうする	運動する	to exercise

え ──────

え	絵	picture
エアコン		air conditioner
えいせいてきな	衛生的な	sanitary
えき	駅	station
エクセル		Excel (software)
えんかい	宴会	enkai; drinking party
エコな		ecological
エコバッグ		eco bag
エスカレーター		escalator
エネルギー		energy
えほん	絵本	picture book
えらぶ	選ぶ	to choose; select

お ──────

おい	甥	nephew
おいだす	追い出す	to kick (someone) out
おいのり	お祈り	prayer
おいはらう	追い払う	to exorcise; drive away
おおあめ	大雨	heavy rain
オーエス		operating system
おおくの	多くの	many; much
おおぜいの	大勢の	a large number of (people)
おかあさん	お母さん	mom
おかし	お菓子	candy; cookie
おくる	送る	to send
おくれる	遅れる	to be delayed; late for
おこす	起こす	to cause (v.t.)
おこっている	怒っている	angry
おこる	起こる	to occur
おさけ	お酒	alcohol
おしえ	教え	instruction; teachings
おじぎ	お辞儀	bow (greeting)
おじさん		uncle; middle-aged man
おしゃべりをする		to have a chat
おす	押す	to push
オセロ		Othello computer game

おせん	汚染	pollution
おそらく	恐らく	perhaps; maybe
おちつく	落ち着く	to calm down
おと	音	sound
おとうさん	お父さん	dad
おとしより	お年寄り	old person
おとす	落とす	to drop (v.t.)
おとずれる	訪れる	to visit
おどる	踊る	to dance
おどろく	驚く	to be surprised
おどろくこと	驚くこと	surprise (noun)
おとをたてる	音を立てる	to make a sound
おなかがすく	お腹が空く	to get hungry
おに	鬼	demon
おにぎり		rice ball
おねがいする	お願いする	to beg
オノマトペ		onomatopoeia
おぼえる	覚える	to memorize; learn
おまいりする	お参りする	to visit and pray
おみやげ	お土産	souvenir
おもい	重い	heavy
おもいで	思い出	memory
おもしろい	面白い	interesting
おやゆび	親指	thumb
およぐ	泳ぐ	to swim
おりたたみがさ	折りたたみ傘	folding umbrella
おりる	降りる	get off/out of (vehicle)
おれ	俺	I (male)
おわる	終わる	to be over; finish; end
おんがく	音楽	music
おんすい	温水	warm water
おんせん	温泉	onsen; spa; hot springs
おんねつ	温熱	warmth
おんねつしき	温熱式	thermal

か ──────

カアカア		cawing (of a crow)
カート		cart
カートリッジ		cartridge
カーナビ		car navigation system
かい	回	counter for times
かいがいへ	海外へ	abroad
かいがん	海岸	seashore
かいぎ	会議	meeting
かいごし	介護士	caregiver
かいしゃ	会社	company
かいてんずし	回転寿司	conveyor-belt sushi
かいばつ	海抜	altitude above sea level
かう	飼う	to keep a pet
かえる	帰る	to return; come back
かかる	掛かる	to hang
かぎをかける	鍵をかける	to lock
かく／えがく	描く	to draw
かぐ	家具	furniture
かくご	覚悟	preparedness; readiness (of mind)
かくにんする	確認する	to confirm

かくやす	格安	super-cheap; discount
がくれき	学歴	academic background; school background
かけい	家計	household budget
かける	掛ける	to put on (glasses)
かご		palanquin
かさたて	傘立て	umbrella stand
かざる	飾る	to decorate
かしこい	賢い	wise
がしつ	画質	picture quality
かす	貸す	to lend
かぞえる	数える	to count
かぜを ひく	風邪を ひく	to catch a cold
ガソリン		gas; gasoline
かた	〜方	how to do something
かたい	堅い	hard
かちょう	課長	section manager
かつ	勝つ	to defeat; win; beat
かつぐ	担ぐ	to shoulder
かっこいい		cool, stylish
かつどう	活動	activity
かていきょうし	家庭教師	tutor
かていゴミ	家庭ゴミ	household garbage
かど	角	corner
かどう	華道	ikebana
かなり		considerably
かのじょ	彼女	girlfriend
カバーする		to cover
カビ		mold (fungus)
かぶ	株	stocks
カプセル		capsule
かふんしょう	花粉症	hay fever
かみ	紙	paper
がめん	画面	screen
がめんタッチ	画面タッチ	touching the screen
かゆい		itchy
カラオケ		karaoke
ガラケー		feature phone
カラス		crow
から		because
からだにわるい	体に悪い	bad for health
〜からです		(it is) because…
かる	刈る	to cut; mow
かれし	彼氏	boyfriend
かれる	枯れる	to wither
カレンダー		calendar
かわ	川	river
かんがえ	考え	idea; thought; opinion
かんがえる	考える	to think
かんけい	関係	relationship
かんげいする	歓迎する	to welcome
かんこう	観光	sightseeing
かんこうきゃく	観光客	tourist
かんじ	感じ	feeling; impression
かんしゃする	感謝する	to thank
かんじる	感じる	to feel
かんせいする	完成する	to be completed

がんたん	元旦	New Year's Day
かんたんな	簡単な	easy
かんちがい	勘違い	mistaken idea
かんぱい（する）	乾杯（する）	(to) toast (with drinks)
がんばる	頑張る	to do one's best
かんるい	缶類	cans (type of trash)

き ————

き	木	wood; tree
キーボード		keyboard
きいろ	黄色	yellow (noun)
ぎおんまつり	祇園祭	Gion Festival
きかい	機械	machine
きかく	企画	project
ききじょうず	聞き上手	good listener
きく	聞く	to listen
きこくする	帰国する	to return to one's country
きじ	記事	article
きせつ	季節	season
ぎだい	議題	agenda
きたえる	鍛える	to train; build up
きたない	汚い	dirty; messy
きちんと		properly
キッチン		kitchen
きって	切手	postage stamp
きっと		surely; certainly
きっぷ	切符	ticket
きどうする	起動する	to be activated
きにする	気にする	to worry; be worried; care
きね		mallet
きぶん	気分	mood; feeling
きぼうする	希望する	to hope
きみ	君	you (informal)
きめる	決める	to determine; decide
きもち	気持ち	feeling; mood
きゃく	客	guest; customer
キャラクター		character
きゅうけいする	休憩する	to have a break
ぎゅうしゃ	牛車	oxcart
ぎゅうどん	牛丼	beef rice bowl
きゅうな	急な	sudden; abrupt
きゅうに	急に	suddenly; all at once
ぎゅうにゅう	牛乳	milk
きゅうりょう	給料	pay; salary
きょうかしょ	教科書	textbook
きょうかする	強化する	to strengthen
きょうしつ	教室	classroom
きょうじゅうに	今日中に	by the end of the day
きょうりょくする	協力する	to cooperate
きょく	曲	song; music
きりすぎる	切りすぎる	to cut too short
ぎりチョコ	義理チョコ	obligation chocolate
きれいな		beautiful
きれいにする		to tidy up; beautify

きをつかう	気を遣う	to care a lot
きをつける	気を付ける	to be careful; take care
きんえん	禁煙	no smoking
ぎんこう	銀行	bank
きんじょのひと	近所の人	neighbor
きんにく	筋肉	muscle

く

くう	食う	to eat; gobble
くうき	空気	air
くうき せいじょうき	空気清浄機	air purifier
くうこう	空港	airport
くうらん	空欄	blank space
くずれる	崩れる	to collapse
ぐっすり		fast (asleep)
くみたてる	組み立てる	to assemble; put together
ぐらい		about; approximately
クラウドサービス		cloud service
グラス		glass (for drinking)
グラフをかく		to plot a graph
グラム		gram
くるまいす	車椅子	wheelchair
クレジット・カード		credit card

け

けいかいな	軽快な	light; agile; with a light touch
けいご	敬語	honorific expression
けいざいてきな	経済的な	economical
けいさん	計算	calculation
けいじ	掲示	notice; sign
げいじゅつ	芸術	art
けいたい	携帯	mobile phone; cellphone
けいだい	境内	the precincts of a temple/shrine
けいたいでんわ	携帯電話	cellphone; mobile phone
けいば	競馬	horse racing
けいやく	契約	contract
ゲーム		game
ゲームき	ゲーム機	game console
げきやす	激安	bargain-priced
けしょうする	化粧する	to wear makeup
けっこう	結構	really; considerably
けっこんする	結婚する	to marry
げひんな	下品な	coarse; vulgar
けむり	煙	smoke
ける	蹴る	to kick
けれども		however
げん	弦	string (of an instrument)
げんいん	原因	cause
けんがく	見学	field trip
げんき	元気	fine; well; healthy
げんご	言語	language

けんこう	健康	health
けんさ	検査	examination
けんさくする	検索する	to do a search
けんじょうご	謙譲語	humble expression
げんだいてき	現代的	modern
けんどう	剣道	kendo
けんどうのしあい	剣道の試合	kendo match
げんぱつ	原発	nuclear power plant
げんぱつじこ	原発事故	nuclear power-plant accident
けんびきょう	顕微鏡	microscope
けんめいな	賢明な	sensible; wise

こ

こいにおちる	恋に落ちる	to fall in love
こいびと	恋人	boy (girl) friend
ごう	号	number (counter suffix)
ごうかくする	合格する	to pass (a test); succeed
こうかんする	交換する	to replace
こうげきする	攻撃する	to attack
こうしょう	交渉	negotiation
こうしん	行進	march
こうしんする	行進する	to march; parade
こうずい	洪水	flood
こうそくどうろ	高速道路	expressway
こうつういはん	交通違反	traffic offense
こうどうする	行動する	to act; behave
こうどけいざい せいちょうき	高度経済 成長期	high economic growth period
こうねつ	高熱	high fever
こうやさん	高野山	Mount Koya
こうりゅうする	交流する	to interact
こうれいしゃ	高齢者	elderly people
こえる	肥える	to get fat
こえる	超える／ 越える	to exceed
コーヒー		coffee
ごかいする	誤解する	to misunderstand
こぐ		to row (a boat)
こくはくする	告白する	to confess; declare one's love
こげる	焦げる	to get burnt
ごじゅうのとう	五重塔	five-story pagoda
こしるい	古紙類	used paper (type of garbage)
こたえる	答える	to respond (to questions)
ことば	言葉	word; language
こども	子供	child
ことわる	断る	to refuse; turn down
こな	粉	powder
コピーき	コピー機	photocopier
こまる	困る	to be annoyed; be in trouble
ゴミ		garbage; trash
ゴミばこ	ゴミ箱	wastebasket
コミュニケー ションする		to communicate

こむ	込む	be fully booked; be crowded
こめ	米	rice
コメディ		comedy
こゆび	小指	little finger
ゴルフ		golf
これから		from now on
コレステロール		cholesterol
こわい	怖い	frightening; scary
こわす	壊す	to break (v.t.)
こわれる	壊れる	to be broken; break down; break (v.i.)
こんかい	今回	this time
こんげつ	今月	this month
こんしゅうまつ	今週末	this weekend
コンテスト		contest
こんど	今度	next time; this time
こんな		such... (this kind of)
コンパ		party; social event
コンビニ		convenience store

さ ———

サービス		service
サーブする		to serve
さいあく	最悪	the worst
さいきん	最近	recently; these days
サイト		site
さいふ	財布	wallet
さいぼう	細胞	cell
サイン		autograph; signature
さがす	探す	to look for; seek; hunt
さかな	魚	fish
さがる	下がる	to go down; drop; move back
さしばし	刺し箸	stabbing chopsticks into food
さしみ	刺身	sashimi
さしみていしょく	刺身定食	sashimi set meal
さす	指す	to point (at)
さす	刺す	to stab; stick
さそう	誘う	to invite; tempt
さつじんはん	殺人犯	murderer
さとう	砂糖	sugar
さどう	茶道	tea ceremony
さなぎ		pupa
サポートする		to support
さら	皿	plate
さわる	触る	to touch
さんかする	参加する	to participate
さんかするひと	参加する人	participant
さんぎょう	産業	industry
さんせいう	酸性雨	acid rain
さんぽする	散歩する	to take a walk

し ———

じ	字	letter; character
しあわせな	幸せな	happy (sustained feeling)

シートベルト		seatbelt
シートベルトをする		to buckle up (seatbelt)
ジェスチャー		gesture
ジェットコースター		roller coaster
しかし		but; however
しかた	仕方	how to do; method; way
しかる	叱る	to scold
じかんがいに	時間外に	off the clock
じかんどおりに	時間通りに	on time
じき	時期	time; period
しきん	資金	funds; capital
じけん	事件	incident; case
しげんゴミ	資源ゴミ	recyclable garbage
じこ	事故	accident
じこにあう	事故にあう	to have an accident
ししょう	師匠	teacher; instructor
じしん	自信	confidence
じしん	地震	earthquake
しずかに	静かに	quietly; silently
しぜん	自然	nature
じだい	時代	age; period; era
したしくなる	親しくなる	to become friendly
しっけ	湿気	moisture; damp; humidity
じっこうする	実行する	to put into practice
しっている	知っている	to know
じつは	実は	in fact; actually; to tell the truth
しっぱいする	失敗する	to fail
しつれんする	失恋する	to have one's heart broken
しどうする	指導する	to instruct
じどうで	自動で	automatically
しとしと		gently (of rain)
しな，しなもの	品，品物	article; goods
しばらく	暫く	for a while; for the time being
じぶん	自分	oneself
じぶんで	自分で	by oneself; for oneself
しまう		to put away; put an end to
しめきり	締め切り	deadline
しゃかい	社会	society
しゃしん	写真	photo
ジャズ		jazz
しゃちょう	社長	company president
シャベル		shovel
しゃみせん	三味線	shamisen
しゃりょう	車両	car; railway car; vehicle
シャワー		shower
シャワーをあびる	シャワーを浴びる	to take a shower
ジャンプをする		to jump
じゅう	銃	gun; pistol
しゅうかん	習慣	custom; habit
しゅうかん	週間	week (counter suffix)
しゅうきょう	宗教	religion

しゅうごうじかん	集合時間	meeting time
しゅうしゅう	収集	collection
じゅうたい	渋滞	traffic jam
じゅうたく	住宅	house; housing
しゅうちゅうする	集中する	to concentrate
じゅうでんする	充電する	to charge
じゅうどう	柔道	judo
じゅうような	重要な	important; essential
しゅっちょう	出張	business trip
しゅみ	趣味	hobby
しゅるい	種類	kind; sort; type
しゅわ	手話	sign language
じゅんきゅう	準急	semi-express train
しょうかいする	紹介する	to introduce
しょうぎ	将棋	shogi (Japanese chess)
じょうし	上司	boss
しょうしか	少子化	declining birth rate
じょうずに	上手に	well; skillfully
じょうだん	冗談	joke
しょうめい	照明	electric lighting
しょか	初夏	early summer
しょくせんき	食洗機	dishwasher
しょっき	食器	dishes
しょり	処理	handling; processing
しらべる	調べる	to examine; research
しり	尻	buttock; hip
しりあう	知り合う	become acquainted with
しりょう	資料	document; material
しるもの	汁物	soup
しんがくする	進学する	to go on to a higher-level school
しんかする	進化する	to develop; evolve
しんかんコンパ	新歓コンパ	welcome drinking party
しんかんせん	新幹線	shinkansen (bullet train)
シングルス		singles (e.g., tennis)
じんこう	人口	population
しんしゃ	新車	new car
じんじゃ	神社	shrine
しんじる	信じる	to believe
じんしんじこ	人身事故	fatal accident
しんせんな	新鮮な	fresh
しんど	震度	seismic intensity
しんとう	神道	Shinto
しんにゅうせい	新入生	new student
しんぶん	新聞	newspaper
しんゆう	親友	best friend; close friend
しんりん	森林	forest

す ───────

すいどう	水道	water supply
すう	吸う	to breathe in; smoke
すうじゅうまん	数十万	hundreds of thousands
スーツケース		suitcase
スーパー		supermarket
すがた	姿	image
スキーする		to ski

すぎる	過ぎる	to go by; pass
すく	空く	to become less crowded
すぐに	直ぐに	at once; soon
すごい		huge; terrible
すごす	過ごす	to spend (time)
すすむ	進む	to advance
ずっと		whole time; all the way
ステージ		stage
すてる	捨てる	dispose of; throw away
スプーン		spoon
スマホ		smartphone
スムーズに		smoothly
すもう	相撲	sumo wrestling
スモッグ		smog
ずるずると		with a slurp
すわる	座る	to sit down; take a seat

せ ───────

せいおん	清音	voiceless sound
せいかくな	正確な	correct; exact; precise
せいかつ	生活	life; daily existence
せいかつする	生活する	to make a living
せいじんしき	成人式	coming-of-age ceremony
ぜいたくな	贅沢な	extravagant; luxurious
せいふ	政府	government
せいぶつ	静物	still life
せおう	背負う	to carry on one's back
せかい	世界	the world; the earth
せき	席	seat
せきゆファンヒーター	石油ファンヒーター	oil fan heater
セキュリティ		security
せきをする	咳をする	to cough
せっかく		specially; expressly
せっけん	石けん	soap
せっすい	節水	water conservation
せってい	設定	setting; setup
せつでん	節電	power saving
せつでんする	節電する	to save electricity
せつめいする	説明する	to explain
せつめいぶん	説明文	explanatory text
せつやく	節約	economizing; saving
せまい	狭い	narrow
せん	線	line
せんじつ	先日	the other day
せんしゅ	選手	player
せんしゅう	先週	last week
ぜんぜん	全然	not ... at all/in the least
せんぞ	先祖	ancestor
せんそう	戦争	war
せんたく	洗濯	laundry
ぜんぶ	全部	all; the whole
せんぷうき	扇風機	electric fan

そ ───────

そうさ	操作	operation; management
そうじ	掃除	cleaning

そうだんする	相談する	to consult		ただ		free (of charge)
ぞく	族	tribe; group		たちぐい	立ち食い	eating while standing
そせん	祖先	ancestor		たつ	経つ	to go by; pass
そつぎょうする	卒業する	to graduate		たっきゅう	卓球	table tennis
そつろん	卒論	graduation thesis		たった		only; just
そと	外	outdoors; outside		たてかえる	建て替える	to rebuild
そのあとに	その後に	after that		たてもの	建物	building
そば		soba (noodles)		たてる	建てる	to build; to found
ソファー		sofa		たてる	点てる	to make tea (for tea ceremony)
ソフト		software				
そぼ	祖母	grandmother		たてる	立てる	to make/raise (a noise)
それから		then; after that; since then		たとえば	例えば	for example
				たな	棚	shelf; rack
それぞれの		each; respective		たのしい	楽しい	enjoyable; pleasant
それに		what's more; besides		たのしみ	楽しみ	fun; pleasure
そんをする	損をする	to lose money		たのむ	頼む	to ask; request
				たばこ	煙草	cigarette; tobacco
				タブー		taboo
た ———				タブレット		tablet
ターゲット		target		たぶん	多分	perhaps; maybe
だいいち	第1	first; no. 1; first of all		だめだ	駄目だ	useless; in vain; no good; doesn't work
たいかい	大会	congress; event				
だいがくいん	大学院	graduate school		ためる		to accumulate
たいき	大気	atmosphere		たよりをもらう	便りをもらう	to hear from
たいくつな	退屈な	dull; boring		たんご	単語	word; vocabulary
たいけん	体験	experience		ダンスホール		dance hall
だいこうぶつ	大好物	favorite food		たんとう	担当	(in) charge
たいさく	対策	countermeasure				
だいじな	大事な	important; serious		**ち** ———		
だいじょうぶ	大丈夫	all right; okay		ち	血	blood
たいしんか	耐震化	making quakeproof		チェックイン		check-in
だいしんさい	大震災	great earthquake		チェロ		cello
たいせつな	大切な	important; precious		ちかい	近い	approaching; near; close
だいたい	大体	approximately; roughly				
				ちがい	違い	difference
たいちょうふりょう	体調不良	bad health		ちかづく	近づく	to approach
				ちかてつ	地下鉄	subway (for trains)
ダイニング		dining room		ちから	力	power; strength; energy
だいぶ		fairly; pretty		ちきゅう	地球	Earth
たいふう	台風	typhoon		ちきゅうおんだんか	地球温暖化	global warming
タイプをする		to type				
たいへん	大変	hard		チケット・ショップ		ticket shop
たいわ	対話	dialogue				
たうえ	田植	rice-planting		ちこくする	遅刻する	to be late for
タオル		towel		ちゃんと		properly; without fail; neatly
たおれる	倒れる	to fall down; collapse				
だから		so; therefore		ちゅうしゃいはん	駐車違反	parking violation
だくおん	濁音	voiced consonant				
たくさん		a lot		ちゅうとはんぱ	中途半端	half-finished/half-baked
タクシー		taxi		ちゅうもんする	注文する	to order (an item)
だけ		only; just; merely; simply		ちょうさする	調査する	to investigate; survey; examine
タコ		octopus		ちょきんする	貯金する	to save money
たこやき	たこ焼き	octopus dumpling		チョコレート		chocolate
だし	山車	festival float		ちょっと		a little; a few
たしかに	確かに	actually; certainly		ちをとる	血をとる	to draw blood
だす	出す	to take out; let out				
ただしい	正しい	right; proper; correct				

つ ───────

つうきんする	通勤する	to commute
つうやくしゃ	通訳者	translator
つかいかた	使い方	how to use
つかいすて	使い捨て	disposable
つかう	使う	to use
つかむ		to take hold (of); grasp
つかれる	疲れる	to be tired; get tired
つき	月	moon
つぎの	次の	next; subsequent
つきあう	付き合う	to keep company (with)
つく	着く	to arrive
つくる	作る	to cook; manufacture
つけっぱなし	つけっ放し	leaving sth turned on
つける	付ける	to put on; add; attach; turn on
つける	浸ける	to soak; dip
つごう	都合	convenience
つづく	続く	to continue (v.i.)
つづける	続ける	to continue (v.t.)
つつみがみ	包み紙	wrapping paper
つつむ	包む	to wrap
つなみ	津波	tsunami
〜っぱな しにする	〜っ放 しにする	to leave something as it is
つまようじ	爪楊枝	toothpick
つまらない		boring; dull
つまらない		trifling
つめたい	冷たい	cold (temperature)
つもり		intention
つゆ	梅雨	rainy season
つゆあけ	梅雨明け	end of the rainy season
つゆいり	梅雨入り	start of the rainy season
つり	釣り	fishing; change (money)
つる	釣る	to fish

て ───────

ていど	程度	degree
ていねいに	丁寧に	politely; carefully
データ		data
でかける	出かける	to go out
てがみ	手紙	letter (correspondence)
デザイン		design
でし	弟子	apprentice
てつだう	手伝う	to help; assist
てのひら	手のひら	palm (of hand)
デパート		department store
てまねきする	手招きする	to beckon
でも		though; even
てら	寺	temple
テレビゲーム		video game
てをぬく	手を抜く	to cut corners
てんいん	店員	salesclerk
てんき	天気	weather
でんき	電気	electricity; electric light
てんじぶつ	展示物	exhibit; item on display
でんしゃ	電車	train

でんしょく	電飾	electric illumination
てんしょくする	転職する	to change job
てんじんまつり	天神祭	Tenjin Festival
てんちょう	店長	shopkeeper
でんとうてきな	伝統的な	traditional
でんどうの	電動の	electric; electromotive
てんぷする	添付する	to attach (to an e-mail)
でんわする	電話する	to telephone
でんわばんごう	電話番号	telephone number

と ───────

ど	度	degree
トイレットペーパー		toilet paper
とう	塔	pagoda
とうき	陶器	pottery
どうぐ	道具	tool
とうじょうする	搭乗する	to board a plane
どうぶつ	動物	animal
どうりょう	同僚	colleague; co-worker
どうろ	道路	road
とうろくする	登録する	to register
とおい	遠い	far; distant
トースター		toaster
どこでも		everywhere
どこも		everywhere
ところ	所	place
どシー	度C	degrees centigrade
とちゅうで	途中で	on one's way
どっかで		somewhere
とっきゅう	特急	limited express (train)
となりで	隣で	beside; next to
となりの	隣の	next; neighboring
とにかく		anyway
どのように		how
とめる	止める	to stop (v.t.)
ドライバー		driver
トラブル		trouble
とりい	鳥居	torii shrine gate
とる	撮る	to take (a picture)
とる	取る	to take; pick up
ドル		dollar
どろみず	泥水	muddy water

な ───────

ナイフ		knife
なおす	直す	to correct
なおす	治す	to fix up; cure
なかがいい	仲がいい	on good terms; close
なかなか〜できない		have a hard time doing
なかに	中に	inside
なかま	仲間	friend; companion
なかゆび	中指	middle finger
ながれる	流れる	to flow
なく	鳴く	to cry (animals/birds)
なくなる		to disappear; be gone
なさすぎる		to have too little
なぜ		why

なぜかというと		because (formal)
なぜなら（ば）		because (written style)
なつかしい	懐かしい	nostaligic feeling
なっとう	納豆	natto; fermented soy-beans
など	等	and so on; and the like
なまビール	生ビール	draft beer
なまもの	生もの	raw food
なやむ	悩む	to worry
ならぶ	並ぶ	to line up
なる	鳴る	to sound; reverberate
なるほど	成る程	I see!; Indeed!
なわとびをする	縄跳びをする	to skip rope
なんでかというと		because (casual)
なんども	何度も	many times

に ─────────

にく	肉	meat; flesh
にげる	逃げる	to escape; flee
にさんぷん	2, 3分	a few minutes
にじかい	二次会	afterparty
にじゅうに	二重に	double
にた	似た	similar
にたいして	に対して	against...; toward...
にっか	日課	daily routine/work
にっけいきぎょう	日系企業	Japanese-affiliated company
にほんじゅう	日本中	all over Japan
にもつ	荷物	baggage; bag; parcel
にゅうがくする	入学する	to enter school
によると		according to...
にわ	庭	garden
にんき	人気	popularity
にんげん	人間	human
にんげんドック	人間ドック	full medical checkup

ぬ ─────────

ぬぐ	脱ぐ	to take off (clothes)

ね ─────────

ねあがり	値上がり	rise in price
ねいろ	音色	sound; tone; timbre
ネクタイ		tie; necktie
ねこむ	寝込む	to be ill in bed
ねだん	値段	price
ねつがある	熱がある	to have a fever
ねつがでる	熱が出る	come down with a fever
ネット		Net; the Internet
ネット・ショッピング		Internet shopping
ネットで		on the Net; on line
ねぼうする	寝坊する	to oversleep
ねむい	眠い	sleepy
ねらう		to aim
ねる	寝る	to go to bed
ねんのため	念のため	just in case

の ─────────

ノート		notebook
ノートパソコン		laptop computer
のせる	乗せる	to give a ride; pick up
〜ので		because...
のぼる	登る	to climb
のぼる	上る	to go up
のりかえる	乗り換える	to change trains
のりほうだい	乗り放題	unlimited ride
のりもの	乗り物	amusement park ride
のる	乗る	to get on; ride
のれる	乗れる	to hold (have room for)

は ─────────

ばあい	場合	case; occasion
バーガー		burger
バーベキュー		barbecue
はい／ぱい／ばい	杯	counter for cups/glasses
はいたつ	配達	delivery
はいてみる		to try on (shoes)
はいる	入る	to come in
はえる	生える	to grow (v.i.)
はかいする	破壊する	to destroy
はがす	剥がす	to tear/peel off; remove
はく	吐く	to vomit; spit
バクテリア		bacteria
はさむ	挟む	to nip
はし	箸	chopsticks
はしづかい	箸使い	how to use chopsticks
はじめ	始め	beginning; start
はじめて	初めて	for the first time
はじめに	始めに	first of all; at the beginning
ばしょ	場所	place; location; site
パソコン		personal computer
はだかで	裸で	in the nude; naked
はたけ	畑	field
はたち	二十歳	twenty years old
はたらく	働く	to work
パチンコ		pachinko
はっきりと		clearly; frankly
パック		pack; package; carton
はっぽうしゅ	発泡酒	low-malt beer
はっぴょうする	発表する	to give a presentation
はなし	話	talk; story
はなしじょうず	話し上手	good talker; conversationist
はなび	花火	fireworks
はなみ	花見	cherry-blossom viewing
はねだくうこう	羽田空港	Haneda Airport
はねる		to splash
はやねはやおきをする	早寝早起きをする	to keep early hours
はらう	払う	to pay
パレード		parade
はれる	晴れる	to clear up (weather)

バレンタインデー		Valentine's Day
パン		bread
ばんこんか	晩婚化	getting married later; late marriage
はんする	反する	to be contrary to; to violate
ばんぜんにする	万全にする	to be fully secure
はんたいする	反対する	to oppose

ひ ——————

ビーフ		beef
ビール		beer
ひかえる	控える	to refrain from
ひきこもる	引きこもる	to remain withdrawn from the outside world
ひく	弾く	to play (a string instrument or piano)
ひく	引く	to pull; to catch (a cold)
ひくい	低い	low
ひこうき	飛行機	airplane
ひさしぶり	久しぶり	long time no see
びじゅつ	美術	art
びじゅつかん	美術館	art gallery
ひっこす	引っ越す	to move house
ひつような	必要な	necessary
ひどい（じこ）	ひどい(事故)	serious (accident)
びとく	美徳	virtue
ひとごみ	人ごみ	crowds
ひとさしゆび	人指し指	forefinger
ひとちがい	人ちがい	mistaking for somebody else
ひなんする	避難する	to take refuge/shelter
ひはんする	批判する	criticize
ひま	暇	free time; spare time
ひょうげんする	表現する	to express (something)
びょうめい	病名	disease name
ひらく	開く	to open
ひろう	拾う	to pick up; gather
びん	瓶	bottle

ふ ——————

ふあん	不安	fear; anxiety; unease
ファンヒーター		fan heater
フィットネス		fitness
フィットネス・クラブ		fitness club
ふうしゃ	風車	windmill
ふうふ	夫婦	married couple
ふえる	増える	to increase
フォーク		fork
ぶか	部下	subordinate (coworker)
ぶかつ	部活	club activity
ふきょう	不況	recession
ふく	吹く	to blow
ふく	福	fortune; luck
ふくざつな	複雑な	complex; complicated
ふくせい	複製	duplication
ふくろ	袋	bag

ふじさん	富士山	Mount Fuji
ふた	蓋	lid; cap
ぶつかる		to hit; bump; collide
ぶっきょう	仏教	Buddhism
ぶつぞう	仏像	statue of Buddha
ふで	筆	calligraphy brush
ぶひん	部品	part; component
ふべんな	不便な	inconvenient
ふむ	踏む	to step on
プラスチック		plastic
プラモデル		plastic model
ブランド		brand
フリーマーケット		flea market
ふる	降る	to rain; snow
プレーする		to play (a game)
ふろ	風呂	bath
プロジェクター		projector
ぶんか	文化	culture
ぶんべつする	分別する	separate and sort (trash)

へ ——————

へいてん	閉店	closed (of a store)
へいわ	平和	peace
へたな	下手な	bad at/poor (at sth)
ペットびよう	ペット美容	pet grooming
ペットボトル		PET/plastic bottle
べつに	別に	separately
へび	蛇	snake
へや	部屋	room
へらす	減らす	to decrease (v.t.); reduce; cut down
へる	減る	to decrease (v.i.)
へんか	変化	change
べんき	便器	toilet bowl; urinal
へんきゃくぐち	返却口	tray return area (cafe)
べんきょうする	勉強する	to study
べんざ	便座	toilet seat
へんじ	返事	reply; answer
べんとう	弁当	bento box; lunch box
へんな	変な	strange; funny; suspicious
べんりな	便利な	convenient

ほ ——————

ほ／ぽ	歩	counter for steps
ポイント		point
ポイントカード		rewards card
ほうそう	包装	packaging; wrapping
〜ほうだい	〜放題	all you can ... (eat, drink, etc.)
ぼうはんカメラ	防犯カメラ	security camera
ほうほう	方法	method
ホーム		platform (of station)
ホームステイ		homestay
ボール		ball
ほかに	他に	another; other; else
ほかんする	保管する	to keep; store

ほちょうき	補聴器	hearing aid
ポテト		potato
ほめる		to praise
ほんとうに	本当に	really
ほんとうの	本当の	true; real; actual
ほんとうのこと	本当のこと	truth
ほんや	本屋	bookstore

ま ───────

まいあさ	毎朝	every morning
まいしゅうまつ	毎週末	every weekend
まいつき	毎月	every month
マイバッグ		reusable shopping bag
マイボトル		reusable bottle
まえに	前に	forward; before...
まかせる	任せる	to leave; entrust
まがる	曲がる	to turn; curve
まく		to scatter; throw (beans)
まける	負ける	to lose (a game)
まける		to reduce a price
まさか		You're kidding!
まず		first of all
まずい		awful
マスクをする		to wear a face mask
ますます		more and more
まぜる	混ぜる	to mix; blend
また		again
まだ		still; not yet
まだまだです		not yet
まちあわせ	待ち合わせ	meeting, rendezvous
まちがう	間違う	to be wrong; make a mistake
マックブック		MacBook
マッサージ		massage
マッサージチェア		massage chair
まっちゃ	抹茶	matcha (green tea)
まつり	祭り	festival
まどぐち	窓口	ticket window/counter
まとめて		as a whole; all together
まどり	間取り	floor plan; room arrangement
まなぶ	学ぶ	to learn; study
まにあう	間に合う	to be in time; catch (train); meet (deadline)
マニアックな		maniacal; crazy
マニュアル・ミッション		manual transmission
まねする	真似する	to mimic; imitate; copy
ママ		mommy
まめ	豆	bean
マラソン		marathon
まるい	丸い	round; circular
まわる	回る	to spin around
まん	万	ten thousand
～まんえん	～万円	(multiple of) ten thousand yen

マンガ	漫画	comic; manga
まんげつ	満月	full moon
マンション		condominium

み ───────

みがく	磨く	to brush (one's teeth)
みぎ	右	right (side)
みこし	御輿	portable shrine
みこんか	未婚化	tendency not to marry
みじかくする	短くする	to abbreviate
ミス		error
みずぶそく	水不足	water shortage
みせさき	店先	storefront
みそしる	味噌汁	miso soup
みつかる	見つかる	to be found; find
みなと	港	port; harbor
みなみぐち	南口	south entrance/exit
ミリメートル		millimeter

む ───────

むかし	昔	long ago; olden days
むく	向く	to face
むく	剥く	to peel
むこう	向こう	over there
むし	虫	insect
むしあつい	蒸し暑い	hot and humid
むしのこえ	虫の声	sound of insects
むすめ	娘	daughter
むだ	無駄	waste; wastage
むりな	無理な	impossible
むりに～する	無理に～する	to try too hard to do (something)
むりをする	無理をする	to try too hard

め ───────

め	目	counter for order
メアド		e-mail address
めいわく	迷惑	trouble; nuisance
めいわくメール	迷惑メール	junk mail; spam e-mail
めぐる	巡る	to go around; tour; travel
メモする		to make a memo; take notes

も ───────

もう		already; anymore; yet (in question)
もうすぐ		soon
もえないゴミ	燃えないゴミ	non-combustible trash
もえるゴミ	燃えるゴミ	combustible trash
もくぞうの	木造の	wooden
もくひょう	目標	goal; objective
もしかしたら		perhaps
もしかすると		perhaps; maybe
もち	餅	rice cake
もちをつく	餅をつく	to pound steamed rice
もったいない		wasteful

もっと		more
もてる	持てる	to be attractive to the opposite sex
もどす	戻す	to put back; return (v.t.)
もとのばしょ	元の場所	original position
もどる	戻る	to return (v.i.)
モバゲー		mobile game
もんだい	問題	problem; question

や ——————

やける	焼ける	to toast; grill (v.i.)
やこうばす	夜行バス	night bus
やさい	野菜	vegetable
やすみ	休み	closed (of a shop)
やすみ	休み	rest; break time; vacation
やすむ	休む	to take a rest
やせる	痩せる	to lose weight
やたい	屋台	food stall (in the street)
やっぱり		after all; as I expected
やぶる	破る	to tear; rip
やぶれる	破れる	to be torn
やめる	辞める	to quit (one's post)
やめる	止める	to give up (doing sth)
やりかた	やり方	how to do; method
やるき	やる気	can-do; motivation
やわらかい	柔らかい	soft

ゆ ——————

ゆ	湯	hot water
ゆうえんち	遊園地	amusement park
ゆうしょうする	優勝する	to win first prize
ゆうじん	友人	friend
ゆうべ	夕べ	last night
ゆうめいな	有名な	famous
ユーモア		humor
ゆか	床	floor
ゆっくり		slowly
ゆぶね	湯船	bathtub
ゆめ	夢	dream

よ ——————

よういする	用意する	to prepare; get ready
ようき	容器	container
ようきゅうする	要求する	to ask (for)
ようご	用語	term; terminology
ようじ	用事	things to do
ようしき	洋式	Western-style
ようす	様子	appearance; situation
ようび	曜日	day of the week
ようをたす	用を足す	to go to the bathroom; use the toilet
よく	よく	well; often
よごれる	汚れる	to get dirty; be polluted
よしん	余震	aftershock
よそうがい	予想外	unexpected
よてい	予定	plan; schedule

よなか	夜中	midnight
よやくする	予約する	to reserve; book; make appointment
(〜に)よる		depending on ...

ら ——————

ラーメン		ramen noodles
らいにちする	来日する	to visit Japan
らいねん	来年	next year
らくな	楽な	comfortable; relaxed; easy (job)
ラジオ		radio
ラッシュアワー		rush hour
ラベル		label
らんぼうな	乱暴な	violent; rough

り ——————

りかいする	理解する	to understand
リサイクルする		to recycle
リズミカルな		rhythmical
リズム		rhythm
リハビリ		rehabilitation
リビング		living room
りゆう	理由	reason; cause
りゅうがくせい	留学生	foreign student
リユースする		to reuse
リュック		backpack
りょうがえする	両替する	to exchange (money)
りょうしゃ	両社	both companies
りようする	利用する	to utilize
りょうほう	両方	both
りょうり	料理	cooking; food; dish
りょこうする	旅行する	to travel; take a trip
リラックスする		to relax

る ——————

ルール		rule
るす	留守	not at home; absence
れいぞうこ	冷蔵庫	refrigerator; fridge
レジ		cash register
レシーブする		to receive (e.g., ball from opponent)
レジぶくろ	レジ袋	plastic checkout bag
レポート		report

れ ——————

れんきゅう	連休	consecutive public holidays
れんしゅうじあい	練習試合	practice game
れんぞくで	連続で	(times) in a row
れんしゅうする	練習する	to practice; train

ろ ——————

ろうどうりょく	労働力	workforce
ろうどうりょくじんこう	労働力人口	labor force population
ろじょうで	路上で	on the street

ロッカー		locker
ロボット		robot

わ ————

わ	輪	circle; ring; loop
わかもの	若者	young people
わからない	分からない	unclear
わかる	分かる	to understand
わかれる	別れる	to part (from a person); break up
わけ	訳	reason
わける	分ける	to divide; share; separate

わしき	和式	Japanese-style (of toilet)
わしょく	和食	Japanese food
わずか	僅か	few; little; slight
わすれがたい	忘れがたい	unforgettable
わたす	渡す	to give; hand; pass (sth to someone)
わら	笑	laughter; LOL; haha
わり	割	ten percent (10%)
わりかん	割り勘	splitting the bill; Dutch reat
わりかんにする		split the bill; go Dutch

English–Japanese Glossary

A ───────

abandon, to	あきらめる	諦める
abbreviate, to	みじかくする	短くする
about...; around...	～ぐらい	
abroad	かいがいへ	海外へ
absence (from home)	るす	留守
absent-mindedly	うっかり	
academic background	がくれき	学歴
accident	じこ	事故
accident, to have an	じこにあう	事故にあう
according to ...	～による	
accumulate, to	ためる	
acid rain	さんせいう	酸性雨
act, to; behave, to	こうどうする	行動する
activated, to be	きどうする	起動する
activity	かつどう	活動
actually	じつは	実は
add, to; attach, to	つける	付ける
advance, to	すすむ	進む
after	あと	後
after all	やっぱり	
afterparty	にじかい	二次会
after that	そのあとに	その後に
again	また	
against; toward	にたいして	に対して
age; period; era	じだい	時代
agenda	ぎだい	議題
agile	けいかいな	軽快な
aim, to	ねらう	
air	くうき	空気
air conditioner	エアコン	
airplane	ひこうき	飛行機
airport	くうこう	空港
air purifier	くうき せいじょうき	空気清浄機
alcohol	おさけ	お酒
alive, to be	いきる	生きる
all; the whole	ぜんぶ	全部
all over Japan	にほんじゅう	日本中
all right; okay	だいじょうぶ	大丈夫
all you can ... (eat, drink, etc.)	～ほうだい	～放題
allergy	アレルギー	
already	もう	
altitude above sea level	かいばつ	海抜
altogether; as a whole	まとめて	
ambiguous	あいまいな	曖昧な
amusement park	ゆうえんち	遊園地
amusement park ride	のりもの	乗り物
ancestor	せんぞ/そせん	先祖/祖先
Android OS	アンドロイド	
and so on; et cetera	など	等
angry	おこっている	怒っている
animal	どうぶつ	動物
animation	アニメ	
anime culture	アニメぶんか	アニメ文化
annoyed, to be	こまる	困る
annoying; noisy	うるさい	
another; other	ほかに	他に
anymore	もう	
anyway	とにかく	
apartment	アパート	
app	アプリ	
appear (in a photo), to	うつる	写る
appear (on TV, in a mirror), to	うつる	映る
appearance; situation	ようす	様子
appointment	アポ	
apprentice	でし	弟子
approach, to	ちかづく	近づく
approaching	ちかい	近い
approximately	だいたい	大体
arm	うで	腕
around...; about...	～ぐらい	
arrive, to	つく	着く
art; fine art	びじゅつ	美術
art; the arts	げいじゅつ	芸術
art gallery	びじゅつかん	美術館
article (newspaper)	きじ	記事
article; goods	しな/しなもの	品/品物
as a whole; altogether	まとめて	
as I expected	やっぱり	
ask, to; request, to	たのむ	頼む
ask (for), to	ようきゅうする	要求する
assemble; put together	くみたてる	組み立てる
at once	すぐに	直ぐに
atmosphere	たいき	大気
attach, to; add, to	つける	付ける
attach (to e-mail), to	てんぷする	添付する
attack, to	こうげきする	攻撃する
attraction	アトラクション	
attractive to the opposite sex	もてる	持てる
autograph; signature	サイン	
automatically	じどうで	自動で
awful	まずい	

B ───────

backpack	リュック	
bacteria	バクテリア	
bad at	へたな	下手な
bad for one's health	からだ にわるい	体に悪い
bad health	たいちょう ふりょう	体調不良
bag	ふくろ	袋
baggage	にもつ	荷物

ball	ボール	
bank	ぎんこう	銀行
barbecue	バーベキュー	
bargain-priced	げきやす	激安
bath	ふろ	風呂
bathtub	ゆぶね	湯船
bean	まめ	豆
beautiful	うつくしい	美しい
beautiful (pretty)	きれいな	
because (casual)	なんでか　というと	
because (formal)	なぜか　というと	
because (written style)	なぜなら（ば）	
because...	～ので／から	
because, it is	からです	
beckon, to	てまねきする	手招きする
become acquainted	しりあう	知り合う
become friendly, to	したしくなる	親しくなる
become full, to	いっぱいになる	
become less crowded	すく	空く
beef	ビーフ	
beef rice bowl	ぎゅうどん	牛丼
beer	ビール	
beg, to	おねがいする	お願いする
beginning, at the	はじめに	始めに
beginning; start	はじめ	始め
believe, to	しんじる	信じる
bento box; lunch box	べんとう	弁当
beside; next to	となりで	隣で
best friend	しんゆう	親友
blank space	くうらん	空欄
blood	ち	血
blow, to	ふく	吹く
board a plane, to	とうじょうする	搭乗する
board, to; get on, to	のる	乗る
bookstore	ほんや	本屋
boring	たいくつな	退屈な
boring; dull; trifling	つまらない	
boss	じょうし	上司
both	りょうほう	両方
both companies	りょうしゃ	両社
bottle	びん	瓶
bow (greeting)	おじぎ	お辞儀
boy/girl friend	こいびと	恋人
boyfriend	かれし	彼氏
brand	ブランド	
bread	パン	
break (v.t.)	こわす	壊す
break (v.i.)	こわれる	壊れる
break, to have a	きゅうけいする	休憩する
break down, to	こわれる	壊れる
break; holiday	やすみ	休み
breakfast	あさごはん	朝ご飯
break up (with s/o)	わかれる	別れ
breathe in; smoke, to	すう	吸う
bright	あかるい	明るい

broken, to be	こわれる	壊れる
brush (teeth), to	みがく	磨く
buckle up (seatbelt)	シートベルト　をする	
Buddhism	ぶっきょう	仏教
Buddhist statue	ぶつぞう	仏像
build, to; found, to	たてる	建てる
building	たてもの	建物
bullet train	しんかんせん	新幹線
bump, to	ぶつかる	
burger	バーガー	
buried, to be	うまる	埋まる
burnt, to get	こげる	焦げる
bury, to	うめる	埋める
business trip	しゅっちょう	出張
but; however	しかし	
buttock; hip	しり	尻
by oneself; in person	じぶんで	自分で
by the end of the day	きょうじゅうに	今日中に

C ——————

calculation	けいさん	計算
calendar	カレンダー	
calligraphy brush	ふで	筆
calm down, to	おちつく	落ち着く
can-do; motivation	やるき	やる気
candy; cookie	おかし	お菓子
cans (type of trash)	かんるい	缶類
capital; funds	しきん	資金
capsule	カプセル	
car; rail car; vehicle	しゃりょう	車両
car navigation system	カーナビ	
care a lot, to	きをつかう	気を遣う
careful, to be	きをつける	気を付ける
caregiver	かいごし	介護士
carry on one's back	せおう	背負う
cart	カート	
carton	パック	
cartridge	カートリッジ	
case; occasion	ばあい	場合
cash register	レジ	
catch a cold, to	かぜを ひく	風邪を ひく
caterpillar	あおむし	青虫
cause	げんいん	原因
cause, to	おこす	起こす
cawing (of a crow)	カアカア	
celebrate, to	いわう	祝う
cell	さいぼう	細胞
cello	チェロ	
cellphone	けいたいでんわ	携帯電話
certainly	たしかに	確かに
change (new thing)	へんか	変化
change (money)	つり	釣り
change job, to	てんしょくする	転職する
change trains, to	のりかえる	乗り換える
character	キャラクター	
(in) charge	たんとう	担当

charge (a device), to	じゅうでんする	充電する
chat, to	おしゃべり をする	
check-in	チェックイン	
cherry-blossom viewing	はなみ	花見
child	こども	子供
chocolate	チョコレート	
cholesterol	コレステロール	
choose, to; select, to	えらぶ	選ぶ
chopsticks	はし	箸
chopsticks, how to use	はしづかい	箸使い
cigarette; tobacco	たばこ	煙草
circle; ring; loop	わ	輪
classroom	きょうしつ	教室
cleaning	そうじ	掃除
clear up (weather), to	はれる	晴れる
clearly; frankly	はっきりと	
climb, to	のぼる	登る
close friend	しんゆう	親友
closed (of a store)	へいてん	閉店
closed; on a break	やすみ	休み
cloud service	クラウドサービス	
club activity	ぶかつ	部活
coarse; indecent	げひん	下品
coarse; rough	あらい	粗い
coffee	コーヒー	
cold (to touch)	つめたい	冷たい
collapse, to	くずれる	崩れる
colleague; co-worker	どうりょう	同僚
collection	しゅうしゅう	収集
collide, to	ぶつかる	
combustible trash	もえるゴミ	燃えるゴミ
come in, to	はいる	入る
comedy	コメディ	
comfortable	らくな	楽な
comic; manga	マンガ	漫画
coming-of-age ceremony	せいじんしき	成人式
communicate, to	コミュニケーションする	
commute, to	つうきんする	通勤する
company	かいしゃ	会社
company president	しゃちょう	社長
completed, to be	かんせいする	完成する
complex; complicated	ふくざつな	複雑な
concentrate, to	しゅうちゅう する	集中する
condominium	マンション	
confess, to	こくはくする	告白する
confidence	じしん	自信
confirm, to	かくにんする	確認する
congress; event	たいかい	大会
consciousness	いしき	意識
consecutive public holidays	れんきゅう	連休
considerably	かなり	

consult, to	そうだんする	相談する
container	ようき	容器
contest	コンテスト	
continue (v.t.)	つづける	続ける
continue (v.i.)	つづく	続く
contract	けいやく	契約
contrary to, to be	はんする	反する
convenience	つごう	都合
convenience store	コンビニ	
convenient	べんりな	便利な
conveyor-belt sushi	かいてんずし	回転寿司
cook, to	つくる	作る
cookie; candy	かし	菓子
cooking; food; dish	りょうり	料理
cool; stylish	かっこいい	
cooperate, to	きょうりょく する	協力する
corner	かど	角
correct, to	なおす	直す
correct; exact	せいかくな	正確な
cough, to	せきをする	咳をする
count, to	かぞえる	数える
countermeasure	たいさく	対策
cover, to	カバーする	
credit card	クレジット・カード	
criticize, to	ひはんする	批判する
crow	カラス	
crowded, to be	こむ	込む
crowds	ひとごみ	人ごみ
cry (animals, birds), to	なく	鳴く
culture	ぶんか	文化
cure, to	なおす	治す
custom; habit	しゅうかん	習慣
customer	きゃく	客
cut (grass, hair), to	かる	刈る
cut corners, to	てをぬく	手を抜く
cut down; decrease, to	へらす	減らす
cut too short, to	きりすぎる	切りすぎる

D ───────

dad	おとうさん	お父さん
daily routine/work	にっか	日課
damp; moisture	しっけ	湿気
dance, to	おどる	踊る
dance hall	ダンスホール	
dangerous	あぶない	危ない
dash, to; hurry, to	いそぐ	急ぐ
data	データ	
day of the week	ようび	曜日
daughter	むすめ	娘
deadline	しめきり	締め切り
decide, to	きめる	決める
declare one's love, to	こくはくする	告白す
declining birth rate	しょうしか	少子化
decorate; adorn, to	かざる	飾る
decrease (v.t.)	へらす	減らす
decrease (v.i.)	へる	減る

defeat, to	かつ	勝つ
degree	ていど	程度
degrees centigrade	どシー	度℃
delayed, to be	おくれる	
delivery	はいたつ	配達
demon	おに	鬼
department store	デパート	
depending on ...	(〜に)よる	
design, to	デザインをする	
designer (adj.)	ブランド	
destination	いきさき	行き先
destroy, to	はかいする	破壊する
determine; decide, to	きめる	決める
develop; evolve, to	しんかする	進化する
dialogue	たいわ	対話
difference	ちがい	違い
different culture	いぶんか	異文化
dining room	ダイニング	
dirty	きたない	汚い
dirty, to get	よごれる	汚れる
disease name	びょうめい	病名
disgusting	いやな	嫌な
dish; cooking; food	りょうり	料理
dishes	しょっき	食器
dishwasher	しょくせんき	食洗機
disposable	つかいすて	使い捨て
dispose of, to	すてる	捨てる
divide, to; share, to	わける	分ける
document	しりょう	資料
dollar	ドル	
do one's best, to	がんばる	頑張る
double	にじゅうに	二重に
doze off, to	うとうとする	
draft beer	なまビール	生ビール
draw, to	かく／えがく	描く
draw blood	ちをとる	血をとる
dream	ゆめ	夢
drinking party; enkai	えんかい	宴会
drive, to	うんてんする	運転する
drive away, to	おいはらう	追い払う
driver	ドライバー	
driver	うんてんしゅ	運転手
drop, to (v.t.)	おとす	落とす
dull; boring; bored	たいくつだ	退屈だ
dump, to	すてる	捨てる
duplication	ふくせい	複製
Dutch treat	わりかん	割り勘

E —————

each; respective	それぞれの	
early summer	しょか	初夏
earthquake	じしん	地震
easy	かんたんな	簡単な
easy (job)	らくな	楽な
eat, to; gobble, to	くう	食う
eating while standing	たちぐい	立ち食い
eco bag	エコバッグ	

ecological	エコ	
economical	けいざいてきな	経済的な
economizing; saving	せつやく	節約
elderly people	こうれいしゃ	高齢者
electric; electromotive	でんどうの	電動の
electric fan	せんぷうき	扇風機
electric illumination	でんしょく	電飾
electricity	でんき	電気
electric light	でんき	電気
electric lighting	しょうめい	照明
e-mail address	メアド	
empty can	あきかん	空き缶
end of rainy season	つゆあけ	梅雨明け
energy	エネルギー	
energy; strength	ちから	力
enjoyable	たのしい	楽しい
enkai; drinking party	えんかい	宴会
enter a Japanese house	あがる	上がる
enter (start) school, to	にゅうがくする	入学する
entrance	いりぐち	入口
entrust, to; leave, to	まかせる	任せる
era	じだい	時代
error	ミス	
escalator	エスカレーター	
escape, to	にげる	逃げる
e-sport	イースポーツ	
et cetera	など	等
even now	いまでも	今でも
every month	まいつき	毎月
every morning	まいあさ	毎朝
every weekend	まいしゅうまつ	毎週末
everywhere	どこでも／どこも	
evolve, to	しんかする	進化する
exact; precise	せいかくな	正確な
examination	けんさ	検査
examine; survey, to	しらべる	調べる
exceed, to	こえる	超える／越える
exchange (money), to	りょうがえする	両替する
exercise	うんどうする	運動する
exhibit; display item	てんじぶつ	展示物
exorcise	おいはらう	追い払う
experience	たいけん	体験
explain	せつめいする	説明する
explanatory text	せつめいぶん	説明文
express	ひょうげんする	表現する
express; indicate, to	あらわす	表す
expressly; specially	せっかく	
expressway	こうそくどうろ	高速道路
extravagance	ぜいたく	贅沢

F —————

face, to	むく	向く
fail, to	しっぱいする	失敗する
faint, to	たおれる	倒れる
considerably	かなり	
fall down; collapse, to	たおれる	倒れる

falling birth rate	しょうしか	少子化
fall in love, to	こいにおちる	恋に落ちる
famous	ゆうめいな	有名な
fan heater	ファンヒーター	
far; distant	とおい	遠い
fast (asleep)	ぐっすり	
fat, to get	こえる	肥える
fatal accident	じんしんじこ	人身事故
favorite food	だいこうぶつ	大好物
fear; anxiety; unease	ふあん	不安
feature phone	ガラケー	
feel, to	かんじる	感じる
feeling; impression	かんじ	感じ
feeling; mood	きもち	気持ち
festival	まつり	祭り
festival float	だし	山車
fever, come down with	ねつがでる	熱が出る
fever, to have a	ねつがある	熱がある
few, a	ちょっと	
few; little; slight	わずか	僅か
few minutes, a	にさんぷん	2，3分
field	はたけ	畑
field trip	けんがく	見学
find, to; be found, to	みつかる	見つかる
fine; well; healthy	げんき	元気
finish, to; end, to	おわる	終わる
fireworks	はなび	花火
first; first of all	だいいち	第1
first of all; at the beginning	まず / はじめに	まず / 始めに
first time, for the	はじめて	初めて
fish, to	つる	釣る
fish	さかな	魚
fishing	つり	釣り
fitness	フィットネス	
fitness club	フィットネス・クラブ	
five-story pagoda	ごじゅうのとう	五重塔
fix up, to; cure, to	なおす	治す
flea market	フリーマーケット	
flee, to	にげる	逃げる
flood	こうずい	洪水
floor	ゆか	床
floor plan	まどり	間取り
flow, to	ながれる	流れる
food; dish; cooking	りょうり	料理
food stall (in street)	やたい	屋台
for a while	しばらく	暫く
forefinger	ひとさしゆび	人指し指
foreign student	りゅうがくせい	留学生
forest	しんりん	森林
for example	たとえば	例えば
for the first time	はじめて	初めて
for the time being	しばらく	暫く
fork	フォーク	
fortune; luck	ふく	福

forward; before	まえに	前に
found, to be	みつかる	見つかる
frankly; clearly	はっきりと	
free (of charge)	ただ	
free time; spare time	ひま	暇
fresh	しんせんな	新鮮な
friend	ゆうじん	友人
friend; companion	なかま	仲間
frightening; scary	こわい	怖い
from now on	これから	
full-fledged	いちにんまえ	一人前
full medical checkup	にんげんドック	人間ドック
full moon	まんげつ	満月
fully booked, to be	こむ	込む
fully secure, to be	ばんぜんにする	万全にする
fun; pleasure	たのしみ	楽しみ
funds; capital	しきん	資金
furniture	かぐ	家具

G ————

game	ゲーム	
game console	ゲームき	ゲーム機
garbage	ゴミ	
garden	にわ	庭
gas; gasoline	ガソリン	
gather up, to	ひろう	拾う
general	いっぱんてき	一般的
gently (of rain)	しとしと	
gesture	ジェスチャー	
get a fever, to	ねつがでる	熱が出る
get burnt, to	こげる	焦げる
get dirty; be polluted	よごれる	汚れる
get fat, to	こえる	肥える
get hungry, to	おなかがすく	お腹が空く
get off (vehicle)	おりる	降りる
get on; board, to	のる	乗る
get out of (vehicle)	おりる	降りる
get ready, to	よういする	用意する
get tired, to	つかれる	疲れる
get warm; warm up	あたたまる	暖まる
getting married later	ばんこんか	晩婚化
Gion Festival	ぎおんまつり	祇園祭
girlfriend	かのじょ	彼女
give, to; hand, to	わたす	渡す
give, to	あげる	上げる
give a ride/lift to, to	のせる	乗せる
give up, to	あきらめる	諦める
give up (doing sth)	やめる	止める
glass (for drinking)	グラス	
global warming	ちきゅうおんだんか	地球温暖化
goal; objective	もくひょう	目標
go (board game)	いご	囲碁
go around; tour, to	めぐる	巡る
go down, to; drop, to	さがる	下がる
golf	ゴルフ	
gone, to be	なくなる	

English	Kana	Kanji
good listener	ききじょうず	聞き上手
good-looking guy	イケメン	
good match	りょうえん	良縁
good talker/ conversationalist	はなし じょうず	話し上手
good terms, to be on	なかがいい	仲がいい
go on to a higher-level school	しんがくする	進学する
go out, to	でかける	出かける
go to bed, to	ねる	寝る
go to the bathroom, to	ようをたす	用を足す
go up, to	のぼる	上る
go up, to; rise, to	あがる	上がる
go well, to	うまくいく	
gossip	うわさばなし	うわさ話
government	せいふ	政府
GPS	カーナビ	
graduate, to	そつぎょうする	卒業する
graduate school	だいがくいん	大学院
graduation thesis	そつろん	卒論
gram	グラム	
grandmother	そぼ	祖母
grasp, to	つかむ	
great earthquake	だいしんさい	大震災
greet, to	あいさつする	挨拶する
grill, to	やく	焼く
grow (v.i.)	はえる	生える
guest	きゃく	客
guide, to	あんないする	案内する
gun; pistol	じゅう	銃

H

English	Kana	Kanji
habit	しゅうかん	習慣
half-finished/-baked	ちゅうとはんぱ	中途半端
handling; processing	しょり	処理
Haneda Airport	はねだくうこう	羽田空港
hang (v.i.)	かかる	掛かる
happy	しあわせな	幸せな
pleasant; enjoyable	たのしい	楽しい
hard (difficult)	たいへん	大変
hard (to the touch)	かたい	堅い
have (bad experience)	あう	遭う
have a break, to	きゅうけいする	休憩する
have a chat, to	おしゃべり をする	
have a fever, to	ねつがある	熱がある
have a headache, to	あたまがいたい	頭が痛い
have an accident, to	じこにあう	事故にあう
have too little, to	なさすぎる	
hay fever	かふんしょう	花粉症
head	あたま	頭
headache, to have a	あたまがいたい	頭が痛い
health	けんこう	健康
healthy; well; fine	げんき	元気
hear from, to	たよりをもらう	便りをもらう
hearing aid	ほちょうき	補聴器
heartbroken, to be	しつれんする	失恋する

English	Kana	Kanji
heavy	おもい	重い
heavy rain	おおあめ	大雨
help, to; assist, to	てつだう	手伝う
high economic growth period	こうどけいざい せいちょうき	高度経済 成長期
high fever	こうねつ	高熱
hit, to; bump, to	ぶつかる	
hobby	しゅみ	趣味
hold (have room for)	のれる	乗れる
holiday; break	やすみ	休
homestay	ホームステイ	
honorific expression	けいご	敬語
hope, to	きぼうする	希望する
horse racing	けいば	競馬
hot and humid	むしあつい	蒸し暑い
hot springs	おんせん	温泉
hot water	ゆ	湯
house	じゅうたく	住宅
household budget	かけい	家計
household garbage	かていゴミ	家庭ゴミ
housing	じゅうたく	住宅
how	どのように	
how to do; method	やりかた/ しかた	やり方/ 仕方
however	けれども/しかし	
huge; terrible	すごい	
human	にんげん	人間
humble expression	けんじょうご	謙譲語
humidity	しっけ	湿気
humor	ユーモア	
hundreds of thousands	すうじゅうまん	数十万
hungry, to get	おなかがすく	お腹が空く
hurry, to	いそぐ	急ぐ
hurt, to	いためる	痛める

I

English	Kana	Kanji
I (male)	おれ	俺
idea; thought	かんがえ	考え
ikebana	かどう	華道
ill in bed, to be	ねこむ	寝込む
illumination (electric)	でんしょく	電飾
image	イメージ	
immediately	すぐに	
important; essential	じゅうような	重要な
important; precious	たいせつな	大切な
important; serious	だいじな	大事な
impossible	むりな	無理な
inch	インチ	
in charge	たんとう	担当
incident; case	じけん	事件
inconvenient	ふべんな	不便な
increase, to	ふえる	増える
indecent; coarse	げひん	下品
Indeed!; I see!	なるほど	
industry	さんぎょう	産業
in fact; in reality	じつは	実は
insect	むし	虫

inside	のなかに	の中に
install, to	インストールする	
instant noodles	インスタントラーメン	
instruct, to	しどうする	指導する
instruction; teachings	おしえ	教え
instructor	ししょう	師匠
intention	つもり	
interact, to	こうりゅうする	交流する
intercultural	いぶんかかん	異文化間
interesting	おもしろい	面白い
intermittent	いちじ	一時
intern	インターン	
Internet shopping	ネット・ショッピング	
in time for, to be	まにあう	間に合う
introduce, to	しょうかいする	紹介する
investigate, to	ちょうさする	調査する
invite, to; tempt, to	さそう	誘う
I see!; Indeed!	なるほど	
itchy	かゆい	
item on display	てんじぶつ	展示物
izakaya	いざかや	居酒屋

J

Japanese-affiliated company	にっけいきぎょう	日系企業
Japanese food	わしょく	和食
Japanese-style (toilet)	わしき	和式
jazz	ジャズ	
joke	じょうだん	冗談
judo	じゅうどう	柔道
jump, to	ジャンプする	
junk mail	めいわくメール	迷惑メール
just in case	ねんのため	念のため

K

karaoke	カラオケ	
keep, to; store, to	ほかんする	保管する
keep (a pet), to	かう	飼う
keep company with, to	つきあう	付き合う
keep early hours, to	はやねはやおきをする	早寝早起きをする
kendo	けんどう	剣道
keyboard	キーボード	
kick, to	ける	蹴る
kick (someone) out, to	おいだす	追い出す
kind; sort; type	しゅるい	種類
kitchen	キッチン	
knife	ナイフ	
knock down, to	うちおとす	打ち落とす
know, to	しっている	知っている

L

label	ラベル	
labor force population	ろうどうりょくじんこう	労働力人口
language	げんご	言語

laptop computer	ノートパソコン	
large number (people)	おおぜいの	大勢の
last night	ゆうべ	夕べ
last week	せんしゅう	先週
late for, to be	おくれる/ちこくする	遅れる/遅刻する
late marriage	ばんこん	晩婚
laughter; LOL; haha	わら	(笑)
laundry	せんたく	洗濯
learn, to; study, to	まなぶ	学ぶ
leave, to; entrust, to	まかせる	任せる
leaving sth turned on	つけっぱなし	つけっ放し
lend, to	かす	貸す
letter (correspondence)	てがみ	手紙
letter; character	じ	字
lid; cap	ふた	蓋
lie	うそ	嘘
life; life force	いのち	命
life; daily existence	せいかつ	生活
lift up, to	あげる	上げる
light touch, with a	けいかいな	軽快な
lighting; illumination	しょうめい	照明
limited express (train)	とっきゅう	特急
line	せん	線
line up, to	ならぶ	並ぶ
listen, to	きく	聞く
little, a	ちょっと	
little finger	こゆび	小指
living room	リビング	
lock, to	かぎをかける	鍵をかける
locker	ロッカー	
long ago	むかし	昔
long time no see	ひさしぶり	久しぶり
longed for; missed	なつかしい	
look for; seek, to	さがす	探す
loop; circle; ring	わ	輪
lorikeet	インコ	
lose (a game), to	まける	負ける
lose money, to	そんをする	損をする
lose weight, to	やせる	痩せる
lot, a	たくさん	
love	あい	愛
love, to	あいする	愛する
low	ひくい	低い
low-malt beer	はっぽうしゅ	発泡酒
luck; fortune	ふく	福
luggage rack	あみだな	網棚
lunch box; bento box	べんとう	弁当
luxurious	ぜいたくな	贅沢な

M

MacBook	マックブック	
machine	きかい	機械
mail address	メアド	
make a circuit, to	いっしゅうする	一周する
make a fool of, to	ばかにする	馬鹿にする
make a living, to	せいかつする	生活する

make a memo, to	メモする	
make a mistake, to	まちがう	間違う
make (a noise), to	たてる	立る
make a sound, to	おとをたてる	音を立てる
make good use, to	うまくつかう	うまく使う
make tea (for tea ceremony), to	たてる	点てる
makeup, to wear	けしょうする	化粧する
making a building earthquake-resistant	たいしんか	耐震化
mallet	きね	
management; handling	そうさ	操作
manga; comic	マンガ	漫画
maniacal; crazy	マニアックな	
manual transmission	マニュアル・ミッション	
manufacture, to	つくる	作る
many; much	おおくの	多くの
many times	なんども	何度も
marathon	マラソン	
march; parade	こうしん	行進
march, to; parade, to	こうしんする	行進する
married couple	ふうふ	夫婦
(face) mask, to wear	マスクをする	
marry, to	けっこんする	結婚す
massage	マッサージ	
massage chair	マッサージチェア	
match; competition	しあい	試合
matcha (green tea)	まっちゃ	抹茶
material	しりょう	資料
meaning	いみ	意味
meat; flesh	にく	肉
meet (deadline, time)	まにあう	間に合う
meeting; rendezvous	まちあわせ	待ち合わせ
meeting	かいぎ	会議
meeting time	しゅうごうじかん	集合時間
memorize; learn, to	おぼえる	覚える
memory	おもいで	思い出
merely; simply	だけ	
messy	きたない	汚い
method	ほうほう	方法
Metro; subway	ちかてつ	地下鉄
microscope	けんびきょう	顕微鏡
middle-aged man	おじさん	
middle finger	なかゆび	中指
midnight	よなか	夜中
mikoshi	みこし	御輿
milk	ぎゅうにゅう	牛乳
millimeter	ミリメートル	
mimic, to; imitate, to	まねする	真似する
mischief	いたずら	悪戯
miso soup	みそしる	味噌汁
missed; longed for	なつかしい	
mistaken idea	かんちがい	勘違い
mistaking for s/o else	ひとちがい	人ちがい
misunderstand, to	ごかいする	誤解する

mix, to; blend, to	まぜる	混ぜる
mobile game	モバゲー	
mobile phone	けいたい	携帯
modern	げんだいてき	現代的
moisture; damp	しっけ	湿気
mold (fungus)	カビ	
mom	おかあさん	お母さん
mommy	ママ	
mood; feeling	きぶん	気分
moon	つき	月
more	もっと	
more and more	ますます	
more than...	いじょう	以上
motion	うごき	動き
Mount Fuji	ふじさん	富士山
Mount Koya	こうやさん	高野山
move, to; transfer, to	うつす	移す
move back/behind, to	さがる	下がる
move house, to	ひっこす	引っ越す
movement; motion	うごき	動き
mow, to	かる	刈る
muddy water	どろみず	泥水
murderer	さつじんはん	殺人犯
muscle	きんにく	筋肉
music	おんがく	音楽

N ———————

naked	はだかで	裸で
narrow	せまい	狭い
natto; fermented soybeans	なっとう	納豆
natural; reasonable	あたりまえの	当たり前の
nature	しぜん	自然
near; close	ちかい	近い
neatly; properly	ちゃんと	
necessary	ひつような	必要な
need, to	いる	要る
negotiation	こうしょう	交渉
neighbor	きんじょのひと	近所の人
nephew	おい	甥
Net; the Internet	ネット	
nevertheless	しかし	
new car	しんしゃ	新車
new student	しんにゅうせい	新入生
New Year's Day	がんたん	元旦
newspaper	しんぶん	新聞
next; subsequent	つぎの	次の
next-door; adjacent	となりの	隣の
next time; this time	こんど	今度
next year	らいねん	来年
night bus	やこうばす	夜行バス
nip, to	はさむ	挟む
no. (counter suffix)	ごう	号
noisy; annoying	うるさい	
non-combustible trash	もえないゴミ	燃えないゴミ
no smoking	きんえん	禁煙

nostalgic feeling	なつかしい	懐かしい
not at all	ぜんぜん	全然
not at home; absence	るす	留守
notebook	ノート	
notice; sign	けいじ	掲示
not in the least	ぜんぜん	全然
not much; not often	あまり/あんまり	余り
not yet	まだ/まだまだです	
nuclear power plant	げんぱつ	原発
nuclear power-plant accident	げんぱつじこ	原発事故
nude; in the nude	はだかで	裸で
number; edition	ごう	号
number 1	だいいち	第1

O

obligation chocolate	ぎりチョコ	義理チョコ
occasion; case	ばあい	場合
occur, to	おこる	起こる
octopus	タコ	
octopus dumplings	たこやき	たこ焼き
off the clock	じかんがいに	時間外に
oil fan heater	せきゆファンヒーター	石油ファンヒーター
okay; all right	だいじょうぶ	大丈夫
old person	おとしより	お年寄り
online shopping	ネット・ショッピング	
oneself	じぶん	自分
online	ネットで	
only; just	たった/だけ	
for/by oneself	じぶんで	自分で
on one's way	とちゅうで	途中で
on the street	ろじょうで	路上で
on time	じかんどおりに	時間通りに
onomatopoeia	オノマトペ	
onsen; hot springs	おんせん	温泉
open (v.t.)	あける	開ける
open (v.i./v.t.)	ひらく	開く
operation; handling	そうさ	操作
operating system	オーエス	
opinion; thought	かんがえ	考え
opponent (of a game)	あいて	相手
oppose, to	はんたいする	反対する
opposing team	あいてチーム	相手チーム
order (v.t.)	ちゅうもんする	注文する
order (v.i.)	ならぶ	並ぶ
original position	もとのばしょ	元の場所
OS	オーエス	
Othello computer game	オセロ	
other; another	ほかに	他に
other day, the	せんじつ	先日
other person	あいて	相手
outdoors; outside	そと	外
over; finished, to be	おわる	終わる

over there	むこう	向こう
overdrink, to	のみすぎる	飲みすぎる
oversleep, to	ねぼうする	寝坊する
overwork (v.i.)	はたらきすぎる	働きすぎる
oxcart	ぎゅうしゃ	牛車

P

pachinko	パチンコ	
pack; package	パック	
packaging; wrapping	ほうそう	包装
pagoda	とう	塔
painful	いたい	痛い
palanquin	かご	
palm (of hand)	てのひら	手のひら
paper	かみ	紙
parade	パレード	
parcel	にもつ	荷物
parking violation	ちゅうしゃいはん	駐車違反
part (from a person)	わかれる	別れる
part; component	ぶひん	部品
part; portion	いちぶ	一部
part-time job	アルバイト	
part-time pay	アルバイトだい	アルバイト代
part-timer	アルバイト	
participant	さんかするひと	参加する人
participate, to	さんかする	参加する
partner	あいて	相手
party; social event	コンパ	
pass (a test), to	ごうかくする	合格する
pass to, to	わたす	渡す
pay, to	はらう	払う
pay; salary	きゅうりょう	給料
peace	へいわ	平和
peel, to	むく	剥く
peel off, to	はがす	剥がす
perhaps	もしかしたら	
perhaps; maybe	おそらく/たぶん	恐らく/多分
perhaps; maybe	もしかしたら/もしかすると	
period; era; age	じだい	時代
personal computer	パソコン	
PET/plastic bottle	ペットボトル	
pet grooming	ペットびよう	ペット美容
photocopier	コピーき	コピー機
photograph	しゃしん	写真
pick up, to; gather, to	ひろう	拾う
pick up (in a car), to	のせる	乗せる
picture	え	絵
picture book	えほん	絵本
picture quality	がしつ	画質
place	ところ	所
place; location; site	ばしょ	場所
plan; schedule	よてい	予定
plastic	プラスチック	

plastic bottle	ペットボトル	
plastic checkout bag	レジぶくろ	レジ袋
plastic model	プラモデル	
plate	さら	皿
platform (of station)	ホーム	
play, to; socialize, to	あそぶ	遊ぶ
play (a game), to	プレーする	
play (strings/piano)	ひく	弾く
player (sportsperson)	せんしゅ	選手
plot a graph, to	グラフをかく	
point	ポイント	
point (at), to	さす	指す
politely; carefully	ていねいに	丁寧に
pollen allergy	かふんしょう	花粉症
polluted, to be	よごれる	汚れる
pollution	おせん	汚染
poor (at something)	へたな	下手な
popularity	にんき	人気
population	じんこう	人口
port; harbor	みなと	港
portable shrine	みこし	御輿
possibly	もしかしたら／もしかすると	
potato	ポテト	
pottery	とうき	陶器
pound steamed rice, to	もちをつく	餅をつく
powder	こな	粉
power; strength	ちから	力
power saving	せつでん	節電
practice, to; train, to	れんしゅうする	練習する
practice game	れんしゅうじあい	練習試合
praise, to	ほめる	
prayer	おいのり	お祈り
precincts (of shrine)	けいだい	境内
precise	せいかくな	正確な
prepaid transport card	アイシーカード	
prepare, to	よういする	用意する
preparedness	かくご	覚悟
(company) president	しゃちょう	社長
presentation, to give	はっぴょうする	発表する
pretty; fairly	だいぶ	
price	ねだん	値段
problem; question	もんだい	問題
processing	しょり	処理
project	きかく	企画
projector	プロジェクター	
promptly	すぐに	
properly; neatly	ちゃんと	
pull, to	ひく	引く
pupa	さなぎ	
push oneself hard, to	むりをする	無理をする
put back, to	もどす	戻す
put in, to	いれる	入れる
put into practice, to	じっこうする	実行する
put on (glasses), to	かける	掛ける
put on, to; add, to	つける	付ける

Q ——————

quakeproof, to make	たいしんかする	耐震化する
quietly; silently	しずかに	静かに
quit, to	やめる	辞める／止める

R ——————

rabbit	うさぎ	
radio	ラジオ	
rail car; vehicle; car	しゃりょう	車両
rain, to; snow, to	ふる	降る
rainy season	つゆ	梅雨
raise, to	あげる	上げる
ramen noodles	ラーメン	
raw food	なまもの	生もの
readiness (of mind)	かくご	覚悟
ready, to get	よういする	用意する
really	ほんとうに	本当に
really; considerably	けっこう	結構
reason	わけ	訳
reason; cause	りゆう	理由
rebuild, to	たてかえる	建て替える
receive, to (e.g., ball from opponent)	レシーブする	
recently; lately	さいきん	最近
recession	ふきょう	不況
recyclable garbage	しげんゴミ	資源ゴミ
recycle, to	リサイクルする	
red	あかい	赤い
reduce; decrease, to	へらす	減らす
reduce a price, to	まける	
refrain from, to	ひかえる	控える
refrigerator	れいぞうこ	冷蔵庫
refuse, to	ことわる	断る
register, to	とうろくする	登録する
rehabilitation	リハビリ	
relationship	かんけい	関係
relax, to	リラックスする	
relaxed; comfortable	らくな	楽な
religion	しゅうきょう	宗教
remaining unmarried	みこんか	未婚化
remove, to; tear off, to	はがす	剥がす
replace, to	こうかんする	交換する
reply; answer	へんじ	返事
report	レポート	
reservation; booking	よやく	予約
reserve, to; book, to	よやくする	予約する
resign onself to, to	あきらめる	諦める
respect, to	うやまう	敬う
respond; answer, to	こたえる	答える
rest; break	やすみ	休み
rest, to take a	やすむ	
return (v.t.)	もどす	戻す
return (v.i.)	もどる	戻る
return; come back, to	かえる	帰る

return to one's country, to	きこくする	帰国する
reusable bottle	マイボトル	
reusable shopping bag	マイバッグ	
reuse, to	リユースする	
rewards card	ポイントカード	
rhythm	リズム	
rhythmical	リズミカルな	
rice	こめ	米
rice ball	おにぎり	
rice cake	もち	餅
rice-planting	たうえ	田植え
ride (amusement park)	のりもの	乗り物
ride, to	のる	乗る
right; proper; correct	ただしい	正しい
right (side)	みぎ	右
rip, to (v.t.)	やぶる	破る
rise in price	ねあがり	値上がり
risky	あぶない	危ない
river	かわ	川
road	どうろ	道路
robot	ロボット	
roller coaster	ジェットコースター	
room	へや	部屋
room arrangement	まどり	間取り
room to let	あきべや	空き部屋
rope skipping	なわとび	縄跳び
round; circular	まるい	丸い
row (a boat), to	こぐ	
row, in a	れんぞくで	連続で
rule	ルール	
rush hour	ラッシュアワー	

S ————

salary	きゅうりょう	給料
sales	うりあげ	売り上げ
salesclerk	てんいん	店員
sanitary	えいせいてきな	衛生的な
sashimi	さしみ	刺身
save electricity, to	せつでんする	節電する
save money, to	ちょきんする	貯金する
saving; economizing	せつやく	節約
saving water	せっすい	節水
scary	こわい	怖い
scatter (beans), to	まく	
school background	がくれき	学歴
scold, to	しかる	叱る
screen	がめん	画面
search, to (e.g., on computer)	けんさくする	検索する
seashore	かいがん	海岸
season	きせつ	季節
seat	せき	席
seatbelt	シートベルト	
section manager	かちょう	課長
security	セキュリティ	

security camera	ぼうはんカメラ	防犯カメラ
seismic intensity	しんど	震度
sell (v.t.)	うる	売る
sell (v.i.)	うれる	売れる
sell well	よくうれる	よく売れる
semi-express train	じゅんきゅう	準急
send, to	おくる	送る
sensible	けんめいな	賢明な
separate, to	わける	分ける
separate and sort trash	ぶんべつする	分別する
separately	べつに	別に
serious (accident)	ひどい（じこ）	ひどい（事故）
serve, to	サーブする	
service	サービス	
set meal with sashimi	さしみていしょく	刺身定食
set off (fireworks), be	あがる	上がる
setting; setup	せってい	設定
several; a few	いくつか	
shamisen	しゃみせん	三味線
shelf; rack	たな	棚
shinkansen	しんかんせん	新幹線
Shinto	しんとう	神道
shogi (Japanese chess)	しょうぎ	将棋
shoot, to	うつ	撃つ
shoot down, to	うちおとす	打ち落とす
shopkeeper	てんちょう	店長
shoulder, to	かつぐ	担ぐ
shovel	シャベル	
shower	シャワー	
shrine	じんじゃ	神社
sightseeing	かんこう	観光
signature; autograph	サイン	
sign language	しゅわ	手話
similar	にた	似た
simply	だけ	
since then; after that	それから	
sing, to	うたう	歌う
singles (e.g., tennis)	シングルス	
sit down, to	すわる	座る
site	サイト	
situation	ようす	様子
skip rope, to	なわとびをする	縄跳びをする
sleepy	ねむい	眠い
slipshod, to be	てをぬく	手を抜く
slowly	ゆっくり	
slurp, with a	ずるずると	
smartphone	スマホ	
smog	スモッグ	
smoke	けむり	煙
smoothly	スムーズに	
snake	へび	蛇
snore, to	いびきをかく	
so; therefore	だから	
soak, to; dip, to	つける	浸ける

soap	せっけん	石けん
soba (noodles)	そば	
society	しゃかい	社会
sofa	ソファー	
soft	やわらかい	柔らかい
software	ソフト	
somewhere	どっかで	
song; music	きょく	曲
soon	もうすぐ / すぐに	
sound; reverberate, to	なる	鳴る
sound; noise	おと	音
sound; tone; timbre	ねいろ	音色
sound; voice	こえ	声
soup	しるもの	汁物
south entrance/exit	みなみぐち	南口
souvenir	おみやげ	お土産
spa; hot springs	おんせん	温泉
spam e-mail	めいわくメール	迷惑メール
spare time	ひま	暇
specialist subject	せんもん	専門
specially; expressly	せっかく	
spend (time), to	すごす	過ごす
spin around, to	まわる	回る
splash, to	はねる	
split the bill, to	わりかん にする	割り勘 にする
splitting the bill	わりかん	割り勘
spoon	スプーン	
stab, to	さす	刺す
stabbing chopsticks into food	さしばし	刺し箸
stable; steady	あんていした	安定した
stage	ステージ	
stall (street food)	やたい	屋台
stamp (postage)	きって	切手
start of rainy season	つゆいり	梅雨入
station	えき	駅
statue of Buddha	ぶつぞう	仏像
step on, to	ふむ	踏む
still; not yet	まだ	
still life	せいぶつ	静物
stocks	かぶ	株
stone	いし	石
stop, to	とめる	止める
storefront	みせさき	店先
storekeeper	てんちょう	店長
strain, to	いためる	痛める
strange; suspicious	へん	変
street, on the	ろじょうで	路上で
strength; energy	ちから	力
strengthen, to	きょうかする	強化する
strike, to	うつ	打つ
string (of instrument)	げん	弦
study, to	べんきょうする	勉強する
stylish; cool	かっこいい	
subordinate (coworker)	ぶか	部下

subsequent; next	つぎ	次
subway; Metro	ちかてつ	地下鉄
such ...	こんな～	
succeed (in a test)	ごうかくする	合格する
sudden; abrupt	きゅうな	急な
suddenly; all at once	きゅうに	急に
sugar	さとう	砂糖
suitcase	スーツケース	
sumo wrestling	すもう	相撲
super-cheap; discount	かくやす	格安
supermarket	スーパー	
support, to	サポートする	
surely; certainly	きっと / かならず	
Surely not!	まさか	
surprised, to be	おどろく	驚く
surprising	おどろくこと	驚くこと
survey; investigate, to	ちょうさする	調査す
suspicious; strange	へんな	変な
sweet	あまい	甘い
swim, to	およぐ	泳ぐ
switch on; turn on, to	つける	付ける

T ————————

table tennis	たっきゅう	卓球
tablet	タブレット	
taboo	タブー	
take (a picture), to	とる	撮る
take, to	とる	取る
take a rest, to	やすむ	休む
take a shower, to	シャワーを あびる	シャワーを 浴びる
take a trip, to	りょこうする	旅行する
take a walk, to	さんぽする	散歩する
take care, to	きをつける	気をつける
take first prize, to	ゆうしょうする	優勝する
take hold, to; grasp, to	つかむ	
take off (clothes), to	ぬぐ	脱ぐ
take out; let out, to	だす	出す
take refuge;	ひなんする	避難する
takoyaki	たこやき	たこ焼き
talk; story	はなし	話
target	ターゲット	
taste	あじ	味
taxi	タクシー	
tea ceremony	さどう	茶道
teacher; instructor	ししょう	師匠
teachings	おしえ	教え
tear, to; rip, to	やぶる	破る
tear off, to	はがす	剥がす
telepathy	いしんでんしん	以心伝心
telephone, to	でんわする	電話する
telephone number	でんわばんごう	電話番号
temple	てら	寺
ten percent	わり	割
ten thousand	まん	万
Tenjin Festival	てんじんまつり	天神祭

English	Kana	Kanji
term; terminology	ようご	用語
textbook	きょうかしょ	教科書
thank, to	かんしゃする	感謝する
then; after that	それから	
therefore	だから	
thermal	おんねつしき	温熱式
these days	さいきん	最近
thickness	あつさ	厚さ
things to do	ようじ	用事
think, to	かんがえる	考える
this month	こんげつ	今月
this time	こんかい	今回
this weekend	こんしゅうまつ	今週末
though; even...	でも	
throw away, to	すてる	捨てる
throw (beans), to	まく	
thumb	おやゆび	親指
ticket	きっぷ	切符
ticket shop	チケット・ショップ	
ticket window	まどぐち	窓口
ticket counter	うりば	売り場
tidy up; beautify, to	きれいにする	
tie; necktie	ネクタイ	
time; period	じき	時期
time being, for the	しばらく	暫く
time of the meeting	しゅうごうじかん	集合時間
tired, to be	つかれる	疲れる
toast (cook), to	やく	焼く
toast (with drinks), to	かんぱいする	乾杯する
toaster	トースター	
together; with	いっしょに	一緒に
toilet bowl; urinal	べんき	便器
toilet paper	トイレットペーパー	
toilet seat	べんざ	便座
tool	どうぐ	道具
toothpick	つまようじ	爪楊枝
torii shrine gate	とりい	鳥居
torn, to be	やぶれる	破れる
to tell the truth (*idiom*)	じつは	実は
touch, to	さわる	触る
touching the screen	がめんタッチ	画面タッチ
tourist	かんこうきゃく	観光客
toward; against	にたいして	に対して
towel	タオル	
traditional	でんとうてきな	伝統的な
traffic jam	じゅうたい	渋滞
traffic offense	こうつういはん	交通違反
train	でんしゃ	電車
train, to; build up, to	きたえる	鍛える
transfer, to (v.t.)	うつす	移す
translator	つうやくしゃ	通訳者
trash	ゴミ	
travel, to	りょこうする	旅行する
travel around (a place)	(〜を) めぐる	(〜を) 巡る

English	Kana	Kanji
tray return area (cafe)	へんきゃくぐち	返却口
tribe; group	ぞく	族
trifling	つまらない	
trouble	トラブル	
trouble; nuisance	めいわく	迷惑
trouble, to be in	こまる	困る
true; real; actual	ほんとうの	本当の
truth	ほんとうのこと	本当のこと
truth is, the	じつは	実は
try on (shoes), to	はいてみる	
try one's best, to	がんばる	頑張る
try too hard, to	むりをする	無理をする
try too hard to do sth	むりに〜する	無理に〜する
tsunami	つなみ	津波
turn, to; curve, to	まがる	曲がる
turn on; switch on, to	つける	付ける
tutor	かていきょうし	家庭教師
twenty years old	はたち	二十歳
type, to	タイプをする	
typhoon	たいふう	台風

U ————

English	Kana	Kanji
udon noodles	うどん	
umbrella stand	かさたて	傘立て
uncle	おじさん	
unclear	わからない	分からない
undergo, to	うける	受ける
understand, to	りかいする	理解する
understand, to	わかる	分かる
undoubtedly	きっと/かならず	必ず
uneasiness	ふあん	不安
unexpected	よそうがい	予想外
unforgettable	わすれがたい	忘れがたい
unlimited ride	のりほうだい	乗り放題
unpleasant	いやな	嫌な
use, to	つかう	使う
use the bathroom (toilet), to	ようをたす	用を足す
used paper (trash type)	こしるい	古紙類
useless; to no avail	やくにたたない	役に立たない
useless; no good	だめだ	駄目だ
utilize, to	りようする	利用する

V ————

English	Kana	Kanji
vacancy; vacant room	あきべや	空き部屋
vacation; break	やすみ	休み
Valentine's Day	バレンタインデー	
various	いろいろな	
variously	いろいろと	色々と
vegetable	やさい	野菜
vehicle; car; rail car	しゃりょう	車両
video game	テレビゲーム	
violate (rules), to	はんする	反する
violent; rough	らんぼうな	乱暴な
virtue	びとく	美徳

visit, to	おとずれる	訪れる
visit; ask; hear (humble verb), to	うかがう	伺う
visit and pray, to	おまいりする	お参りする
visit Japan, to	らいにちする	来日する
voice; sound	こえ	声
voiced consonant	だくおん	濁音
voiceless sound	せいおん	清音
vomit, to; spit, to	はく	吐く
vulgar	げひんな	下品な

W ────────

wallet	さいふ	財布
war	せんそう	戦争
warm	あたたかい	暖かい
warm up, to	あたたまる	暖まる
warmth	おんねつ	温熱
warm water	おんすい	温水
wash, to	あらう	洗う
waste; wastage	むだ	無駄
wastebasket	ゴミばこ	ゴミ箱
wasteful	もったいない	
water conservation	せっすい	節水
water shortage	みずぶそく	水不足
water supply	すいどう	水道
wear makeup, to	けしょうをする	化粧をする
weather	てんき	天気
week (counter suffix)	しゅうかん	週間
welcome, to	かんげいする	歓迎する
welcome party	しんかんコンパ	新歓コンパ
well; healthy; fine	げんき	元気
well; skillfully	うまく/ じょうずに	うまく/ 上手に
Western-style	ようしき	洋式
what's more/besides	それに	
wheelchair	くるまいす	車椅子
while, for a	しばらく	暫く

whole, the; all	ぜんぶ	全部
whole time, the	ずっと	
win, to; beat, to	かつ	勝つ
why	なぜ	
win first prize, to	ゆうしょうする	優勝する
windmill	ふうしゃ	風車
window-shopping	ウィンドー・ ショッピング	
Windows 10	ウィンドウズテン	
wise	かしこい	賢い
wise; sensible	けんめいな	賢明な
withdrawn from the outside world, to be	ひきこもる	引きこもる
wither, to	かれる	枯れる
without fail	ちゃんと	
wood	き	木
wooden	もくぞうの	木造の
word; language	ことば	言葉
word; vocabulary	たんご	単語
work, to	はたらく	働く
workforce	ろうどうりょく	労働力
world	せかい	世界
worried, to be	なやむ	悩む
worry, to; care, to	きにする	気にする
worst, the worst	さいあく	最悪
Wow!	うわ	
wrap, to	つつむ	包む
wrapping; packaging	ほうそう	包装
wrapping paper	つつみがみ	包み紙
wrong, to be	まちがう	間違う

Y ────────

yellow (noun)	きいろ	黄色
yet (in question)	もう	
you	きみ	君
young people	わかもの	若者
You're kidding!	まさか	

Answer Key

PRELIMINARY REVIEW
Page 15 • EXERCISE SET 1

1. 会って　　　atte
2. 泣いて　　　naite
3. こいで　　　koide
4. 指して　　　sashite
5. 立って　　　tatte
6. 学んで　　　manande
7. 込んで　　　konde
8. 走って　　　hashitte
9. 寝て　　　　nete
10. 勉強して　　benkyō shite
11. 高くて　　　takakute
12. なくて　　　nakute
13. 食べなくて　tabenakute
14. おいしくなくて　oishikunakute
15. 元気で　　　genki de

Page 16 • EXERCISE SET 2

❶ よく 音楽を 聞いて 歩きます。
Yoku ongaku o kīte arukimasu.
❷ ボールを ねらって 打ちます。
Bōru o neratte uchimasu.
❸ 試験は むずかしくて 答えが 分かりません。
Shiken wa muzukashikute kotae ga wakarimasen.
❹ 僕は 歯を 磨いて お姉さんは 化粧を します。
Boku wa ha o migaite onēsan wa keshō o shimasu.

Page 17 • EXERCISE SET 3

❶ はじめて アルバイトを して みました。
Hajimete arubaito o shite mimashita.
❷ 顕微鏡で 細胞を 見て みました。
Kenbikyō de saibō o mite mimashita.
❸ 医者に 相談 して みました。
Isha ni sōdan shite mimashita.

Page 19 • EXERCISE SET 4

❶ 花粉症に なって しまいました。
Kafunshō ni natte shimaimashita.
❷ 肩を 痛めて しまいました。
Kata o itamete shimaimashita.
❸ 疲れて 寝て しまいました。
Tsukarete nete shimaimashita.

Page 20 • Reading Comprehension Questions

1. 自転車に 乗って 行きます。
Jitensha ni notte ikimasu.
He goes by bike.
2. うっかり 弁当を 忘れて しまいました。
Ukkari bentō o wasurete shimaimashita.
He carelessly forgot his packed lunch.
3. 練習試合を やって みました。負けて しまいました。
Renshū jiai o yatte mimashita. Makete shimaimashita.
He tried playing a practice game. He ended up losing.

CHAPTER 1
Page 23 • EXERCISE SET 1

1. 旅行する　　**ryokō suru**
2. 読む　　　　**yomu**
3. 走る　　　　**hashiru**
4. 起きる　　　**okiru**
5. 寝る　　　　**neru**
6. 食べる　　　**taberu**
7. 作る　　　　**tsukuru**
8. 買う　　　　**kau**
9. 飲む　　　　**nomu**
10. 予約する　　**yoyaku suru**

Page 24 • EXERCISE SET 2

❶ 友だちと 毎週する スポーツは テニスです。
Tomodachi to maishū suru supōtsu wa tenisu desu.
The sport I play with my friend every week is tennis.
❷ 夜中に ネットで 聞く 音楽は ジャズです。
Yonaka ni netto de kiku ongaku wa jazu desu.
The music I listen to at midnight on the internet is jazz.
❸ 彼女に あげる おみやげは チョコレートです。
Kanojo ni ageru omiyage wa chokorēto desu.
The souvenir I'll give my girlfriend is chocolate.
❹ よく 読む マンガは ドラゴンボールです。
Yoku yomu manga wa doragonbōru desu.
The comic I usually read is Dragon Ball.
❺ ときどき 食べる 和食は 寿司です。
Tokidoki taberu washoku wa sushi desu.
The Japanese food I sometimes have is sushi.

Page 26 • EXERCISE SET 3

❶	❷	❸	❹	❺	❻	❼	❽
イ	ウ	ク	カ	オ	エ	ア	キ

Page 27 • EXERCISE SET 4

❶ 父が 買った パソコンは ウィンドウズテンです。
Chichi ga katta pasokon wa windōzu ten desu.
The computer my father bought is a
Windows 10 one.
❷ 彼らが 毎日 練習した スポーツは 剣道です。
Karera ga mainichi renshū shita supōtsu wa kendō desu.
The sport they practiced every day was kendo.
❸ けんじが 写真を 撮った 電車は 新幹線です。
Kenji ga shashin o totta densha wa shinkansen desu.
The train Kenji took a photo of was a shinkansen.
❹ 東京で 私たちが 訪れたお寺は 浅草寺です。
Tōkyō de watashitachi ga otozureta otera wa sensōji desu.
The temple we visited in Tokyo was Sensoji.
❺ 毎日 食べたうどんは きつねうどんです。
Mainichi tabeta udon wa kitsune udon desu.
The udon I ate every day was kitsune udon.

Page 29 • EXERCISE SET 5

❶ タコが とても 大きい たこ焼きを 食べました。
Tako ga totemo ōkī takoyaki o tabemashita.
❷ 私たちは 桜が きれいな 公園に 行きました。
Watashitachi wa sakura ga kirei na kōen ni ikimashita.

Page 31 • Reading Comprehension Questions

1. 羽田空港に 来ました。東京 近くて 便利です。
Haneda kūkō ni kimashita. Tōkyō ni chikakute benri desu.
She or he came to Haneda Airport. It is close to Tokyo and
convenient.
2. 銀座で ウィンドーショッピングを 楽しみました。
Ginza de windō shoppingu o tanoshimimashita.
She or he enjoyed window-shopping in Ginza.
3. ジャパン・レール・パス と言います。JRの電車に 乗り
放題の 切符です。でも，のぞみは だめです。観光客が
買います。
Japan rēru pasu to īmasu. Jeiāru no densha ni norihōdai no kippu desu. Demo, nozomi wa dame desu. Kankōkyaku ga kaimasu.
It's called the Japan Rail Pass. It's an unlimited-ride ticket
for JR trains. But you cannot ride on the Nozomi. Tourists
can buy it.
4. 格安チケット売り場で 少し 安く 売っているものです。
Kakuyasu chiketto uriba de sukoshi yasuku utte iru mono desu.
It is the one which is sold at cheap ticket counters at a
slightly lower price.

CHAPTER 2
Page 35 • EXERCISE SET 1

1. 読めます   **yomemasu**
2. 走れます   **hashiremasu**
3. 起きられます   **okiraremasu**
4. 行けます   **ikemasu**
5. 買えます   **kaemasu**
6. 出られます   **deraremasu**
7. 入れます   **hairemasu**
8. 歩けます   **arukemasu**
9. 持てます   **motemasu**
10. 予約できます   **yoyaku dekimasu**

Page 36 • EXERCISE SET 2

1. 出発することができる   **shuppatsu suru koto ga dekiru**
2. 読むことができる   **yomu koto ga dekiru**
3. 起きることができる   **okiru koto ga dekiru**
4. 行くことができる   **iku koto ga dekiru**
5. 出ることができる   **deru koto ga dekiru**
6. 持つことができる   **motsu koto ga dekiru**
7. 予約することができる   **yoyaku suru koto ga dekiru**

Page 36 • EXERCISE SET 3

❶ (a) ユキさんは 100回 連続で なわとびが できます。
    Yuki san wa hyakkai renzoku de nawatobi ga dekimasu.
  (b) ユキさんは100回 連続でなわとびをすることができます。
    Yuki san wa hyakkai renzoku de nawatobi o suru koto ga dekimasu.
    Yuki can skip rope 100 times in a row.
❷ (a) 私は エクセルで うまく グラフが かけます。
    Watashi wa ekuseru de umaku gurafu ga kakemasu.
  (b) 私はエクセルでうまくグラフをかくことが できます。
    Watashi wa ekuseru de umaku gurafu o kaku koto ga dekimasu.
    I can plot a graph well in Excel.
❸ (a) けんじは シングルスの試合で 太郎に 勝てました。
    Kenji wa shingurusu no shiai de taro ni katemashita.
  (b) けんじはシングルスの試合で太郎に勝つことができました。
    Kenji wa shingurusu no shiai de taro ni katsu koto ga dekimashita.
    Kenji was able to win the singles against Taro.

Page 37 • EXERCISE SET 4

❶ 電車の中で 携帯電話を 使うことができますか。
  Densha no naka de keitai denwa o tsukau koto ga dekimasu ka.
  いいえ，使うことはできません。
  Īe, tsukau koto wa dekimasen.
❷ 美術館で 展示物の 写真を 撮ることができますか。
  Bijutsukan de tenjibutsu no shashin o toru koto ga dekimasu ka.
  いいえ，撮ることはできません。
  Īe, toru koto wa dekimasen.
❸ ペットボトルを ゴミ箱に 捨てることができますか。
  Petto botoru o gomibako ni suteru koto ga dekimasu ka.
  いいえ，捨てることはできません。
  Īe, suteru koto wa dekimasen.

Page 38 • EXERCISE SET 5

❶ きれいな 満月が 見えますね。
  Kirei na mangetsu ga miemasu ne.
  A beautiful new moon can be seen.
❷ チェロの 美しい音色が 部屋から 聞こえます。
  Chero no utsukushī neiro ga heya kara kikoemasu.
  The beautiful sound of the cello can be heard coming from the room.

Page 39 • EXERCISE SET 6

1. 現在では 日本の アニメ文化は 産業(だ)と言える。
  Genzai de wa nihon no anime bunka wa sangyō (da) to ieru.
  It can be said that Japanese animation culture is an industry.
2. 余震は しばらく 続くと 考えられる。
  Yoshin wa shibaraku tsuzuku to kangaerareru.
  It is believed the aftershocks will continue for the time being.
3. 新聞は なくなると 思われる。
  Shinbun wa nakunaru to omowareru.
  It is thought that newspapers will disappear.

Page 42 • Reading Comprehension Questions

1. 今は 1日に 3つ 覚えられます。
  Ima wa ichi nichi ni mittsu oboeraremasu.
  Now he or she can memorize three a day.
2. いいえ，読めなくても いいです。
  Īe, yomenakutemo ī desu.
  No, he or she does not have to.
3. 人間の 気持ちや 様子や 音を 表す オノマトペという 言葉が むずかしいです。
  Ningen no kimochi ya yōsu ya oto o arawasu onomatope to iu kotoba ga muzukashī desu.
  The words called "onomatopoeia," which express human feelings, a situation or sound, are difficult.

CHAPTER 3
Page 44 • EXERCISE SET 1

1. 読みながら   **yominagara**
2. 走りながら   **hashirinagara**
3. 行きながら   **ikinagara**
4. 入りながら   **hairinagara**
5. 持ちながら   **mochinagara**
6. 食べながら   **tabenagara**
7. 見ながら   **minagara**
8. 練習しながら   **renshū shinagara**

Page 45 • EXERCISE SET 2

❶ けんじは スキーを しながら ジャンプが できます。
  Kenji wa sukī o shinagara janpu ga dekimasu.
  Kenji can jump while skiing.
❷ 侍は 歌いながら 踊っています。/
  侍は 踊りながら 歌っています。
  Samurai wa utainagara odotte imasu. /
  Samurai wa odorinagara utatte imasu.
  The samurai is dancing while singing. /
  The samurai is singing while dancing.
❸ 選手は ボールを 蹴りながら 走っています。/
  選手は 走りながら ボールを 蹴っています。
  Senshu wa bōru o kerinagara hashitte imasu /
  Senshu wa hashirinagara bōru o kette imasu.
  The player is running while kicking the ball. /
  The player is kicking the ball while running.

Page 46 • EXERCISE SET 3

❶ タバコを 吸って 道路を 歩かないで 下さい。
  Tabako o sutte dōro o arukanaide kudasai.
  Don't smoke while walking in the street, please.
❷ 電車の中で 大きな 声を 出して 電話しない方が いいです。
  Densha no naka de ōkina koe o dashite denwa shinai hō ga ī desu.
  On the train, you shouldn't speak loudly on the phone.
❸ アルバイトを して 留学を 続けています。
  Arubaito o shite ryūgaku o tsuzukete imasu.
  They are continuing their study while working part time.

Page 47 • EXERCISE SET 4

1. 読まないで／読まずに   **yomanaide / yomazuni**
2. 走らないで／走らずに   **hashiranaide /hashirazuni**
3. 待たないで／待たずに   **matanaide / matazuni**

4. 持たないで／持たずに **motanaide / motazuni**
5. 食べないで／食べずに **tabenaide / tabezuni**
6. 見ないで／見ずに **minaide / mizuni**
7. 練習しないで／練習せずに **renshū shinaide / renshū sezuni**

Page 47 • EXERCISE SET 5

❶ お菓子を 食べないで（食べずに） 野菜を 食べましょう。
Okashi o tabenaide (tabezuni) yasai o tabemashō.
Let's eat vegetables instead of candy.

❷ たばこを 吸わないで（吸わずに） コーヒーを 飲みましょう。
Tabako o suwanaide (suwazuni) kōhī o nomimashō.
Let's have coffee without smoking.

❸ エアコンを つけないで（つけずに） 扇風機を 使いましょう。
Eakon o tsukenaide (tsukezuni) senpūki o tsukaimashō.
Let's use the fan instead of the air-conditioner.

❹ テレビを 見ないで（見ずに） 本を 読みましょう。
Terebi o minaide (mizuni) hon o yomimashō.
Let's read books instead of watching TV.

Page 49 • EXERCISE SET 6

❶ 三味線は 弦が 三本しか ありません。
Shamisen wa gen ga sanbon shika arimasen.
A shamisen only has three strings.

❷ かごは 一人しか 乗れません。
Kago wa hitori shika noremasen.
Only one person can ride in a palanquin.

Page 53 • Reading Comprehension Questions

1. それは 分かりません。人に よります。
Sore wa wakarimasen. Hito ni yorimasu.
It is unclear. It depends on the person.

2. スマホを しながら 歩いたり 自転車を 運転したり します。
Sumaho o shinagara aruitari jitensha o unten shitari shimasu.
They walk or ride a bicycle while using a smartphone.

3. 本屋で 立ちながら 本を 読むことです。
Hon'ya de tachinagara hon o yomu koto desu.
It means reading a book while standing in a bookstore.

CHAPTER 4

Page 57 • EXERCISE SET 1

1. 戦争は（or が） 終わった が／
戦争は（or が） 終わりました が
sensō wa (or ga) owatta ga / sensō wa (or ga) owarimashita ga

2. 雨は（or が） 降っているが／
雨は（or が） 降っていますが
ame wa (or ga) futte iru ga / ame wa (or ga) futte imasu ga

3. 安かったが／安かったですが
yasukatta ga / yasukatta desu ga

4. 大事だが／大事ですが
daiji da ga / daiji desu ga

Page 57 • EXERCISE SET 2

❶ 手を 洗いましたが、まだ かゆいです。
Te o araimashita ga, mada kayui desu.
I washed my hands, but they're still itchy.

❷ 急ぎましたが、電車に 間に合いませんでした。
Isogimashita ga, densha ni maniaimasen deshita.
I hurried, but I missed the train.

❸ 早く 帰りたいですが、会議が とても 長いです。
Hayaku kaeritai desu ga, kaigi ga totemo nagai desu.
I want to go home early, but the meeting is really long.

Page 58 • EXERCISE SET 3

❶ 彼女から メッセージを もらいましたが、とても 懐かしいです。
Kanojo kara messēji o moraimashita ga, totemo natsukashī desu.
I got a message from her and I felt really nostalgic.

❷ マラソンに 出ましたが、優勝 しました。
Marason ni demashita ga, yūshō shimashita.
I was in the marathon and I won.

Page 59 • EXERCISE SET 4

1. それを 買った けれども **sore o katta keredomo**
2. 天気は（が） 悪い けれども **tenki wa (ga) warui keredomo**
3. 彼は 親切だ けれども **kare wa shinsetsu da keredomo**

Page 59 • EXERCISE SET 5

❶ 結婚したけれども、あまり 幸せではありません。
Kekkon shita keredomo, amari shiawase dewa arimasen.
"結婚しましたけれども" is redundant, so the dictionary form + **keredomo** is common.

❷ 去年洗濯機を 買ったけど、今は 壊れてる。
Kyonen sentakuki o katta kedo, ima wa kowareteru.
The whole sentence is informal, so **kedo** or **keredo** is fine.

Page 60 • EXERCISE SET 6

❶ 新車を 買ったのに ひどい事故に 遭いました。
Shinsha o katta noni hidoi jiko ni aimashita.
Though I bought a new car, I had a terrible accident.

❷ 空が きれいなのに、汚い煙が 出ています。
Sora ga kirei na noni, kitanai kemuri ga dete imasu.
Though the sky is clear, there is dirty smoke coming out.

Page 60 • EXERCISE SET 7

1. 雨が 降っているし、バスが 来ないし
Ame ga futte iru shi, basu ga konai shi
2. 疲れたし 眠いし
Tsukareta shi, nemui shi
3. のどがかわいたし、頭が 痛いし
Nodo ga kawaita shi, atama ga itai shi
4. 暑いし行きたくないし
Atsui shi, ikitaku nai shi
5. もう 食べたし、お金がないし
Mō tabeta shi, okane ga nai shi

Page 61 • EXERCISE SET 8

❶ 今日は 祭りだし、面白いし、行こう。
Kyō wa matsuri da shi, omoshiroi shi, ikō.
There's a festival today, it looks interesting, let's go!

❷ 二十歳になったし、お酒が 飲めるし、居酒屋に 行こう。
Hatachi ni natta shi, osake ga nomeru shi, izakaya ni ikō.
I'm 20 now, I can drink alcohol, let's go to the izakaya!

❸ 暑いし、疲れたし、帰りたいよ。
Atsui shi, tsukareta shi, kaeritai yo.
It's hot and I'm tired and I want to go home.

❹ 天気が 悪いし 道が 狭いし、大変です。
Tenki ga warui shi, michi ga semai shi, taihen desu.
The weather's bad, the road is narrow, it's awful.

Page 62 • EXERCISE SET 9

1. （私が／あなたが） 行っても
(watashi ga / anata ga) ittemo
2. （私が／あなたが） 飲んでも
(watashi ga / anata ga) nondemo
3. （私が／あなたが） やっても／しても
(watashi ga / anata ga) yattemo / shitemo
4. （それが） 高くても
(sore ga) takakutemo
5. （それが） よくなくても
(sore ga) yoku nakutemo
6. （それが） 不便でも
(sore ga) fuben demo

Page 63 • EXERCISE SET 10

❶ いくら 忙しくても、メールを チェックします。
Ikura isogashikutemo, mēru o chekku shimasu.
However busy I am, I check my mail.

② いくら 大変な 仕事でも，任せてください。
Ikura taihen na shigoto demo, makasete kudasai.
You can trust me with no matter what kind of difficult work.
③ いくら 教えても 分かりません。
Ikura oshietemo wakarimasen.
However much he teaches him, he doesn't understand.
④ いくら 考えても うまく 書けません。
Ikura kangaetemo umaku kakemasen.
No matter how hard I think, I can't write it well.

Page 66 • Reading Comprehension Questions
1. 燃えるゴミと 燃えないゴミを 分けます。
Moeru gomi to moenai gomi o wakemasu.
We should separate burnable and non-burnable garbage.
2. 瓶から ラベルを はがして 別に 捨てます。
Bin kara raberu o hagashite betsu ni sutemasu.
We should remove the label from bottles and throw them away separately.
3. 部屋が ゴミで いっぱいになる 人が います。
Heya ga gomi de ippai ni naru hito ga imasu.
Some people let their rooms become full of garbage.

CHAPTER 5
Page 69 • EXERCISE SET 1
① ママ，あれ ほしいから 買って。
Mama, are hoshī kara katte.
② 危ないから シートベルトを して。
Abunai kara shīto beruto o shite.
③ 血を とりますから（orとるので）動かないで
ください ね。
Chi o torimasu kara (or toru node) ugokanaide kudasai ne.
④ 手伝いますから 心配しないでくださいね。
Tetsudaimasu kara shinpai shinaide kudasai ne.

Page 70 • EXERCISE SET 2
① 計算ミスのために 仕事を 休むことができません。
Keisan misu no tame ni shigoto o yasumu koto ga dekimasen.
Because of the calculation errors I can't take a break.
② 不況のために，タクシーの お客さんが 減りました。
Fukyō no tame ni takushī no okyakusan ga herimashita.
Because of the recession, there are fewer taxi customers.
③ うまく 行かない ために，ボスは 悩んでいます。
Umaku ikanai tame ni, bosu wa nayande imasu.
The boss is worried because things aren't going well.
④ 水不足 のために，水を もらっています。
Mizubusoku no tame ni, mizu o moratte imasu.
Due to the water shortage, we are being given water.

Page 71 • EXERCISE SET 3
① 迷惑メールが たくさん 来る ん です。
Meiwaku mēru ga takusan kuru n desu.
(It's because) I'm getting a lot of junk mail.
② 仕事が 締め切りに 間に合わない ん です。
Shigoto ga shimekiri ni mani awanai n desu.
(It's because) I'm behind on the deadline.
③ 今日は 太郎の 誕生日な ん です。
Kyō wa tarō no tanjōbi na n desu.
(It's because) it's Taro's birthday.
④ 津波から 逃げる ん です。
Tsunami kara nigeru n desu.
(It's because) they're running from the tsunami.

Page 73 • EXERCISE SET 4
① A: どうして腕が 赤い ん ですか。
Dōshite ude ga akai n desu ka.
Why is your arm red?
B: なぜかというと 私は アレルギーがあるからです。
Nazeka to iu to watashi wa arerugī ga aru kara desu.
Because I've got an allergy.

② A: どうして 入院した ん ですか。
Dōshite nyūin shita n desu ka.
Why is he in the hospital?
B: なぜかというと 足を 折った から です。
Nazeka to iu to ashi o otta kara desu.
Because he broke his leg.
③ A: どうして ドライバーは 困っている ん ですか。
Dōshite doraibā wa komatte iru n desu ka.
Why is the driver annoyed?
B: なぜかというと ガソリンが 高くなったからです。
Nazeka to iu to gasorin ga takaku natta kara desu.
Because the gas became expensive.
④ A: どうして 機械で 草を 刈っている ん ですか。
Dōshite kikai de kusa o katte iru n desu ka.
Why is he using a machine to cut the grass?
B: なぜかというと 手で 刈るのが 難しいからです。
Nazeka to iu to te de karu no ga muzukashī kara desu.
Because it's difficult to cut it by hand.

Page 74 • EXERCISE SET 5
① 実は 歯が 痛い ん です。
Jitsu wa ha ga itai n desu.
Actually, I've got toothache.
じゃあ，今は食べられない ん ですね。
Jā, ima wa taberarenai n desu ne.
Then that's why you're not eating, then.
② 実は タブレットは/を 初めて 使う ん です。
Jitsu wa taburetto wa/o hajimete tsukau n desu.
Actually it's my first time using a tablet.
じゃあ，まだ できない ん ですね。
Jā, mada dekinai n desu ne.
Right, so you can't do it yet.
③ 実は カメラを 買った ん です。
Jitsu wa kamera o katta n desu.
Actually, I bought a camera.
じゃあ，いい 写真が 撮れる ん ですね。
Jā, ī shashin ga toreru n desu ne.
Right, so you can take nice photos, can't you.

Page 75 • EXERCISE SET 6
① 牛丼を 食べに 行きましょう。
Gyūdon o tabe ni ikimashō.
Let's go to eat a beef rice bowl.
② 公園へ バーベキューを しに 行きます。
Kōen e bābekyū o shi ni ikimasu.
(They're) going to have a barbecue.
③ ダンスホールへ 踊りに 行きます。
Dansu hōru e odori ni ikimasu.
He's going dancing at the dance hall.

Page 76 • EXERCISE SET 7
1. 働きすぎます　　hatarakisugimasu
2. 買いすぎます　　kaisugimasu
3. 休みすぎます　　yasumisugimasu
4. 寝すぎます　　nesugimasu
5. 見すぎます　　misugimasu
6. 練習しすぎます　　renshū shisugimasu
7. 安すぎます　　yasusugimasu
8. 遅すぎます　　ososugimasu
9. 退屈すぎます　　taikutsu sugimasu

Page 77 • EXERCISE SET 8
① このソフトは むずかしすぎて うまく 使えません。
Kono sofuto wa muzukashisugite umaku tsukaemasen.
This software is so difficult that I can't use it well.
② 太郎はゲームが おもしろすぎて やめられません。
Taro wa gēmu ga omoshirosugite yameraremasen.
Taro is so interested in his game that he can't stop.
③ 疲れすぎて 朝まで ぐっすり 寝られます。
Tsukaresugite asa made gussuri neraremasu.
I'm so tired that I'll sleep soundly till morning.

Page 78 • EXERCISE SET 9

❶ 海岸は ゴミを 全部 拾うには 広すぎます。
Kaigan wa gomi o zenbu hirou ni wa hirosugimasu.
The beach is too big for us to pick up all the trash.

❷ 先生の 説明は 理解するには むずかしすぎます。
Sensei no setsumei wa rikai suru ni wa muzukashisugimasu.
The teacher's explanation is too difficult to understand.

Page 79 • EXERCISE SET 10

❶ お菓子を ちょっと 買いすぎですね。
Okashi o chotto kaisugi desu ne.
You've bought too many cakes, don't you think?

❷ ゲームの しすぎですね。
Gēmu no shisugi desu ne.
You play games too much, don't you think?

Page 81 • Reading Comprehension Questions

1. たくさん ありすぎて 数えられません。
Takusan arisugite kazoeraremasen.
There are too many to count.

2. 子どもから お年寄りまで 来ます。
Kodomo kara otoshiyori made kimasu.
Those from children to old people come.

3. 港や 川から 上がります。
Minato ya kawa kara agarimasu.
They are set off from a harbor or a river.

CHAPTER 6

Page 84 • EXERCISE SET 1

1. 走ろう   **hashirō**
2. 食べよう   **tabeyō**
3. 買おう   **kaō**
4. 起きよう   **okiyō**
5. 確認しよう   **kakunin shiyō**

Page 86 • EXERCISE SET 2

❶ 私は 彼女と ダンスを 練習しようと 思います。
Watashi wa kanojo to dansu o renshū shiyō to omoimasu.
I think I'll practice dancing with her.

❷ ピアノの 練習を やめようと 思います。
Piano no renshū o yameyō to omoimasu.
I think I'm going to give up piano practice.

❸ 花子は 神様に お願いしようと 思っています。
Hanako wa kamisama ni onegai shiyō to omotte imasu.
Hanako will try praying to the gods.

❹ バレンタインデーに 彼氏に チョコレートを あげようと 思います。
Barentain dē ni kareshi ni chokorēto o ageyō to omoimasu.
I'm planning to give my boyfriend chocolate for Valentine's day.

Page 87 • EXERCISE SET 3

❶ 今日も 仕事を（or で）頑張る つもりです。
Kyō mo shigoto o (or de) ganbaru tsumori desu.
I intend to do my best at work today.

❷ これから 両社は 協力する 予定です。
Kore kara ryōsha wa kyōryoku suru yotei desu.
From hereon both companies plan to cooperate.

❸ 銀行に 百万円 貯金する つもりです。
Ginkō ni hyakuman en chokin suru tsumori desu.
I intend to save a million yen in the bank.

❹ 車に 乗る つもりは ありません。
Kuruma ni noru tsumori wa arimasen.
車に 乗らない つもりです。
Kuruma ni noranai tsumori desu.
I have no intention of using a car.

❺ 人間ドックで 検査する 予定です。
Ningen dokku de kensa suru yotei desu.
I'm scheduled to have a full medical checkup.

Page 88 • EXERCISE SET 4

❶ 休んだ 方が いいです よ。
Yasunda hō ga ī desu yo.
You should take a break.

❷ 無理に 食べない 方が いいです よ。
Muri ni tabenai hō ga ī desu yo.
You shouldn't force yourself to eat.

❸ お父さん！もっと お母さんと 話した 方が いいです よ。
Otōsan! Motto okāsan to hanashita hō ga ī desu yo.
Dad! You should talk to Mom more!

Page 89 • EXERCISE SET 5

1. 書き方   **kakikata**
2. 読み方   **yomikata**
3. 見方   **mikata**
4. しかた（仕方） **shikata**

Page 90 • EXERCISE SET 6

❶ 日本語での 手紙の 書き方
nihongo de no tegami no kakikata
how to write a letter in Japanese

❷ ホテルの 予約の しかた
hoteru no yoyaku no shikata.
how to reserve a hotel

❸ ソフトの インストールの しかた
sofuto no insutōru no shikata
how to install the software

❹ 新幹線の 乗り方
shinkansen no norikata
how to take a shinkansen

❺ 漢字の 覚え方
kanji no oboekata

❻ 日本の お風呂の 入り方
nihon no ofuro no hairikata

❼ 東京での 暮らしかた
tōkyō de no kurashikata
東京での 生活の しかた
tōkyō de no seikatsu no shikata

❽ 荷物の 海外への 送り方
nimotsu no kaigai e no okurikata

Page 91 • EXERCISE SET 7

❶ 私は 泳ぐ 方法を 知りません。
Watashi wa oyogu hōhō o shirimasen.
I don't know how to swim.

❷ 東京駅の 八重洲 南口へ 行く 方法が わかりません。
Tōkyō eki no yaesu minamiguchi e iku hōhō ga wakarimasen.
I don't know the way to the Yaesu south exit of Tokyo Station.

❸ 日本人と 付き合う 方法は ちょっと むずかしいです。
Nihonjin to tsukiau hōhō wa chotto muzukashī desu.
(The way of) socializing with Japanese people is a bit difficult.

❹ 箸を 使う 方法を いつ 覚えましたか。
Hashi o tsukau hōhō o itsu oboemashita ka.
When did you learn how to use chopsticks?

Page 92 • EXERCISE SET 8

❶ タブレットの 操作の 仕方が 分かりました。
Taburetto no sōsa no shikata ga wakarimashita.
I know how to operate the tablet.

❷ 花の デザインの 仕方を 覚えました。
Hana no dezain no shikata o oboemashita.
I learned how to do flower designs.

❸ 花子は 田植えの 仕方を よく 知っています。
Hanako wa taue no shikata o yoku shitte imasu.
Hanako really knows how to plant rice.

1. それは 仏教の 教えで，食べ物の命を もらう からです。
   Sore wa bukkyō no oshie de, tabemono no inochi o morau kara desu.
   It's because it's the teaching of Buddhism and they receive the life of food.
2. 箸で 刺して 食べない 方が いいです。（箸から 箸に 食べ物を 渡さない 方が いいです。）
   Hashi de sashite tabenai hō ga ī desu. (Hashi kara hashi ni tabemono o watasanai hō ga i desu.)
   It is better not to eat stabbing food with chopsticks. (It is better not to pass food from chopsticks to chopsticks.)
3. うどんや ラーメンを 食べながらです。
   Udon ya rāmen o tabenagara desu.
   (They make sounds) while eating udon or ramen.

CHAPTER 7
Page 99 • EXERCISE SET 1

❶ 石油ファンヒーターを つけて おきました。
   Sekiyu fan hītā o tsukete okimashita.
❷ 100円ショップで 買い物を して おきます。
   Hyaku en shoppu de kaimono o shite okimasu.
❸ ぐっすり 寝て おきます。
   Gussuri nete okimasu. (Note: an intransitive verb may occasionally take **-TE OKIMASU** when there is no object.)
❹ シャベルで 雪を 屋根から 下ろして おきます。
   Shaberu de yuki o yane kara oroshite okimasu.

Page 100 • EXERCISE SET 2

❶ パソコンが 壊れて います。
   Pasokon ga kowarete imasu.
   The computer is broken.
❷ 店が 閉まって います。
   Mise ga shimatte imasu.
   The store is closed.
❸ パンが 焼けて います。
   Pan ga yakete imasu.
   The bread is toasted.
❹ あそこに 防犯 カメラが 付いて います。
   Asoko ni bōhan kamera ga tsuite imasu.
   A security camera has been installed over there.

Page 101 • EXERCISE SET 3

❶ 資料が 印刷して あります。
   Shiryō ga insatsu shite arimasu.
❷ スマホにアプリが たくさん インストールして あります。
   Sumaho ni apuri ga takusan instōru shite arimasu.
❸ ロッカーの 鍵が かけて あります。
   Rokkā no kagi ga kakete arimasu.
❹ ドルは/が 円に 替えて あります。
   Doru wa/ga en ni kaete arimasu.

Page 103 • EXERCISE SET 4

❶ 資料を コピー機に 置きっぱなしに して います。
   Shiryō o kopīki ni okippanashi ni shite imasu.
   (She's) left the papers on the photocopier.
❷ 本を 開きっぱなしに して 寝て しまいました。
   Hon o hirakippanashi ni shite nete shimaimashita.
   (I) fell asleep with (my) book still open.
❸ テレビを つけっぱなしに しないで ください。
   Terebi o tsukeppanashi ni shinaide kudasai.
   Don't leave the TV on, please.

Page 103 • EXERCISE SET 5

❶ 携帯電話を 充電しっぱなしで 忘れて います。
   Keitai denwa o jūden shippanashi de wasurete imasu.
   I forgot about my phone and left it charging.
❷ 本を 開きっぱなしで 寝て しまいました。
   Hon o hirakippanashi de nete shimaimashita.
   (I) fell asleep with (my) book still open.

❶ 風車が 止まった まま（で）回りません。
   Fūsha ga tomatta mama (de) mawarimasen.
❷ 運転手が 配達の 荷物を 置いた ままです。
   Untenshu ga haitatsu no nimotsu o oita mama desu.
❸ 電気を つけた ままに しないでください。
   Denki o tsuketa mama ni shinaide kudasai.
❹ 食器を 洗った ままに しないでください。
   Shokki o aratta mama ni shinaide kudasai.

Page 109 • Reading Comprehension Questions

1. 品物が 新しい 包み紙で 二重に 包んで あったり，新しい 袋に 入れて あったりします。
   Shinamono ga atarashī tsutsumigami de nijū ni tsutsunde attari, atarashī fukuro ni irete attari shimasu.
   The article is double wrapped in a new wrapping paper or is put into a new bag.
2. 原発 事故の 問題が あって 節電した からです。
   Genpatsu jiko no mondai ga atte setsuden shita kara desu.
   It's because there was the problem of a nuclear power plant accident and electricity was being saved.
3. 昔の弁当は容器がリユースできましたが，今の弁当は使い捨ての容器です。
   Mukashi no bentō wa riyūsu dekimashita ga, ima no bentō wa tsukaisute no yōki desu.
   Lunch boxes could be reused in the old days but these days lunch boxes are disposable containers.

CHAPTER 8
Page 113 • EXERCISE SET 1

❶ 花を 生けるのは 芸術 です。
   Hana o ikeru no wa geijutsu desu.
   Flower arrangement is an art.
   彼女の 趣味は 花を 生ける ことです。
   Kanojo no shumi wa hana o ikeru koto desu.
   Her hobby is flower arrangement.
❷ ダンスを するのは 楽しい です。
   Dansu o suru no wa tanoshī desu.
   Dancing is fun.
   男の子たちの 部活は ダンスを する ことです。
   Otoko no ko tachi no bukatsu wa dansu o suru koto desu.
   The boy's club activity is dancing.

Page 115 • EXERCISE SET 2

❶ けんじさんが 好きなのは 猫です。
   Kenji san ga suki na no wa neko desu.
❷ 私が よく 飲むのは 日本酒 です。
   Watashi ga yoku nomu no wa nihonshu desu.

Page 116 • EXERCISE SET 3

❶ けんじが タブレットで 音楽を 聞いている のを 見ました。
   Kenji ga taburetto de ongaku o kite iru no o mimashita.
   I saw Kenji listening to music on the tablet.
❷ 花子が 発表するのを 聞きました。
   Hanako ga happyō suru no o kikimashita.
   I listened to Hanako give the presentation.
❸ けんじが 迷惑メールで 困っている のを 見ました。
   Kenji ga meiwaku mēru de komatte iru no o mimashita.
   I saw that Kenji was annoyed by the junk mail.
❹ 娘は お母さんが お皿を 洗うのを 手伝います。
   Musume wa okāsan ga osara o arau no o tetsudaimasu.
   The daughter helps the mother wash the dishes.

Page 117 • EXERCISE SET 4

❶ 来週 バーベキューを しに 行くのを 楽しみに して います。
   Raishū bābekyū o shini iku no o tanoshimi ni shite imasu.
   I'm looking forward to going to a barbecue next week.
❷ お寺の 写真を 撮る のを 楽しみに して います。
   Otera no shashin o toru no o tanoshimi ni shite imasu.
   I'm looking forward to taking photos of the temple.

❸ 赤ちゃんは 出かけるのを 楽しみに して います。
Akachan wa dekakeru no o tanoshimi ni shite imasu.
The baby is looking forward to going out.

Page 117 • EXERCISE SET 5
❶ お父さんの 日課は 毎朝 ジョギングする こと です。
Otōsan no nikka wa mai asa jogingu suru koto desu.
Dad's daily morning routine is jogging.
❷ お母さんの 日課は 激安 商品を 探す こと です。
Okāsan no nikka wa gekiyasu shōhin o sagasu koto desu.
Mom's daily routine is looking for bargain-priced goods.
❸ 私たちの 担当は ゴミを 分別する こと です。
Watashitachi no tantō wa gomi o bunbetsu suru koto desu.
Our job is to separate the trash.
❹ クラウドサービスは ネットで データを 利用する こと です。
Kuraudo sābisu wa netto de dēta o riyō suru koto desu.
Cloud service lets us utilize data via a network.

Page 120 • Reading Comprehension Questions
1. 部屋が 2つと リビング, ダイニング, キッチンが ある 住宅です。
Heya ga futatsu to ribingu, dainingu, kitchin ga aru jūtaku desu.
It is a house with two rooms, a living room, a dining room and a kitchen.
2. 木造の 一戸建てに 住む の が 好きです。
Mokuzō no ikkodate ni sumu no ga suki desu.
They like to live in a wooden detached house.
3. 洋式 便器が 一般的に なりました。
Yōshiki benki ga ippanteki ni narimashita.
The Western-style toilet gained popularity.

CHAPTER 9
Page 123 • EXERCISE SET 1
❶ けんじは ギターが 弾ける ように なりました。
Kenji wa gitā ga hikeru yō ni narimashita.
Kenji is now able to play the guitar.
❷ 私は 陶器が 作れる ように なりました。
Watashi wa tōki ga tsukureru yō ni narimashita.
Now I can make pottery.
❸ 補聴器で よく 聞こえる ように なりました。
Hochōki de yoku kikoeru yō ni narimashita.
I am now able to hear with a hearing aid.
❹ スマホが 起動 しなく なりました。
Sumaho ga kidō shinaku narimashita.
My smartphone became unable to be activated.
❺ ガソリンが 高すぎて 買えなく なりました。
Gasorin ga takasugite kaenaku narimashita.
Gas is so expensive that I can't afford it any more.

Page 124 • EXERCISE SET 2
❶ みなさんが 分かる ように よく 説明 します。
Minasan ga wakaru yō ni yoku setsumei shimasu.
I give a good explanation so that everyone understands.
❷ 自分で 立てる ように サポート します。
Jibun de tateru yō ni sapōto shimasu.
I'll help you so that you can stand by yourself.
❸ 本が きちんと 並ぶ ように 置いて います。
Hon ga kichinto narabu yō ni oite imasu.
She is placing the books so that they line up in order.
❹ 風邪を ひかない ように マスクを します。
Kaze o hikanai yō ni masuku o shimasu.
I wear a mask so that I don't catch a cold.

Page 125 • EXERCISE SET 3
❶ 家を 建て替える ために 荷物を 移して います。
Ie o tatekaeru tame ni nimotsu o utsushite imasu.
We're moving boxes so that we can rebuild our house.

❷ 鬼を 追い払う ために 豆を まきます。
Oni o oiharau tame ni mame o makimasu.
We're scattering beans to chase away the devil.

Page 126 • EXERCISE SET 4
❶ 父の ために ネクタイを 買います。
Chichi no tame ni nekutai o kaimasu.
I bought a necktie for my father.
❷ 熱の ために 寝込んでいます。
Netsu no tame ni nekonde imasu.
I'm ill in bed because of a fever.
❸ 明日の 発表の ために レポートの 準備を して います。
Ashita no happyō no tame ni repōto no junbi o shite imasu.
I'm preparing the report for tomorrow's presentation.

Page 127 • EXERCISE SET 5
❶ 発表 する のに プロジェクターが 必要 です。
Happyō suru no ni purojekutā ga hitsuyō desu.
A projector is necessary for giving a presentation.
❷ それを 決める のに 会議が 重要です。
Sore o kimeru no ni kaigi ga jūyō desu.
In order to decide, a meeting is important.

Page 127 • EXERCISE SET 6
❶ けんじは よく 学校に 遅刻 する ように なりました。
Kenji wa yoku gakkō ni chikoku suru yō ni narimashita.
Kenji has gotten into the habit of being late for school.
❷ おばあさんは カートを 押して 歩く ように なりました。
Obāsan wa kāto o oshite aruku yō ni narimashita.
The old woman has gotten into the habit of walking with a cart.
❸ 最近 マイボトルを使う ように なりました。
Saikin maibotoru o tsukau yō ni narimashita.
Recently I've started using a reusable bottle.

Page 128 • EXERCISE SET 7
❶ 先生に 挨拶 する ように して います。
Sensei ni aisatsu suru yō ni shite imasu.
I'm trying to get into the habit of greeting the teacher.
❷ 先生の 質問に すぐに 答える ように して います。
Sensei no shitsumon ni sugu ni kotaeru yō ni shite imasu.
I'm trying to answer the teacher's questions quickly.
❸ お風呂の 水を 洗濯に 使う ように して います。
Ofuro no mizu o sentaku ni tsukau yō ni shite imasu.
I'm trying to use the bathwater in the washing machine.

Page 129 • EXERCISE SET 8
❶ エアコンを つけずに 扇風機を 使う ことに して います。
Eakon o tsukezu ni senpūki o tsukau koto ni shite imasu.
❷ 電車の 中でも 勉強 する ことに して います。
Densha no naka de mo benkyō suru koto ni shite imasu.

Page 133 • Reading Comprehension Questions
1. 千語 程度 覚えたら いいです。
Sen go teido oboetara ī desu.
It will be okay if you learn about one thousand words.
2. [k] や [t] の 音を 使ったら できます。
[k] ya [t] no oto o tsukattara dekimasu.
You can do it if you use the sound [k] or [t].
3. 「ころころ」は 明るくて リズミカルな イメージを 表し, 「ごろごろ」は 粗くて 重い ものを 表します。
"Korokoro" wa akarukute rizumikaru na imēji o arawashi, "gorogoro" wa arakute omoi mono o arawashimasu.
"Korokoro" expresses a bright and rhythmical image and "gorogoro" expresses something coarse and heavy.

CHAPTER 10
Page 136 • EXERCISE SET 1
1. 読まれます   yomaremasu
2. 壊されます   kowasaremasu

3. 売られます　　　　　　uraremasu
4. 食べられます　　　　　taberaremasu
5. 作られます　　　　　　tsukuraremasu
6. 聞かれます　　　　　　kikaremasu
7. 飲まれます　　　　　　nomaremasu
8. 知られています　　　　shirarete imasu
9. 攻撃されます　　　　　kōgeki saremasu
10. 批判されます　　　　　hihan saremasu

Page 138 • EXERCISE SET 2

❶ 弟は 兄に 顔を 殴られました。
Otōto wa ani ni kao o naguraremashita.

❷ 相手 チームに ボールを レシーブ されました。
Aite chīmu ni bōru o reshību saremashita.

❸ 男の子は 知らない人に 腕を つかまれました。
Otoko no ko wa shiranai hito ni ude o tsukamaremashita.

❹ 勉強中に 彼女に 隣で 寝られました。
Benkyō chū ni kanojo ni tonari de neraremashita.

Page 139 • EXERCISE SET 3

❶ くれました　　　　　　　　　kuremashita
❷ くれました　　　　　　　　　kuremashita
❸ あげました　　　　　　　　　agemashita
❹ あげました　　　　　　　　　agemashita
❺ もらいました／あげました　moraimashita/agemashita

Page 140 • EXERCISE SET 4

❶ 教えてくれますか ／ 教えてくれませんか
oshiete kuremasu ka / oshiete kuremasen ka

❷ 買って あげました
katte agemashita

❸ 教えて もらいました。
oshiete moraimashita

Page 140 • EXERCISE SET 5

❶ 学生が 教室を 掃除 して くれました。
Gakusei ga kyōshitsu o sōji shite kuremashita.
学生に 教室を 掃除 して もらいました。
Gakusei ni kyōshitsu o sōji shite moraimashita.

❷ 家庭教師が 数学を 教えて くれました。
Katei kyōshi ga sūgaku o oshiete kuremashita.
家庭教師に 数学を 教えて もらいました。
Katei kyōshi ni sūgaku o oshiete moraimashita.

❸ 介護士が 車椅子を 押して くれました。
Kaigoshi ga kuruma isu o oshite kuremashita.
介護士に 車椅子を 押して もらいました。
Kaigoshi ni kuruma isu o oshite moraimashita.

❹ 時間外に 医者が 子どもを 診て くれました。
Jikangai ni isha ga kodomo o mite kuremashita.
時間外に 医者に 子どもを 診て もらいました。
Jikangai ni isha ni kodomo o mite moraimashita.

Page 142 • EXERCISE SET 6

❶ 教えて いただけませんか
oshiete itadakemasen ka

❷ 教えて いただきました
oshiete itadakimashita

❸ 上げて くださいました
agete kudasaimashita

Page 145 • Reading Comprehension Questions

1. 予想外の トラブルを 起こしたり いやな 気持ちを 与えた り します。
Yosōgai no toraburu o okoshitari iya na kimochi o ataetari shimasu.
Unexpected trouble may be caused or unpleasant feelings may be aroused.

2. 異文化間でも 楽しい コミュニケーションが うまく でき る ように なります。
Ibunkakan demo tanoshī komyunikēshon ga umaku dekiru yō ni narimasu.

We will be able to have pleasant and skillful communication between foreign cultures.

3. 自分の 文化を うまく 説明 できる ことが 必要です。
Jibun no bunka o umaku setsumei dekiru koto ga hitsuyo desu.
It is necessary to be able to properly explain one's culture.

CHAPTER 11
Page 150 • EXERCISE SET 1

❶ タバコは やめやすい ですが, アルコールは 控えにくい です。
Tabako wa yameyasui desu ga, arukōru wa hikaenikui desu.

❷ 猫は 飼いやすいですが, 蛇は 飼いにくいです。
Neko wa kaiyasui desu ga, hebi wa kainikui desu.

❸ 筆は 書きにくい ですが, タブレットは タイプ しやすい です。
Fude wa kakinikui desu ga, taburetto wa taipu shiyasui desu.

❹ カプセルは 飲みやすい ですが, 粉は 飲みにくい です。
Kapuseru wa nomiyasui desu ga, kona wa nominikui desu.

Page 151 • EXERCISE SET 2

❶ 花粉症に なった かもしれません。
Kafunshō ni natta kamo shiremasen.
I might have got hay fever.

❷ バーガーが 大きすぎて 口に 入らない かもしれません。
Bāgā ga ōkisugite kuchi ni hairanai kamo shiremasen.
The burger is so big, it might not fit in my mouth.

❸ 地震で 岩が 家に ぶつかる かもしれません。
Jishin de iwa ga ie ni butsukaru kamo shiremasen.
Because of the earthquake, rocks might crash into the houses.

Page 152 • EXERCISE SET 3

❶ きっと よく なる はずです。
Kitto yoku naru hazu desu.
I believe he will get well.

❷ 新聞は トイレット ペーパーに リサイクル される／する はずです。
Shinbun wa toiretto pēpā ni risaikuru sareru/suru hazu desu.
Newspapers should be recycled into toilet paper.

❸ おいしい 餅が できる はずです。
Oishī mochi ga dekiru hazu desu.
It looks like they're making delicious mochi rice cakes.

❹ この レールパスで どの 電車にも 乗れる はずです。
Kono rēru pasu de dono densha ni mo noreru hazu desu.
You should be able to board any train with this rail pass.

Page 153 • EXERCISE SET 4

❶ ここから 入れない にちがいありません。
Koko kara hairenai ni chigai arimasen.
You mustn't be able to enter from here.

❷ ここで タクシーに 乗れる にちがいありません。
Koko de takushī ni noreru ni chigai arimasen.
You must be able to get a taxi here.

❸ 今日は 天気が 晴れる にちがいありません。
Kyō wa tenki ga hareru ni chigai arimasen.
Today the weather is sure to clear up.

❹ 父は 怒って いる にちがいありません。
Chichi wa okotte iru ni chigai arimasen.
Dad must be angry.

Page 156 • EXERCISE SET 5

❶ A: どんな 味 かしら？
Donna aji kashira?
What does it taste like?
B: すごく おいしいん じゃない？
Sugoku oishī n ja nai?
I guess it's really delicious.

❷ A: あの 車 どうした の かな？
Ano kuruma dō shita no ka na?
I wonder what's wrong with that car?

B: 駐車違反 な ん じゃない？
Chūsha ihan na n ja nai?
It's a parking violation, isn't it?
❸ A: 久しぶり。
Hisashiburi.
Long time no see.
B: 人ちがい な ん じゃない？
Hito chigai na n ja nai?
You are mistaking me for somebody else, aren't you?
❹ A: よく 寝て いる ね。
Yoku nete iru ne.
They're sleeping well.
B: 気持ち いい ん じゃない？
Kimochi ī n ja nai?
They're feeling good, aren't they?

Page 159 • Reading Comprehension Questions

1. 言いにくい ことを 言わずに 理解 して もらう ことを 美徳 と している から かもしれません。
   Īnikui koto o iwazuni rikai shite morau koto o bitoku to shite iru kara kamo shiremasen.
   It may be because they make it a virtue to let you understand what is hard to say without saying it.
2. どれぐらい はっきり 言ったら いいか 分かりにくい こと です。
   Dore gurai hakkiri ittara ī ka wakarinikui koto desu.
   It is that they find it difficult to know how directly they should express themselves.
3. 少し はっきりと 話して くれる ように 頼んだら いい か もしれません。
   Sukoshi hakkiri to hanashite kureru yō ni tanondara ī kamo shiremasen.
   It would be better to ask them to speak a little more directly.

CHAPTER 12

Page 163 • EXERCISE SET 1

❶ 今日は 雨が 降る そう（らしい）です。
Kyō wa ame ga furu sō (rashī) desu.
It's supposed to rain today.
❷ ペット美容は 一回 一万円 かかる そう（らしい）です。
Petto biyō wa ikkai ichi man en kakaru sō (rashī) desu.
I hear it's ten thousand yen for one session of pet grooming.
❸ けんじは 自分で 弁当を 作る そう（らしい）です。
Kenji wa jibun de bentō o tsukuru sō (rashī) desu.
Apparently Kenji makes his own bento lunch.

Page 164 • EXERCISE SET 2

❶ 外は 風が 強い よう（みたい）です。
Soto wa kaze ga tsuyoi yō (mitai) desu.
Looks like it's windy outside today.
❷ 雪が やまない よう（みたい）です。
Yuki ga yamanai yō (mitai) desu.
It doesn't look like the snow's going to stop.
❸ 魚が 焼けて いるよう（みたい）です。
Sakana ga yakete iru yō (mitai) desu.
It smells like the fish is grilled.

Page 166 EXERCISE SET 3

1. 空きそうです **sukisō desu**　空いてそうです **suitesō desu**
2. 着きそうです **tsukisō desu**　着いてそうです **tsuitesō desu**
3. 勝ちそうです **kachisō desu**　勝ってそうです **kattesō desu**
3. 来そうです **kisō desu**　来てそうです **kitesō desu**

Page 166 • EXERCISE SET 4

❶ 宴会は 楽しそうです。
Enkai wa tanoshisō desu.
The drinking party looks fun.
❷ 私たちはだいぶ 遅れそうです。
Watashitachi wa daibu okuresō desu.
It looks like we'll be pretty late.
❸ もうすぐ 完成しそうです。
Mōsugu kansei shisō desu.
It seems like it will be completed soon.

Page 167 • EXERCISE SET 5

❶ 寒くて 風邪を ひきそうです。
Samukute kaze o hikisō desu.
It's so cold I may catch a cold.
❷ スモッグの 雨が ひどくて 環境を 破壊しそうです。
Sumoggu no ame ga hidokute kankyō o hakai shisō desu.

Page 172 • Reading Comprehension Questions

1. 女性の 学歴が 高くなったこと，晩婚化，未婚化などの ためです。
   Josei no gakureki ga takaku natta koto, bankonka, mikonka nado no tame desu.
   Because women's educational backgrounds have improved, there is a tendency to marry late, not to marry, etc.
2. 女性が 会社の 仕事と 家の 仕事が 両立 できない こと です。
   Josei ga kaisha no shigoto to ie no shigoto ga ryōritsu dekinai koto desu.
   It is that it is difficult for women to work in companies and do housework.
3. 経済的 理由の ために 家族が 持てないことや，一人で自分らしく過ごしたい からの ようです。
   Keizaiteki riyū no tame ni kazoku ga motenai koto ya, hitori de jibun rashiku sugoshitai kara no yō desu.
   It seems to be because they can't support a family for economic reasons or like to spend time on their own.